To PASTOR

WITH O

FOR YOUR MINISTRY.

— Ted & Hester Redoll

Jan 23, 2009

1 Heb. 2:3

SO GREAT SALVATION

The History and Message of the
Keswick Convention

by

STEVEN BARABAS

B.A., TH.D.

Associate Professor of Theology, Wheaton College

WITH A FOREWORD BY

FRED MITCHELL

Chairman of the Keswick Convention Council 1948–51

Wipf & Stock
PUBLISHERS
Eugene, Oregon

Wipf and Stock Publishers
199 W 8th Ave, Suite 3
Eugene, OR 97401

So Great Salvation
The History and Message of the Keswick Convention
By Barabas, Steven
Copyright©1952 by Barabas, Steven
ISBN: 1-59752-171-X
Publication date 5/5/2005
Previously published by Fleming H. Revell Company, 1952

PREFACE

Every year, during the month of July, thousands of Christians from all parts of the world gather for a Convention for the deepening of the spiritual life, lasting one week, in the little town of Keswick, which nestles at the foot of Skiddaw mountain and beside beautiful Lake Derwentwater, in the Lake District of northern England, a region famous by association with the Lake poets—Wordsworth, Coleridge, and Southey—and for picturesque and fascinating scenery unsurpassed in all England, if not in all Europe.

Since 1875, when the first of these Conventions was held, the influence of what is taught there has been increasingly felt in the Christian world, until Keswick teaching has come to be regarded as one of the most potent spiritual forces in recent Church history. The "Keswick movement" has become historic. There are those who regard it as a sort of modern Pentecost. Its influence, far from being spent, seems to be increasing, so that today there are probably few countries in the world that have not Conventions of their own, similar to it in the things for which it stands.

A movement that has affected the modern Christian Church so vitally has naturally had its critics. These critics are not so numerous or so vociferous today as they were at its beginning, when some of the foremost leaders of the Church attacked it as being dangerously heretical. It is strange, therefore, that no attempt has ever been made, by either friends or foes of the movement, to set forth and examine its teaching in the light of Scripture.

Books on Keswick have indeed been written. Five of them have appeared—four of them by leaders of the Convention. The first of these, *The Keswick Movement in Precept and Practice,* by A. T. Pierson, the well-known American Presbyterian preacher and writer, appeared almost fifty years ago, in 1903. It is a little book, of almost vest-pocket size, but in its small compass it sets forth, with succinctness and clarity, the message for which Keswick stands. In 1907, Charles F. Harford, a son of the founder of the Convention, edited a book entitled *The Keswick Convention: Its Message, It. Method, and Its Men.* The contributors to this volume were some of the outstanding Keswick leaders of the day, and their chapters give much helpful and interesting information on the most important aspects of the Keswick movement—its history, teaching, method, leaders, and influence. Two other books, *Keswick from Within*, by J. B. Figgis, and *These Sixty Years*, by Walter B. Sloan, which appeared, respectively, in 1914 and 1935, do not pretend to be more than running commentaries on the yearly Conventions, sketchily describing some of the outstanding events, personalities, and addresses of each Convention. The fifth, *The Message of Keswick*, is an anonymous publication, but with a Foreword by the Rev. W. H. Aldis, then Chairman of the Keswick Convention Council. Published in 1939, it sets forth with sympathy and understanding the teaching of Keswick, but not with the fulness or systematic fashion of the present volume. None of these books tries to examine and evaluate the Keswick message from the standpoint of the teaching of Scripture. That is the aim of this book.

There are three parts to the book. The first is introductory, and consists of a historical sketch of the movement and an exposition of the Keswick method of presenting its message, which is as important and as distinctive as its teaching.

In the second part an endeavour is made to ascertain and to examine what is actually taught at Keswick during the week of the Convention and in the many books written by its leaders. During the five days in which the teaching of the Convention is presented, Keswick follows a certain sequence, a different subject being dealt with each day: on Monday, sin; on Tuesday, God's provision for sin; on Wednesday, consecration; on Thursday, the Spirit-filled life; and on Friday, Christian service. This order, in a general way, with variations depending upon the response of the Convention-goers to the message being presented, is followed year after year. Each of the five chapters in this second part of the book deals with the particular subject considered on the corresponding day of the Convention.

In the third part are given some biographical notes on a number of Keswick leaders, with the aim of illustrating how men are introduced to Keswick teaching and come to accept it, and the result of its acceptance in their lives. Their experiences are not to be thought of as being in any sense unique, but as representative and typical, not unlike those of thousands who regard themselves as adherents of Keswick teaching.

I have chosen to quote rather extensively from the addresses and books of the Keswick leaders, as in a volume of this kind, dealing with a subject that is still debated, I have thought it only fair to let Keswick speak for itself, in its own words. Moreover, while source material on the subject is abundant, unfortunately not much of it is readily available, even our large theological libraries containing relatively little of it.

The primary source material consists of the annual Reports of the Convention, published, since 1892, under various titles, but usually *The Keswick Week* and *The Keswick Convention;* a weekly paper, *The Life of Faith,* which, with its predecessor, *The Christian's Pathway of Power,* has been closely associated with the Convention from the beginning, and in which most of the addresses were reported from 1875 to 1891; and the many books—most of them of a devotional character—written by Keswick leaders, many of whom wrote very prolifically. Biographies of Keswick leaders, a large number of whom were among the outstanding religious leaders of their time, are abundant and of great help. And then there are the five books on Keswick to which I have just referred.

Here, then, we have the teaching of Keswick, one of the most interesting religious phenomena of our time.

FOREWORD

by Fred Mitchell
Chairman of the Keswick Convention Council, 1948–51

I have read the following pages twice, once in manuscript form and later at the proofs stage. I well remember the first impressions which the earlier reading made on me; they caused me to ask how an American author, who has never visited Britain, much less attended Keswick, could have become acquainted with the Convention, both as to its spirit, teaching and literature, as Dr. Barabas has evidently become. On reading the book for the second time I can only say that my admiration for the author's gifts has been increased.

The Keswick Convention, which began so simply and spontaneously in 1875, has had a most remarkable influence on evangelical thought and life. Its teaching has been made a blessing to thousands; ministers have entered into a new experience of fellowship with God, and their congregations have been affected as a result. At Keswick individuals have met God face to face, and returned to home, church and office with a new testimony; while thousands have been called to missionary service during the Convention week. Moreover, the literature of the Convention, and principally the report of the Convention week's meetings, have circulated far and wide, bringing healing and refreshment throughout the world. The ecumenical value of Keswick (and I use the word ecumenical in its pure form) has been of the greatest value, gathering together as it has done men and women of many countries and almost all Protestant denominations.

But, as Dr. Barabas remarks, the literature about Keswick has been surprisingly scarce and obviously inadequate. One reason for this has been that the men who ministered at the Convention have, for the most part, been men with pastoral responsibilities and who were not free to give themselves to the research demanded for such a history, and were so pressed that the preparation of addresses for the Convention were as much as they could do in addition to their other work.

It was with great joy, therefore, that one received Dr. Barabas's manuscript. It is a book which is faithful and accurate; it is well annotated with sources of his information; it is saturated with an appreciative spirit, for he himself has been so much helped by Keswick. The book will form a text-book and a reference book on this unique movement which has been reproduced with more or less similarity in every continent. It will, I believe, be the means in God's hands of leading many who read it, not to appreciate a Convention or a movement, but to appreciate the risen Lord who by His Spirit is able to do so much more for us than we have yet realized or experienced. Its reading has quickened my own personal desires to be more holy, and I am persuaded that a like result will appear in many readers.

Some will necessarily criticize the book, as Keswick itself has been and is still criticized; but that is of no serious consequence. The truth of God is bigger than any one view or school of thought. If other theologies of holiness help some others to be holy more than Keswick, then we rejoice; but Dr. Barabas's book will certainly help many to experience yet more fully the "so great salvation" which grace has provided, and which is waiting for the appropriation of faith.

CONTENTS

PART I

THE HISTORY AND METHOD OF KESWICK

PART II

THE SEQUENCE OF TEACHING AT KESWICK

xi

PART III

BIOGRAPHICAL SKETCHES OF SOME KESWICK LEADERS

THE HISTORY AND METHOD OF KESWICK

CHAPTER I

THE HISTORY OF KESWICK

In the early 1870s, when the Keswick movement had its rise in England, several powerful religious influences were at work in the land. There were, first, the three parties within the Anglican Church. The High Church party, which had been given new life by the Oxford movement, attacked the growing laxity of the Church in matters of doctrine and polity, and tried to bring about a revival of spiritual life by a return to Catholic ritualism. The Broad Church party sought to make the Established Church as comprehensive as possible, took a special interest in the social reforms of the nation, and by adopting some of the liberal tendencies of German theological scholarship and the Darwinian ideas on evolution departed from the traditional orthodoxy of the Church. The Low Church or Evangelical party was strongly influenced by English Methodism. It strongly advocated simplicity of worship and stressed the necessity of a real experience of conversion. It gave the sermon a more important place in the religious service, and put strong emphasis on the use of the Bible.

Of the Dissenting Churches perhaps the Plymouth Brethren, although few in number, had the most far-reaching influence, extending through both the Established Church and most of the dissenting bodies, far beyond the limits of their own group. They combined a highly Calvinistic impulse with a strict, literal interpretation of and obedience to the Word of God. They also did much to stimulate diligent Bible study and a return to the simplicities of the faith..

The evangelistic campaign of D. L. Moody and Ira D. Sankey in the British Isles, in the years 1873–4, was of unprecedented magnitude and far-reaching influence. They held meetings in the largest cities of England, Scotland, and Ireland, and the response to the message they brought was overwhelming. Not only were many hundreds converted, but Christians throughout the land had their spiritual life quickened, and interest in missions received a new impulse. '

In addition to the above, a new influence, coming from America, was making itself felt in the land—the influence of Higher Life teaching. In a sense, this was not entirely new, for the possibility of fellowship with Christ closer than that enjoyed by the generality of Christians had been taught by Walter Marshall in his book *The Gospel Mystery of Santification*,[1] and by William Romaine, in his books, *The Life of Faith, The Walk of Faith,* and *The Triumph of Faith*;[2] but these books, although regarded as religious classics by some, nevertheless did not have a widespread influence upon the Church. It was the books of the American religious leaders, T. C. Upham[3] and Asa Mahan,[4] that first seriously aroused the interest of the Church in the subject of sanctification and the Spirit-filled life.

But it was not, however, until the publication, in 1859, of W. E. Boardman's *The Higher Christian Life*, that interest in the subject really became widespread. Mark Guy Pearse says of this book that it was "perhaps the first popular treatise on this subject that won its way among all denominations; and its vast circulation, both in America and England, not only melted the prejudices of hosts against this subject, but made it possible for other writers to follow in the paths which he had opened, and led multitudes of timid souls out of the misty dawn into the clear shining of the sun."[5]

Interest in the subject became even more marked through the publication, in 1870, of Robert Pearsall Smith's book, *Holiness through Faith*, which was followed, in 1873, by another book of his, *Walk in the Light*, and by one by his wife, *The Record of a Happy Life*, all of which had a large circulation in England and provoked keen discussion in Evangelical circles.

---

[1] This came out originally in 1692. W. H. Griffith Thomas says in C. F. Harford's *The Keswick Convention*, p. 223, that the essential theology of the Keswick movement is clearly seen in this book. For the story of how Marshall came to write it, see Dr. Alexander Smellie's *Lift Up Your Heart*, pp. 73–5.

[2] These were published respectively in 1764, 1771, and 1795.

[3] *Life and Religious Experiences of Madame Guyon* (1847), *The Life of Faith* (1848), *Principles of the Interior or Hidden Life* (1848), *Treatise on the Divine Union* (1851).

[4] *Scripture Doctrine of Christian Perfection* (1839), *Out of Darkness into Light* (1875).

[5] Mrs. W. E. Boardman, *Life and Labours of the Rev. W. E. Boardman* (New York, 1887), preface, p. vii.

A. Higher Life Meetings and Conferences held by the Pearsall Smiths

Mr. and Mrs. Robert Pearsall Smith, in whom the Keswick movement had its genesis, were born in Philadelphia, he in 1827 and she in 1832. Both were born and bred Quakers, although Mr. Pearsall Smith was through most of his active life a member of the Presbyterian Church. It was not, however, until 1858, eight years after they were married, that they were converted, both, by a happy coincidence, on the same day.

At first the joys of their new-found salvation carried them over everything, but as the years passed they became dissatisfied with their Christian attainments. The religion they had found seemed to provide perfectly for their *future* deliverance from sin, but did not seem to give them *present* deliverance from its power. They were continually sinning and repenting, making good resolutions and breaking them, longing for victory over sin and sometimes getting it, but more often failing.[1]

Mrs. Pearsall Smith says that she knew herself to be a child of God, but was unable to act like one, and this made her wonder whether she had not missed something which would have given her victory. She determined to find out, if possible, what that something was. Older Christians whom she questioned about it all told her the same thing: she had not missed anything; a life of sinning and repenting was inevitable because of the weakness of the flesh, and was all she could ever hope for. She continually cried out with the apostle, "O wretched man that I am, who shall deliver me from the body of this death?" Yet the fact stared her in the face that Paul had not only asked that question but answered it and said triumphantly, "I thank God, through Jesus Christ our Lord." In her discouragement she began to be afraid that she would lose every bit of religion she possessed. She and her husband, she says, had "learned thoroughly the blessed truth of justification by faith, and rejoiced in it with great joy. But here we had stopped. The equally blessed twin truth of sanctification by faith had not yet been revealed to us."[2]

This new revelation came to Mrs. Pearsall Smith about 1867,

[1] Hannah Whitall Smith, *The Unselfishness of God* (New York, Fleming H. Revell Co., 1903), p. 228.
[2] Hannah Whitall Smith, *The Record of a Happy Life* (Philadelphia, J. B. Lippincott & Co., 1873), p. 37.

B

through a young Baptist theological student who was living in her home as a tutor,[1] and a Methodist dressmaker who lived in the little New Jersey village of Millville to which they had removed. From the tutor she learned that the way of victory was by faith; and from the dressmaker, that there was an experience called the "second blessing," which brought one into a place of victory.[2] She says that she now learned a secret of the Christian life which she had never learned before—the secret of committing her daily life as well as her future destiny to Christ; and she found that when she did that, He gave her deliverance from the power of sin, as well as from its guilt.

At first her husband, thinking she had gone off into heresy, was somewhat frightened. He came into her experience when she called his attention to Rom. vi. 6, "Knowing this, that our old man is crucified with him, that the body of sin might be destroyed, that henceforth we should not serve sin." "It was not," she writes, "that either he or I considered ourselves to have become sinless, or that we never met with any further failures. We had simply discovered the 'secret of victory,' and knew that we were no longer the 'slaves of sin' and therefore forced to yield to its mastery, but that we might, if we would, be made more than conquerors through our Lord Jesus Christ. But this did not mean that temptations ceased to come; and when we neglected to avail ourselves of the 'secret' we had discovered, and, instead of handing the battle over to the Lord, took it into our own hands as of old, failure inevitably followed."[3]

Both of them, with characteristic enthusiasm, gave themselves to the zealous propagation of their new views. Being gifted writers and persuasive speakers, they frequently addressed holiness meetings and wrote magazine articles and books. Neither of them had any training in theology, and Mr. Pearsall Smith was a business man by profession; but they had unusual ability in making abstract religious truths appear practical; indeed, those who heard Mrs. Pearsall Smith say that as a Bible teacher she was second to none. The combined mercantile and evangelistic exertions of Mr. Pearsall Smith became so strenuous that his health became seriously affected. A period of rest and change was recommended by his doctor, and it was thought that this rest and change could be best procured in England. In 1872 he and his family therefore went to England. On

[1] Hannah Whitall Smith, *The Record of a Happy Life* (Philadelphia, J. B. Lippincott & Co., 1873), p. 37.
[2] Hannah Whitall Smith, *The Unselfishness of God*, p. 240.
[3] Ibid., p. 267.

their arrival they found that their fame had preceded them. Before long they were invited to hold some drawing-room meetings in London.

The following spring Mr. Pearsall Smith and the Rev. W. E. Boardman, who also was then in Europe for his health, were asked to speak on the subject of the Higher Christian Life to the Evangelical ministers and other Christian workers of London in groups of thirty or forty, at a series of breakfasts.[1] Twenty-four hundred preachers thus heard their message.

After these breakfasts were over, meetings were held by Mr. Pearsall Smith in various parts of London and vicinity, and then in other parts of England and on the Continent. One of those who accepted the new teaching at this time was the Rev. Evan H. Hopkins, later to become one of the most influential of Keswick leaders. He writes as follows of the effect on Christians of these early meetings: "The result was that very many of God's children both at home and abroad were brought to a deep sense of their need in the sphere of the practical life, and awakened to a more believing expectation that a truer and more triumphant life was possible. The spiritual up-lifting that so many experienced as the result of a clear and definite setting forth of the believer's present privileges, and the possibilities of faith, produced a profound impression upon Christians generally. So sudden and striking were the transformations that took place in the experiences and life of some of God's most earnest workers that even those who regarded the movement with suspicion, were unable to gainsay the reality of the blessings that followed." [2]

(1) THE BROADLANDS CONFERENCE

In the summer of 1874, in response to the request of a number of University men who had found partial blessing in some meetings for consecration held at Cambridge during term time, the Rt. Hon. W. Cowper-Temple (later Lord Mount Temple) opened his country seat, "Broadlands," widely known as the residence of the former Lord Palmerston, for a Conference of six days. About a hundred people attended, all by invitation, among them some of such different outlook as Canon Wilberforce, George Macdonald, Andrew Jukes, Theodore Monod, Madame Antoinette Sterling, Mrs. Amanda

[1] Mrs. W. E. Boardman, op. cit., pp. 156–9.
[2] Charles F. Harford, *The Keswick Convention* (London, Marshall Bros., 1907), pp. 25–26.

Smith, and Ion Keith-Falconer. The purpose of the Conference, we are told, was to "have a few days of quiet prayer and meditation upon the Scriptural possibilities of the Christian life, as to maintained communion with the Lord and victory over all known sin."[1]

Describing these meetings afterwards, Mr. Pearsall Smith, who acted as Chairman, said, "We began with the negative side, renunciation of discerned evil, and even of doubtful things which are not of faith, and therefore sin. For some days the company was held under the searching light of God, to see and to remove any obstacles to a divine communion, aught that frustrated the grace of God. We sought to have that which was true in God as to our judicial standing in a risen Christ also true in personal appropriation and experience. Many secret sins, many a scarcely recognized reserve as to *entire* self-renunciation, were here brought up into the light of consciousness, and put away in the presence of the Lord. We desired to make *thorough* work, so as to leave no known evil or self-will unyielded; and we have reason to hope that those present did so, and that we took the position of solemn purpose to renounce instantly everything in which we should find ourselves 'otherwise minded,' as from time to time 'God shall reveal even this unto us'. . . .

"The provisions in the indwelling Holy Ghost, the exceeding great promises of the Word, the separating power of the cross, the risen Saviour, the life more abundantly, were then set before us in various aspects, and pressed upon us as realities, to be grasped by faith and held with unfaltering grasp. . . .

"In the intervals of the meetings, it was interesting to see groups gathered, in the more secluded places in the wood by the river, on their knees, praying, searching the Scriptures, or speaking earnestly to each other of the all-absorbing subjects of our meetings. Someone had proposed to have reading at meal-times, so as to concentrate our minds; but no such plan was needed to keep the company, even at times of refreshment, to the one engrossing subject."[2]

(2) The Oxford Convention

At the close of the Broadlands Conference it was proposed that the meetings be repeated on a larger scale, so that all who desired could attend. Sir Arthur Blackwood, a well-known Christian layman who at that time was head of the Post-Office in England, thereupon sug-

[1] *Account of the Union Meeting for the Promotion of Scriptural Holiness, held at Oxford, August 29 to September 7, 1874* (Chicago, F. H. Revell, 1875), pp. 19–20.
[2] Ibid., pp. 21–4.

gested that the proposed Convention be held at Oxford, in vacation time. This memorable Conference was accordingly held from August 29th to September 7th, 1874. Although there were but three weeks between the call and the Convention, a large and representative number of clergy and laymen came from all parts of the United Kingdom, and even from the Continent. The invitation announced that it was to be a "Union Meeting for the Promotion of Scriptural Holiness," and opened with this statement, "In every part of Christendom the God of all grace has given to many of His children a feeling of deep dissatisfaction with their present spiritual state, and a strong conviction that the truths they believe might and should exercise a power over their hearts and lives, altogether beyond anything they have as yet experienced. They have been brought to see that personal holiness is God's *purpose* for them as well as His *command* . . . They see with deep distress the grievous gap there is between what they *know* of Scriptural truth, and how they *live*. This is not a reaching out toward new forms of doctrine or of ecclesiastical system, but the felt need of more vitality in what has been already accepted." [1]

The Chairman and principal speaker was Robert Pearsall Smith. Other speakers included Mrs. Pearsall Smith, who gave daily Bible Readings which no one missed hearing; Pasteur Theodore Monod, of Paris; Pastor Otto Stockmayer, from Switzerland; the Revs. Evan H. Hopkins and Filmer Sulivan, of England; while the American Higher Life leaders, Dr. Asa Mahan and Dr. W. E. Boardman also took some part in the meetings.

One of those present at the Convention was the Rev. T. D. Harford-Battersby, Vicar of St. John's, Keswick, who was to become one of the founders of the Keswick Convention. It was the first time he had attended any of Mr. Pearsall Smith's meetings, and for the first few days he was perplexed and uncertain as to the scripturalness of the teaching; but before the Convention ended he not only accepted the teaching but came into a new experience with God which years later he described as follows: "I got a revelation of Christ to my soul, so extraordinary, glorious, and precious, that from that day it illuminated my life. I found *He* was *all* I wanted; I shall never forget it; the day and hour are present with me. How it humbled me, and yet what peace it brought." [2]

[1] *Account of the Union Meeting for the Promotion of Scriptural Holiness, held at Oxford, August 29 to September 7, 1874* (Chicago, F. H. Revell, 1875), pp. 29, 30.
[2] W. B. Sloane, *These Sixty Years* (London, Pickering & Inglis, n.d.), p. 17.

A few weeks later Canon Battersby delivered an address on the Oxford Convention to the members of the Evangelical Union for the Diocese of Carlisle, at their annual conference. It is valuable as being an eye-witness account of one who went there suspicious, but came away convinced. The following are a few excerpts from it:

" I had the great privilege of taking part in that ten days' 'Union Meeting for the promotion of Scriptural holiness,' and language fails me to tell of the richness and fulness of the blessing which was poured out upon us during those wondrous gatherings. We were taken out of ourselves; we were led step by step, after deep and close searchings of heart, to such a consecration of ourselves to God, as in the ordinary times of a religious life hardly seemed possible, and we were brought, hundreds of us, clergy and laymen, men and women, to the enjoyment of a peace in trusting Christ for present and future sanctification which exceeded our utmost hopes. These things were testified openly, evening after evening, as the days went on, by clergymen of the Established Church in the presence of many hundreds of Christian people, and so deep and solemn was the impression produced by these testimonies, and by the faithful teaching of those who were chosen to address the assemblies, that persons who had failed in the earlier days to receive the blessing, a blessing which they saw reflected on the very countenances of their more favoured brethren, were stirred up with intenser earnestness to seek for the same benefit, and, I may add, in the great majority of instances, failed not to find it. I can never forget those happy days. . . . And yet there was nothing whatever of fleshly excitement in the meetings; there were no impassioned addresses; no excited prayers; a still, calm, sober, though deeply earnest spirit, seemed to animate both speakers and hearers. We often knelt in silent prayer, and it was then, perhaps, that the presence of the divine 'Comforter' was most felt, and that our souls were most awed under a sense of His holy yet gracious operations in our hearts. . . .

"In one respect there was no difference between these meetings and others of a religious character which are commonly attended by Evangelical Christians, in that no new or peculiar doctrines were enforced, and that the Word of God and prayer, with the singing of simple hymns, were the sole instruments employed for securing the desired end.

"In another respect, however, there was a difference. There was a definiteness of purpose at these meetings, and a directness of aim in the speakers, which were very remarkable. That purpose was, as expressed in the circular which announced the meetings, 'the promotion of Scriptural holiness.' The aim of the speakers therefore was to bring about this result by an ordered scheme of teaching out of the Holy Scriptures. There was a gradual progress in the truths brought forth. The promises of a condition of abiding holiness; examples of the manner in which it had been sought and attained; the contrast between such a state, and that of the larger portion of the professing Church at the present day; the satisfaction and peace enjoyed by those who have attained to the one, and the unsatisfied state of soul of those who stop short of it; these, and other kindred topics, were pressed home, with every variety of appeal to the hearts of the hearers, and each person was invited to self-examination as to his and her state; to a renunciation of all idols of the flesh and spirit, and to a willing surrender of all to Christ, with a full trust in Him for the bestowal of the blessing asked. Such was the character of the teaching employed; whilst, besides this, opportunity was given daily for clergymen and others, who had come into the enjoyment of that condition of soul which was aimed at, to confess what the Lord had done for them, and bear witness to the results of it in their own experience." [1]

(3) THE BRIGHTON CONVENTION

Within nine months of the great Oxford Convention a still larger series of meetings was held at Brighton. About one thousand attended the former; eight thousand the latter. It was held from May 29th to June 7th, 1875, a period of ten days. People came from many parts of the world to attend it. When, in one of the meetings, the Chairman asked those from other lands to stand, it was found that representatives from twenty-three different countries were present.

During the time of the Convention D. L. Moody was just closing his great evangelistic campaign in Covent Garden, London, and on the opening day of the Convention he said to his audience, "Let us lift up our hearts to seek earnestly a blessing on the great Convention that is now being held in Brighton, perhaps the most important meeting ever gathered"; and he sent the following telegram, "Moody and 8,000 persons at the closing meeting at the

[1] *Account of the Union Meeting for the Promotion of Scriptural Holiness, held at Oxford, August 29 to September 7*, 1874 (Chicago, F. H. Revell, 1875), preface, pp. i–vii.

Opera House have specially prayed for the Convention, that great results may follow." And Mr. Pearsall Smith, the Brighton Chairman, said, "Let us ask an answering blessing upon our beloved brother, Mr. Moody, a man who walks with God."[1]

All the large meeting places in Brighton—the Town Hall, the Corn Exchange, the Dome, and the Royal Pavilion were placed at the disposal of the Committee by the town Corporation, free of charge. Although some of these buildings accommodated several thousand people, it was found that none could hold all those who came to the Convention, so that meetings had to be held simultaneously in different halls. The meetings for prayer held each morning in the Corn Exchange at seven o'clock were attended by about three thousand people, and on most days an overflow meeting had to be arranged in another building. The foreign pastors had frequent meetings by themselves, conducted alternately in French and German.

Mr. and Mrs. Pearsall Smith again took a leading part in the speaking. Other important speakers included Stevenson A. Blackwood, Evan H. Hopkins, Henry Varley, Theodore Monod, H. W. Webb-Peploe, Asa Mahan, and E. W. Moore.

The climax of the Convention was reached in two united Communion services, simultaneously held; Dr. Prochnow, of Berlin, presiding in one, and Pastor Rappard, of St. Chrischona, Basle, in the other, while a number of Continental pastors assisted in the administration. After the Benediction had been pronounced, the Chairman said, "The Brighton Convention has now ended, and the blessings from the Convention have begun."

B. The Keswick Convention

In our account of the Oxford Convention, the Rev. T. D. Harford-Battersby was mentioned as having received great blessing at the meetings. Mr. Battersby was a cultured Balliol man, amongst whose contemporaries at Oxford were Matthew Arnold, Lord Coleridge, and Archbishop Frederick Temple. He was brought up an Evangelical, but while at the university came under the spell of John Henry Newman, and adopted his Tractarian views. Following his graduation, he became curate to one who held Anglo-Catholic views, at Gosport. High-Churchism did not satisfy him, however,

---

[1] Sloan, op. cit., p. 19; and J. B. Figgis, *Keswick from Within* (London, Marshall Bros., 1914), p. 34.

and in two years he exchanged it for the Broad-Churchism of the Rev. Frederick W. H. Myers, author of *Catholic Thoughts* and of the well-known poem, *St. Paul,* in whom he seemed "to find a guide and a prophet," [1] and whose curate he became. The one satisfied him no more than the other, and it was not long before he returned to the Evangelical fold. In two years Mr. Myers died, and Mr. Battersby succeeded him at Keswick.

But although he served his parish at Keswick conscientiously and faithfully, and became a leader of the Evangelicals in the diocese of Carlisle, he still was not fully satisfied with his Christian attainments. In 1873 he wrote in his diary, "At this moment I am feeling much inward struggle and questioning about this 'higher Christian life' which is so much talked of and written about. . . . What I have been reading of the experience of others, Mr. Pearsall Smith and his excellent wife and their wonderful boy, 'Frank,' has made me utterly dissatisfied with myself and my state. I feel that I am dishonouring God and am wretched myself by living as I do; and that I *must* either go backwards or forwards, reaching out towards the light and the glory which my blessed Saviour holds out to me, or falling back more and more into worldliness and sin." [2] It was at the Oxford Convention that he found the more satisfactory experience he was looking for.

At the Brighton Convention Canon Battersby and a friend of his, Mr. Robert Wilson, a Quaker who also was specially blessed at Oxford, desiring that others should share what now meant so much to them, decided to hold a Convention at Keswick, where similar teaching should be given. They accordingly invited some of the leading speakers at Brighton to take part, among them Mr. and Mrs. Pearsall Smith. Mr. Pearsall Smith promised to preside. The meetings were to begin on June 29th, only three weeks after the close of the Brighton Convention. The invitation was headed, "Union Meetings for the Promotion of Practical Holiness," and Christians of every section of the Church of God were invited to attend.

Within a few days of the opening of the Convention it was suddenly announced that all of Mr. Pearsall Smith's engagements were cancelled, and that he was returning to America. No explanation was given; but at the Oxford Convention Mr. Pearsall Smith

[1] *Memoir of T. D. Harford-Battersby*, by Two of His Sons. (London, Seeley & Co., 1890), p. 58.
[2] Ibid., p. 151,

had told of a fall from a horse that he had had in 1861 which had been followed by congestion of the brain and long-continued distressing nervous symptoms,[1] and it was said by some that a return of this disorder now rendered a complete rest necessary. His unexpected and dramatic withdrawal, however, created a most trying situation for the promoters of the Keswick meetings, as disquieting rumours filled the land that the real reasons for his withdrawal were erroneous teaching and immoral conduct. Other expected speakers also withdrew, and for a while there was question whether the Conference would not have to be called off. Canon Battersby quickly got in touch with other speakers, however, and it was decided to hold the meetings.

The Conference was held in a tent with about three hundred or four hundred people attending. The speakers were the Revs. H. W. Webb-Peploe, George R. Thornton, and T. Phillips; Mr. H. F. Bowker, Mr. T. M. Croome, and Mr. Murray Shipley (an American). Canon Battersby occupied the chair at all the meetings, and every evening he would apportion next day's work to the speakers.

When the meetings were over, Canon Battersby wrote to *The Record* of the blessing that had been received in them, and said, in part, "Hundreds attended from all parts of the United Kingdom, and it was, I believe, the universal feeling of those who came together that our loss was in reality our gain." Then after acknowledging the debt which he and thousands more owed to Mr. Pearsall Smith, he added, "The Lord has been showing us, in a wonderful way, that if He chooses to lay aside one instrument, He can and will find others to testify of His truth, and to carry on His work."[2]

Before the end of the year Mr. Pearsall Smith's friends were compelled to issue an explanation regarding his departure. It ran as follows, "Rumours of an exceedingly painful character with regard to a prominent teacher, which had for some time been in private circulation having now had currency given to them in your and other papers, we consider it right, in the interests of truth, and in justice to the person in question, to make the following statement: Some weeks after the Brighton Convention, it came to our knowledge that the individual referred to had, on some occasions in personal conversation, inculcated doctrines which were most unscriptural and dangerous. We also found there had been conduct

---

[1] *Account of the Union Meeting for the Promotion of Scriptural Holiness, held at Oxford, August 29 to September 7*, 1874 (Chicago, F. H. Revell, 1875), pp. 134 ff.
[2] W. B. Sloan, op. cit., p. 22.

which, although we were convinced that it was free from evil intention, was yet such as to render action necessary on our part. We therefore requested him to abstain at once from all public work, and when the circumstances were represented to him in their true light, he entirely acquiesced in the propriety of this course, and recognized with deep sorrow the unscriptural and dangerous character of the teaching and conduct in question. In addition to the above, a return of the distressing attacks of the brain, from which he had previously suffered, rendered the immediate cessation from work an absolute necessity." [1]

Although Mr. Pearsall Smith lived almost a quarter of a century more, his public career as a leader of conferences was over, and the rest of his life was spent in quiet seclusion.

The whole movement was subjected to such violent criticism and opposition, that it was uncertain at first whether the Keswick Convention would be held again the next year. To identify oneself with the Higher Life teaching meant to be willing to be separated from the leaders of the Evangelical Church. Canon Battersby felt it necessary carefully to review his position before deciding to call another Convention at Keswick. In his diary there appears the following note, written at this time, 'There must be a thorough sifting of my motives, opinions, and conduct before God. If I feel that I have erred, let me acknowledge it. If not, to God let me commit my cause, and stand fast as a rock, trusting in Him!" [2] He decided definitely and deliberately that there could be no retracing of his steps. The following spring he and Mr. Wilson decided to hold another Convention. After that there was never any doubt that it should be held yearly. Since then it has grown year by year, until now those who attend, coming from many parts of the world, number in the thousands.

C. Other "Keswick" Conventions

Although the Convention at Keswick has come to be associated in a unique way with a particular kind of religious teaching and experience, it must not be thought that it is the only one of its kind. At first it was only one of many similar Conventions held in the British Isles, some of them also annual. There was nothing

---

[1] B. B. Warfield, *Perfectionism* (New York, Oxford University Press, 1931), pp. 506-7.
[2] W. B. Sloan, op. cit., p. 23.

to distinguish it from them. Before many years, however, it grew to be the largest and came to be regarded as the most prominent of them. It became the mother of similar Conventions in Scotland, Ireland, and other parts of England, at which its leaders became the principal speakers.

We have seen that at the Oxford and Brighton Conventions there were pastors present from many different lands. Some of them, when they returned to their own people, started Conferences of a similar type among them. Moreover, before Mr. Pearsall Smith dropped out of conference work, he was enthusiastically received by Christian leaders in various countries on the Continent, and held meetings there almost rivalling in size and interest those he held in England.

Almost from the beginning, the Keswick Convention has sent some of its leaders to other countries to hold conventions or missions on the Keswick plan. These missioners have carried the Keswick message to almost every corner of the world. Today, there are probably few countries that do not have a "Keswick" convention of their own.

CHAPTER II

THE METHOD OF KESWICK

The methods characteristic of the Keswick Convention are quite as important as what is actually taught there, and bear quite as distinct a stamp of peculiarity and individuality. Indeed, it is doubtful if the teaching can be accurately understood and evaluated apart from a knowledge of the methods of the Convention. The two cannot be dissociated.

Bible-centred

The first and perhaps most important particular of the Keswick method is that it is Bible-centred. The Convention stands for no particular brand of denominational theology. It could not, and have on its platform men of many different denominational affiliations. There is only one thing that deeply concerns the Keswick leaders, and that is what God has to say. One of the first things that strikes a person who hears or reads the addresses given at the Convention is the evident effort of the speakers to make the Bible alone their criterion of what is truth. One may agree or disagree with their interpretation of the Scriptures under consideration, but there is never any doubt that central in their thought is what God has to say.

Problems of Higher Criticism are never brought up at any of the meetings. It is not that the speakers are not interested in, or are ignorant of them, for not a few have been scholars of high rank, but simply that there is no question in their minds that the whole Bible is God's word to us. They never argue about or try to defend it. Yet the attitude towards the Bible is not the obscurantist one found in so much of modern fundamentalism.

Keswick holds that God's Word must be taken seriously, for it is God speaking to us. A fundamental reason for the spiritual deadness and ineffectiveness of the Christian Church is that too often the Bible is regarded merely as a book of doctrines which must be believed, or a religious textbook with which Christians must become familiar. Christians give little more than mental assent to what it teaches. It is not regarded as having very much practical value. Early Keswick meetings were called Conventions "for the promotion of *practical* holiness." Keswick teaches that the Bible is first of all a practical book, and that when it is taken seriously life is revolutionized.

Christians admit that the Bible is literally full of promises for them, but they admit that only a small proportion are believed and claimed. For Keswick the gravest sin of the Church is unbelief, for it makes God to be a liar.

A saying frequently heard at Keswick is this, "God's commandment is His enablement," meaning that God never issues a command that He does not give us grace to fulfil. And so Keswick tells us that the divine commandments must be taken as seriously as God's promises. They are not merely ideals which we are to strive to carry out to the best of our ability.

For many years Keswick meetings have been called Conventions "for the promotion of *scriptural* holiness." It is admitted by all that Christians are commanded to be holy, and yet the frank admission is universally made that few Christians are holy. Why is this failure so prevalent? Keswick says, Let us get back to the Scriptures and see what they have to say.

A Spiritual Clinic

Keswick popularized Bible conferences and conventions. Before the founding of Keswick, the United States had its holiness camp meetings, and England had a small but influential conference at Mildmay, founded by the Rev. William Pennefather; but today there are probably hundreds of Bible conferences in the two countries. Yet, with a few exceptions, there is a fundamental difference between them and Keswick. They aim to impart Bible knowledge and to give some spiritual inspiration. People who attend them come away knowing more of what the Bible teaches. Cold facts have been learned in academic fashion. Fellowship with other Christians has a quickening effect; but in a short time this wears off, and in another year they are back for more knowledge and inspiration.

Keswick, on the other hand, is more like a spiritual clinic. The Church should be an army on the march; instead, it is a hospital full of wounded soldiers. Keswick frankly recognizes that many who attend the Convention, especially for the first time, are spiritual casualties of one sort or another. Addresses on the Bible, whether factual or inspirational, will not put wounded Christians on their feet and into the spiritual conflict again. The problem is much more serious than that. Sin is a spiritual disease, bringing paralysis, blindness, deafness, and lameness of soul. Only drastic treatment dealing with the root of the trouble will effect a cure. Mild sedatives and soothing medicines accomplish nothing permanent. Bones out of joint need adjustment before the patient can walk in God's ways and march in His army. And so Keswick, in its diagnosis of the state of the Church, finds it in a dangerously unhealthy condition, and looks upon the Convention as a place where health may be restored and the Christian may learn how health may be maintained. The aim of the Conference is therefore a very practical one, just as a hospital is a very practical place. One deals with soul, the other with physical, cures.

Keswick is sometimes called a mission to Christians, just as evangelistic meetings are a mission to the unsaved. It is true that people are frequently converted at the meetings, but the messages are addressed primarily to Christians, with the purpose just given.

A good deal of the best work of the Convention is done not in the meetings by means of the addresses, but in personal dealings with souls by the leaders. It is understood that any of the speakers may be consulted without the formality of an introduction, and many interviews take place during the week, "almost like patients consulting physicians as to their spiritual ailments."[1] Explanations are asked, difficulties settled, and objections met.

The effectiveness of the Keswick method of dealing with spiritual problems is shown by the fact that during the week of the Convention many letters have been written and telegrams sent making confession of wrong done. Emotionalism has no place in the meetings, but on occasions the Holy Spirit comes down in such power that the effect is overwhelming. Dr. A. T. Pierson relates such an incident which took place during the 1905 Convention.

"While Rev. E. W. Moore was giving an address on 1 Cor. iii. 2–15, on 'The Ordeal of Fire,' I, who was to follow him, felt God's refining fire going through me, revealing the wood, hay, and stubble of work and motive. So humbling and overwhelming was this conviction, that when called upon to lead in prayer and address the meeting, it was quite involuntary first of all to make

[1] J. Elder Cumming, *The Blessed Life* (Stirling, Drummond Tract Depot, n.d.), p. 180.

a confession and ask others, who likewise had felt conscious of
God's direct dealing, to stand before God as those who then and
there besought Him to refine us now. In response to that invitation
practically the whole tent-full of people rose as one man, and, while
prayer were being offered, many joined in an audible 'Amen.' Not
one word of my proposed address was ever delivered, nor was the
subject even indicated. There was no need of leadership. Another
and greater One was in control, invisibly present and presiding.

"The prayer was scarcely concluded, when a spirit of penitent
confession broke out in every quarter, and I stood there on my feet
for about two hours and a half, witnessing the Holy Spirit's won-
derous working. A soldier acknowledged desertion and theft, and
left the tent to write out his confession, and some of us, later on,
saw the letters that he had written. A commander in the navy
declared his purpose to make his ship a floating Bethel. No less
than fifty clergymen, evangelists and leaders in Christian work,
confessed to sins of avarice, ambition, appetite, lust of applause,
neglect of the Word, of prayer, of souls; hundreds of other individuals confessed various sins of omission and commission, sometimes a half-dozen or more on their feet at once.

"No improper word was spoken. All was subdued, but deep,
intense, searching. The meeting might have gone on without decline
of interest, had not motives of expediency and consideration for
others prevailed. When we closed with old 'Coronation' at 10.30,
there had been no disturbance. Penitence, confession, prayer, self-
surrender, holy resolve, had led up to praise and adoration. Then
the great throng quietly separated with the profound sense that
God had visited His people." [1]

It is said that no man can attend a Keswick Convention and be
the same afterwards: he is either a better or a worse man for it.
Why this should be so will be seen when it is kept in mind that
the object of the Convention is to deal with the problem of sin from
the scriptural standpoint. When a Christian is faced with God's
view of sin, he is faced with a crisis. If he chooses not to part with
his sin, he will inevitably be a worse man for it; if he surrenders
it, his life will of necessity be transformed. Keswick proposes to
help him in this fundamental problem.

[1] D. L. Pierson, *A. T. Pierson* (New York, Fleming Revell Company 1912), pp.
292–3.

A Witnessing Platform

It follows from the practical nature of the Convention that its speakers should be men specially equipped and fitted to accomplish its end. As long ago as 1879 Canon Battersby spoke the following words regarding the Keswick standard for its speakers, "Our desire is to let those speak to us and lead us, not who are able to make the most eloquent speeches, but whom God has manifestly led into the secret of the divine life, and who are willing to be nothing, and let Him speak through them; men who will be faithful with us and not spare us, but set forth very plainly our sins, and the things that hinder our full enjoyment of God's peace and our growth in holiness."[1] Evan H. Hopkins bears similar testimony, "It cannot be too clearly stated that those who are asked to speak at this and other similar conventions are those, only, who can bear testimony to a definite experience of the fulness of blessing."[2]

Dr. A. T. Pierson describes more in detail the basis of choosing Keswick speakers. "To an unusual extent, at Keswick, God is magnified, and, as an inevitable consequence, it continues to be true that little deference is paid to men, as such. Great learning and scholarship, rhetorical and oratorical gifts and accomplishments, high social and ecclesiastical position, while not undervalued or depreciated, are by no means overrated. Keswick stands for a peculiar type, both of spiritual teaching and living, and to this all else is consistently subordinated. Those who by conviction hold these truths, and by experiment have tested them, are asked to take part, and no others. It is held that all spiritual truth demands for effective teaching the authority found in *testimony*. Christ sent out as *heralds* only those who were also *witnesses*. The most renowned theological professor, eloquent preacher, or successful evangelist, who might be in a Keswick meeting, would not be asked to speak on its platform, apart from some personal knowledge of the peculiar truth there held and taught. There is a certain witness to the reality of a truth which, even though it finds no direct utterances in the narration of definite experience, gives a strange and unmistakable air of confidence and a peculiar sanction of authority; and such speech, with the whole man behind it, is what

[1] A. T. Pierson, *The Keswick Movement* (New York and London, Funk & Wagnalls Co., 1903), pp. 46–7.
[2] A. T. Pierson, *Forward Movements of the Last Half Century* (New York and London, Funk & Wagnalls Co., 1900), p. 30.

c

is coveted at Keswick. It is a noticeable seal of the Holy Spirit on this unwritten rule and standard that very seldom any man who speaks on this platform gives the impression that he is exploiting himself. This is not the place where 'star sermons' and brilliant rhetorical efforts would find a congenial atmosphere or a sympathetic hearing. There is something indescribable and indefinable in these assemblies which would go far to stifle an ambitious orator. Almost all the addresses are simple expositions of the Word of God, and impress the hearer as quite devoid of attempts at mere literary effect." [1]

From all this it is evident that only those speakers are chosen for the Keswick platform who know experimentally the doctrine of sanctification by faith, and who know how to bring others into the enjoyment of this blessing. Keswick leaders speak not as advocates but as witnesses, as those who have personally experienced the power of the teaching they inculcate. A witnessing platform is distinctive of the Keswick Convention, and is as characteristic as any part of its teaching.

It is because the leaders speak as witnesses of a definite experience, that an impressive feature of their teaching is *definiteness*. They aim at inducing definite personal dealing with God in regard to deliverance from the power of sin, consecration to God, and apprehension of the fulness of the Spirit. It is believed that one of the most important reasons for the unsatisfactoriness of so much Christian living is that Christian experience is indefinite and vague. Keswick speakers must therefore have had a definite experience of the blessing they try to lead others into. It is obvious that where spiritual ill-health is present, good and eloquent speaking with the aim merely of giving an academic study of some portion of the Bible or of inducing a nice religious feeling will accomplish little in the way of healing. "Physician, heal thyself," will be said to such doctors of the soul.

Unity of Spirit

Over the main entrance to the large tent in which the meetings are held at Keswick, and also over the platform, is a large sign with the words, ALL ONE IN CHRIST JESUS. This has been the watchword of the Convention from the beginning, and may be said to be the foundation stone of the harmony, brotherly love, and fellowship that have always characterized it. The unity of spirit that

[1] A. T. Pierson, *The Keswick Movement*, pp. 55–8.

prevails at the Convention is one of its most impressive features. When it is remembered that the speakers come from many different denominations, this is a remarkable fact.

One writer has said, "After attending the Keswick Convention for over twenty-five years, I consider that its most striking feature is the marvellous oneness of spirit which exists among all Christians. We meet in a realm above what we might call earthly divisions, and find ourselves one in Christ Jesus. In my judgment it is the nearest answer to our Lord's Prayer 'That they all might be one'." [1]

Speakers are not permitted to discuss controversial matters at the Convention. They consider themselves pledged (so far as possible) not to teach during the course of any Keswick Convention any doctrines or opinions but those upon which there is general agreement among the promoters of the Convention. The Convention is organized for the purpose of setting forth the truths of scriptural holiness, and all speakers are expected to be one on these, although they may differ on other matters.

Because of the unity of spirit that prevails at the Convention, the movement has never been found to cause divisions in churches. Dr. A. T. Pierson says that no man or woman has ever been known, through its influence or under its teaching, to leave one communion for another. [2] On the contrary, those who accept the Keswick teaching and enter into the experience of a fuller life which it proclaims as the privilege of Christians, incline to remain where they are, and infuse new life into moribund or dead churches.

Progressive Nature of the Teaching

Since the Keswick Convention has a definite aim and purpose to accomplish in its meetings, it is to be expected that the subjects of the addresses will not be haphazardly chosen. The teaching given at the Convention has a beginning, middle, and culmination, and follows a definite, progressive order. The teaching moves on, step by step, with definite results aimed at. It leads first to a negative step, the renunciation of all known sin, and then to a positive step, surrender to Christ for the infilling of the Holy Spirit.

Since the cause of spiritual ill-health is always sin, whether known or unknown, on the first day of the Convention the searchlight of God's Word is focused on sin, and an effort is made to bring the

[1] C. F. Harford, op. cit., p. 112.
[2] A. T. Pierson, *Forward Movements of the Last Half Century*, p. 41.

Christian to its immediate abandonment. On the second day the speakers consider the subject of God's provision for sin, and it is taught that God through Christ has dealt with the whole problem of sin in so final a way that it need not be a continued source of trouble. The consecration of the Christian is the topic of the third day. On the fourth day the addresses are on the fulness of the Spirit. Christian service, including missionary responsibility, is the topic of the last day.

It must not be thought, however, that this is a mechanical, cast-iron pattern, allowing no flexibility or variation, for the general outline is never filled in twice alike. The order of Keswick teaching has been shaped, not by conscious design, but half-unconsciously and without deliberation; because it was observed that there are these successive stages of experience through which believers generally pass who enter into the Spirit-filled life. At the basis of the whole is the conviction that the average Christian life is lacking in real spiritual power, and the belief that God has made it possible for all Christians to live, in the power of Christ's resurrection, a life of consistent victory and effective service.

Types of Meetings

About half a dozen different meetings a day are held during the week of the Convention. The day begins with two early morning prayer meetings, held simultaneously—one of a general character, and one for missionary work. These are followed by a Bible Reading, which is generally given by the same speaker all through the week. There are three general meetings, in the morning, afternoon, and evening; the latter was formerly followed by an after-meeting, in which Christians were urged and helped to come to a definite decision regarding the spiritual problem that faced them—which may have to do with the giving up of some sin, consecration, the infilling of the Holy Spirit, or surrender for service: but these after-meetings have been discontinued as a practice; though they are held when thought needful. Besides these meetings of a general character, there are special meetings—for young people, for ministers, for missionaries and overseas visitors, and sometimes also for women. Besides these official meetings others are held, not sponsored by the Convention, but by different missionary organizations and by other special groups, such as university men, who are in Keswick for the Convention, and these are frequently addressed by the Convention speakers.

In all these meetings there is no attempt to use devices for attracting large crowds. There are no paid singers and no elaborate music, sacred song being solely of the congregational type, and used only as an aid to worship and teaching. There is a marked absence of anything tending to emotionalism. All the meetings are characterized by simplicity.

From early days suggestions were issued by the conveners to those attending the Convention, to help them in fulfilling their object in coming:

"We have met as Christians to wait upon the Lord for the fulfilment in us of those promises of grace which He has made to us in Jesus Christ. For the better securing of this end particular attention is requested to the following suggestions:

1. Come waiting on the Lord, desiring and expecting blessing to your own soul individually.

2. Be ready to learn whatever God may teach you by His word, however opposed to human prejudices and traditions.

3. Heartily renounce all known evil and even doubtful things 'not of faith.'

4. Lay aside for the time all reading except the Bible.

5. Avoid conversation which has a tendency to divert your mind from the object of the meetings. Do not dispute with any, but rather pray with those who differ from you.

6. Eat moderately, dress simply, retire to rest early." [1]

The Holy Spirit Exalted

From the very beginning of the Keswick Convention, the Holy Spirit has been regarded as the real Leader of the meetings. In all that pertains to the Convention—the choice of speakers, the topics chosen by the speakers, the conduct of the meetings, the administration of the Convention as a whole—the Holy Spirit is looked to as the divine Guide and Governor. This is done consciously, with full expectation that He who has been given by the Father as the Director of the affairs of the Church, knows what is best for it. Consequently, prayer is emphasized as the condition of all success and blessing. There is a habitual waiting on God in prayer, both in the meetings and in preparation for them. It may be said, of course, that the leaders of every Bible conference look to God in

[1] C. F. Harford, op. cit., p. 8.

prayer and take it for granted that wisdom will be given by the
Holy Spirit for the direction of its affairs, but it may be doubted
whether in every such conference there is the same conscious waiting in prayer that the Holy Spirit, and He alone, may lead and
have His way. One has to go back to the Book of Acts for a parallel
to the exaltation of the Holy Spirit found in the meetings at
Keswick.

PART II

THE SEQUENCE OF TEACHING
AT KESWICK

CHAPTER III

THE EXCEEDING SINFULNESS OF SIN

We have said that Keswick does not regard itself primarily as a Bible Conference in the usual sense—that is, as a place where Christians come together for fellowship, spiritual uplift, and an increased knowledge of the Bible; but rather as a spiritual clinic to which Christians come to have the great Physician, the Lord Himself, diagnose and heal their spiritual ailments. Keswick is indeed more than a clinic; it is also a place of revelation and challenge—a place where Christians come to a realization of the wealth of their spiritual inheritance in Christ, and are challenged to enter into possession of this heritage, that they may be fitted for Christ's service;[1] but there is no doubt of the truth of a statement often made by Dr. F. B. Meyer, "Keswick is a spiritual clinic."

Another Keswick speaker said, "In a clinic, the first need is accurate diagnosis, and therefore it is not surprising that the first aim proposed at Keswick is the discovery and acknowledgement of 'the sin that doth so easily beset us.' "[2] People therefore come together, he says, that they might know "what the Lord has to say concerning their besetments and weaknesses."[3]

On the opening day of the Convention the topic dealt with by the various speakers is the exceeding sinfulness of sin. It is a day of deep heart-searching, when the searchlight of God's Word is turned upon the inmost recesses of the soul, and sin is laid bare.

It is often said that the one great heresy which afflicts a large part of the Church and keeps back the conquest of the world for

[1] *The Keswick Convention*, 1938, pp. 53, 54.
[2] *The Keswick Convention in Print*, 1941, p. 15.
[3] Ibid., p. 14.

Christ, is a defective view of sin. From the first, opponents of Keswick have accused it of holding a shallow view of sin. The charge is a serious one, and if true would lend great weight to another charge made against the Convention, that it is perfectionist. If one's view of sin were only shallow enough, sinless perfection would not be an impossible attainment.

Keswick holds that its view of sin is not different from that held by Evangelical Christians generally. Is that true? In considering this question it is important to keep in mind that the speakers of the Convention represent many denominations, and that in many cases they are outstanding leaders in their own denominations. Dr. F. B. Meyer was for years regarded as perhaps the outstanding Baptist in the world. Dr. A. T. Pierson had an international reputation as an American Presbyterian clergyman. No writer of devotional literature was better known in the Dutch- and English-speaking world than Dr. Andrew Murray, who was also a leader in the Dutch Reformed Church of South Africa. J. Elder Cumming and George H. C. Macgregor were Presbyterians of wide renown in Scotland. No other clergy in the Evangelical branch of the Anglican Church were held in higher esteem than Dr. H. C. G. Moule, Bishop of Durham, Prebendary H. W. Webb-Peploe, Principal W. H. Griffith Thomas, and Dr. J. Stuart Holden. It is difficult to see how such men could have remained denominational leaders while holding shallow views of sin.

In this chapter we shall do two things. First we shall examine the Keswick view of sin, in order to see whether or not the charges sometimes made against it that it is shallow are valid; and then, since the Keswick message is directed primarily to Christians, we shall seek to discover what the Convention has to say about the sin of Christians.

A. The Keswick View of Sin

Before proceeding to an investigation of the Keswick view of sin, let us briefly set forth some definitions of sin given by Protestant scholars the adequacy of whose views no one ever questions, in order that we may see whether Keswick's teaching is at variance with the generally accepted Protestant viewpoint.

Writing on the Protestant doctrine of sin, Charles Hodge says, "The Protestant Churches at the time of the Reformation did not attempt to determine the nature of sin philosophically. . . . Founding their doctrine on their moral and religious consciousness and upon the Word of God, they declared sin to be the transgression of, or want of conformity to, the divine law. In this definition all classes of theologians, Lutheran and Reformed, agree. . . .

"It is included in these definitions: (1) That sin is a specific evil, differing from all other forms of evil. (2) That sin stands related to law. The two are correlative, so that where there is no law, there can be no sin. (3) That the law to which sin is thus related, is not merely the law of reason, or of conscience, or of expediency, but the law of God. (4) That sin consists essentially in the want of conformity on the part of a rational creature, to the nature or law of God. (5) That it includes guilt and moral pollution." [1]

A. H. Strong's definition of sin is similar to that of Charles Hodge. "Sin is lack of conformity to the moral law of God, either in act, disposition, or state." [2]

R. C. Trench in his classic book, *Synonyms of the New Testament*,[3] says that sin is represented in the New Testament under a large number of aspects, but chiefly under eight. It is chiefly regarded, he says, as the missing of a mark or aim, the overpassing or transgressing of a line, the disobedience to a voice, the falling where one should have stood upright, ignorance of what one ought to have known, diminishing of that which should have been rendered in full measure, non-observance of a law, and a discord in the harmonies of God's universe.

The definitions of sin by Charles Hodge and A. H. Strong are universally regarded as adequate. No one has ever charged them with being shallow or of falling short of the scriptural estimate of sin. And while R. C. Trench does say that it would be easy to give more than the eight New Testament synonyms for sin he mentions, no one questions that the eight he does give are the principal ones in the New Testament. But every Keswick speaker I know of would subscribe without question to the definitions of Hodge and Strong, and would accept Trench's remarks on the New Testament conception of sin.

In proceeding to a careful investigation of the Keswick view of sin, we are confronted with two difficulties. The first is that since no Keswick speaker has ever given us a treatise of Keswick teaching,

[1] Charles Hodge, *Systematic Theology* (New York, Charles Scribner's Sons, 1888), II, pp. 180-1.
[2] A. H. Strong, *Systematic Theology* (Philadelphia, Judson Press, 1946), p. 549.
[3] R. C. Trench, *Synonyms of the New Testament* (London, Macmillan & Co., 1880), pp. 239-40.

there exists no complete and authoritative presentation of the Keswick view of sin. The second is that Keswick is interested in the practical application of religious truth rather than in doctrinal or dogmatic theology. For this reason the Keswick view of sin must be gleaned from the annual Convention reports and the many volumes of devotional literature the speakers have written. One of the best of the latter is Evan H. Hopkins's *The Law of Liberty in the Spiritual Life*, which has a chapter on sin which is the nearest thing to a Keswick definition of sin we can find. It summarizes excellently most of what Mr. Hopkins had to say in his Convention addresses on the subject over a period of many years, and there is nothing in it at variance with what other Convention speakers have taught. Let us examine this chapter.

Mr. Hopkins begins by asking, What is sin? He replies that there are two things it certainly is not: it is not "an inseparable adjunct to our human nature,"[1] for it was not a part of man as originally created, nor is it "a necessary constituent of our moral progress"[2] or spiritual advancement. Mr. Hopkins rejects both the idea of Greek philosophy that matter is inherently evil and that therefore, since our bodies are made of matter, sin is an inseparable part of man, and the idea of modern evolutionary philosophy that in the upward progress of man he will some day come to the place where he will outgrow the need of sinning. He says that it is only as we look at sin in relation to God that we can understand its real character. It has, moreover, many aspects and must be considered from various points of view. He then deals with six of its most important aspects.

(1) Sin is an Offence against God

In its essential character, sin is rebellion against God and want of conformity to the will of God, which the law reveals. Essentially, it is lawlessness. Man has trangressed God's law. His sin must be punished and atoned for. It cannot simply be overlooked. The fact that it is only through Christ's atoning death that sin can be put away shows what an awful offence against God sin is.

Mr. Hopkins certainly does not minimize sin's heinousness as an offence against God.

---

[1] Evan H. Hopkins, *The Law of Liberty in the Spiritual Life* (London, Marshall Bros., 1905), p. 3.
[2] Ibid., p. 4.

According to the Scriptures, God created man completely good, with no bias or tendency to act contrary to the wishes of his Creator. He was created an essentially dependent being, his principle of existence lying not in himself but in God. He was also created with self-awareness. He was conscious that he was a being separate and distinct from God and that he had the power, as a free moral being, of making choices displeasing to God. From the moment that he became aware of these facts there was opened to him the terrible alternative of making God or self the centre of his life. Everything in his make-up and experience told him that true happiness for him lay in continued dependence upon and obedience to God, and that only so could he fulfil the end of his being.

But the time came when he thought he could increase his happiness if he ceased directing his life to God and lived a life independent of Him. He rebelled against his Maker. St. Augustine describes this sin as the result of pride, as a movement whereby a creature decided to set up on his own and live for himself. It was an act of lawlessness, a refusal to conform to the will of God for him. This act of self-will constituted an utter falseness to his true creaturely position, and resulted in the Fall. Scripture teaches that man's rebellion was an offence against God's sovereignty. Such an offence could not be overlooked by God, for that would be contrary to His holy nature. Man is therefore guilty before God who created him, and his sin has to be punished and atoned for. The awfulness of this offence against God is shown by two facts—by the fact that as a result of it fellowship between God and man was broken, and by the fact that only Christ's atoning death could heal the breach between them.

(2) Sin is a Ruling Principle in Man

Although Scripture calls specific outward acts of rebellion against God sin, it does not limit transgression to such outward violations of God's law. Transgression, Mr. Hopkins says, "includes all those *inner* activities of the soul which are opposed to the mind and character of God."[1] Man is a slave to sin, and every part of his nature—his mind, his emotions, his will—is brought under its sway.

"Consider what it is that the fall has involved. It has not only brought upon man the penalty due to sin as an offence, it has en-

[1] Evan H. Hopkins, *The Law of Liberty in the Spiritual Life* (London, Marshall Bros., 1905), p. 8.

slaved him under sin as a ruling principle. Sin is a power that has entered into the central citadel of a man's being, and, establishing itself there, has brought every part of his nature under its sway. Sin is a principle that is essentially opposed to God, and by taking possession of man's will and affections, makes him an enemy of God, and leads him out into open rebellion against Him. Man has thus become a slave to sin." [1]

Certainly this aspect of sin considered by Mr. Hopkins is one of the most important in the New Testament, where the fact is stressed that as a result of the Fall man's whole psycho-physical constitution became corrupted. Romans vi and vii, especially, deal with sin as a ruling principle in man. Our old nature was crucified with Christ, that we might be freed from the service of sin (Rom. vi. 6), that we might be freed from its power (Rom. vi. 7), and that it might have no more dominion over us (Rom. vi. 9).

Perhaps nowhere in Scripture is man's helplessness in the grip of sin more powerfully described than in Romans vii, where Paul, after confessing that the things he wanted to do he found himself unable to do, and the things he did not want to do he found himself compelled to do, cried out in utter despair, "O wretched man that I am! who shall deliver me from the body of this death" (verse 24).

It is this aspect of sin as a ruling principle in man's heart that caused Amiel, himself not a Christian, to say, "The cardinal question is that of sin." He meant man's innately sinful nature, which has been his major problem ever since the Fall, and has been the root of all wicked acts. Man's insistence on his right to himself, when he first rebelled against God, became a ruling principle in him.

There is no doubt that Mr. Hopkins has a thorough grasp of this aspect of sin, and that he goes as far as Scripture permits him to do.

(3) SIN IS MORAL DEFILEMENT

Besides being an offence that has brought upon man penal consequences, and a ruling principle reigning from the central part of his nature over the whole man, sin is also an uncleanness that makes him unfit for God's presence. Man is conscious not only of guilt and moral helplessness, but of defilement. God's holiness cannot tolerate any spiritual uncleanness or pollution in His children. One

[1] Evan H. Hopkins, *The Law of Liberty in the Spiritual Life* (London, Marshall Bros., 1905), p. 18.

purpose of the death of Christ was to "purify unto Himself a peculiar people" by separating them from sin's defilement.

Every reader of the Scriptures is aware that they have much to say about sin as moral defilement. Spiritual uncleanness makes man unfit for God's presence. When man stands before God and gets a vision of His holiness, he is overwhelmed with a sense of his sinfulness and falls down prostrate before Him. We see this again and again in Scripture, as when Isaiah cried out in the temple, "Woe is me! for I am undone; because I am a man of unclean lips, and I dwell in the midst of a people of unclean lips: for mine eyes have seen the King, the Lord of hosts" (Isa. vi. 5). Even non-Christians have an innate sense of the pollution of sin. Perhaps one of the most vivid illustrations in literature of this aspect of sin is found in *Macbeth*, where Lady Macbeth, trying vainly to wash the stain of blood from the hand that murdered the king, pathetically weeps, "Not all the perfumes of Arabia can sweeten this little hand."

(4) SIN IS A SPIRITUAL DISEASE

"Sin is to the soul," says Mr. Hopkins, "what disease is to the body. The effect of disease on our physical organism is just a picture of what sin produces in our spiritual nature." [1]

Mr. Hopkins says that it will help us to understand what sin is in this special aspect, and what it is to be freed from its disabling effects, if we look at our Lord's miracles of healing as illustrations of what He is now doing in the way of spiritual healing upon the souls of men. The physical ailments Jesus cured may be looked upon as setting forth different aspects of sin as a disease that He cures.

For example, take paralysis, which is the loss of the power of voluntary muscular motion, attacking sometimes the whole body, sometimes only a part of it. "Sin has precisely the same effect on our souls. Though there is spiritual life, there may be lack of spiritual vigour. The effect of sin may be traced in the impairment of voluntary power, and in the enfeebling of all moral energy, as well as in the hardening and deadening of the spiritual sense. And the result is the whole tone of the spiritual life is lowered. Sin thus robs us of the power by which alone we are able to perform the functions that belong to our renewed being. And it not only under-

---

[1] Evan H. Hopkins, *The Law of Liberty in the Spiritual Life* (London, Marshall Bros., 1905), p. 8.

mines our strength, it hinders our growth. . . . The new birth may have taken place, the great change of conversion to God may have been clear and unmistakable, and yet sin may have been allowed to come in and produce its paralysing effects. It not only robs us of all spiritual energy, it retards our progress, it hinders our growth." [1]

But sometimes disease has consequences upon the body which are not paralysing. It may affect harmfully particular organs, such as the eyes and the organs of speech. In the same way, sin may impair the spiritual organs of our moral being so that in course of time they will cease to function properly. Then the words, "Having eyes, see ye not? and having ears, hear ye not?" (Mark viii. 18) becomes actually fulfilled. Sin may rob a man of his power of hearing God's voice, of seeing Him when He appears to him, of giving praise to God, and of calling upon Him in prayer.

Except by Keswick speakers, not much is usually made of sin as a spiritual disease by those who discuss the subject of sin. And yet Scripture has much to say about it. For example, Isaiah describes apostate Israel in the following words, "The whole head is sick, and the whole heart faint. From the sole of the foot even unto the head there is no soundness in it; but wounds, and bruises, and putrifying sores: they have not been closed, neither bound up, neither mollified with ointment" (Isa. i. 5, 6).

Sin, Scripture informs us, has harmfully affected every faculty of man. Man's eyes are full of adultery (2 Pet. ii. 14); they are covetous (Jer. xxii. 17), idolatrous (Ezek. xx. 24), evil (Mark vii. 22). His mouth is full of cursing and bitterness (Rom. iii. 14); it speaks iniquity and deceit (Ps. xxxvi. 3), and pours out evil things (Prov. xv. 28). The tongue is deceitful (Rom. iii. 13), a fire, a world of iniquity, full of deadly poison (Jas. iii. 5, 6, 8), and under it are mischief and vanity (Ps. x. 7). Man's ears are dull in hearing spiritual things (Matt. xiii. 15). His feet are swift in running to mischief (Pro. vi. 18). His mind is reprobate (Rom. i. 28), corrupt (1 Tim. vi. 5), blinded (2 Cor. iii. 14). His understanding is darkened (Eph. iv. 18). His conscience is seared (1 Tim. iv. 2), defiled (Titus i. 15), needs purging (Heb. ix. 14). It would be easy to go on almost indefinitely. This is a very important aspect of sin, and affects Christians as well as non-Christians. Many children of God are dull of hearing when God speaks and are slow to

[1] Evan H. Hopkins, *The Law of Liberty in the Spiritual Life* (London, Marshall Bros., 1905), p. 20.

obey when He commands, and this is always due to the impairment of the spiritual faculties by the disease of sin. Keswick rightfully makes much of it.

(5) Sin is an Acquired Habit

We are not born with evil habits; they are acquired; though we are born with the sinful tendencies which give rise to them. It is very important that we recognize the difference there is between inherent tendencies and acquired habits.

Mr. Hopkins tells us too that such "respectable" sinful habits as worry and temper are as inexcusable and as heinous in the eyes of God as habits of theft and corrupt speech, and that they can and must be put away. Such sins as Paul lists in Ephesians iv. 25–32—falsehood, theft, corrupt speech, bitterness, wrath, anger, clamour, railing, malice—may gain such dominion over us that we forfeit our freedom, and if repeated often enough, they become like a second nature. The apostle tells us that they are to be entirely laid aside—stripped off as one puts off old clothes. Here is an aspect of sin often overlooked today by the Church; and the result is impairment of testimony and stunting of spiritual growth.

(6) Sin is an Indwelling Tendency

The Scriptures speak of the indwelling tendency to sin that exists in all human beings as the "law of sin" (Rom. vii. 23, 25; viii. 2). It is as fixed and constant as any of the laws of nature—the law of gravitation, for instance. This is something different from our *liability* to sin, which, of course, also exists in all human beings, not even Adam in his originally sinless and innocent condition having been free from it, although he was free from the tendency to sin.

Mr. Hopkins recognizes that there are people who think we may be freed in this life from all tendency to sin. He says this is unscriptural, as it would involve the eradication of sin and the possibility of the attainment of a *state* of purity. Purity can become a maintained condition, he says, but never a state. As long as we live, we will never be absolutely free from the presence of evil, and consequently the tendency to sin will ever be present with us.

Church history shows that Christians who belong to "holiness groups" are greatly tempted to adopt erroneous views of sin as an indwelling tendency. They admit that every human being is born with a bias to sin—a tendency to have his own way, even though it conflicts with the will of God for him. But sometimes they become convinced that the Lord can so cleanse their heart from evil, that they will have no more tendency to sin. Like Adam, they are *liable* to sin but have no bent to sin—so they say.

Keswick, like other groups interested in practical holiness, has not been free from this temptation, but from the very beginning of the Convention its leaders saw this danger and warned against it. Mr. Hopkins, especially as editor of *The Life of Faith,* returned to the subject again and again. The subject is so crucial that we might well permit Mr. Hopkins further to clarify the Keswick position by quoting from some editorials in which he dealt with the subject.

"It is asked," he says in an editorial, "how can sin and holiness dwell together in the same heart—how can evil remain within when the Holy One enters and takes full possession? Can a man be sick and well at one and the same time? Is he not freed from disease when he is in perfect health? And may it not be said of the soul on whom Christ has laid His healing hand that, being made 'whole,' sin as a disease is entirely removed? The inference therefore is that all sin—not only as transgression, but as a principle—is eradicated when the blessing of 'full salvation' is realized. The law of sin then, it is said, no longer exists, and the very *tendency* to evil is destroyed.

"To entertain such notions, is, to say the least, to have a very superficial knowledge of the true condition of things. In a similar way one who is ignorant of the laws of natural life might conclude that a plant whilst manifesting the activity of vigorous growth is absolutely free from the influence of those powers which tend to reduce it to a condition of death and decay. In other words, that so long as the plant is in the vigour of life all tendency to die is destroyed, or non-existent—that the only power then in operation in fact is the power of life. This would be the popular view of the matter. But it would not be an accurate conclusion.

"Now, when a similar mistake is made in the matter of our spiritual condition, the consequences, as we can well perceive, are most serious.

"Never in this life are we absolutely free from the presence of sin—the tendency to sin and death is ever with us. As with the plant so with the holiest saint, the vital principle has only to be withdrawn for a moment, and the natural tendency is at once apparent. Apart from Christ as our In-dwelling Life even the most advanced believer would at once relapse into his former condition, because the tendency to evil would no longer be counteracted.

"This teaches us that in ourselves we have nothing to glory in—that our holiness does not consist in a *state* of purity which we can possess apart from Christ. Nor that our blessedness arises from any supposed freedom from the natural tendency to sin, but rather from the glorious fact that Christ is stronger than Satan and sin, and that when He takes full possession of the soul He so completely overcomes all the evil and meets the force of its power that the believer is no longer hindered in his progress, or robbed of his peace." [1]

Two years later, in another editorial, Mr. Hopkins returned to this subject again. "When a balloon with a car attached to it is ascending from the earth its tendency is upward—it has no tendency at all downwards, it has lost its tendency to fall. So when the Lord cleanses my heart from all evil—gives me a 'clean heart'—I have no tendency to sin. I am *liable* to sin, but I have no *tendency* to sin.

"Is this the reasoning of any of our readers? The illustration is a good one, but the inference is fallacious, and most misleading in its spiritual application.

"First, as to the balloon, we would say it has not lost its tendency downwards, though it continues to rise. We must remember that its movement upwards is but the resultant of opposing forces. Suppose we say the weight of the materials of which it is composed, or, in other words, its tendency downwards, is equal to four, and the lifting power of the gas by which it is filled is equal to six. As these two forces are diametrically opposed, the power by which it actually ascends is only equal to two.

"Now to say that the balloon has lost all tendency downwards, because it has ceased to move in that direction, but on the contrary is steadily moving upwards, would be to talk after the popular mind, but it would not be an accurate statement of fact. Its tendency to sink, equal to four, remains the same, though it is counteracted by the superior power of six in the opposite direction.

"The very fact that 'the law of the Spirit of Life in Christ Jesus' must be ever in force as a continual necessity, is a proof that the tendency to sin is not extinct, but is simply counteracted.

[1] *The Life of Faith*, September 1883, pp. 161–2.

D

"On the other hand, this does not imply that I need be *conscious* of that tendency. If we walk in the Spirit, the strain is borne by the Spirit. The privilege of the believer is this, that he may so live in the Spirit, and be filled with the Spirit, that, speaking from his consciousness, he may be tempted to say the flesh no longer exists; that he has now only one nature. But let us not be ignorant of Satan's devices. It is then that we are in danger of being shunted off the rails of soberness and truth on to the line of spiritual delusion, which sooner or later terminates in disaster." [1]

It seems to me that nothing can be clearer than that Keswick not only fully understands but has successfully avoided the danger Mr. Hopkins points out. An unscriptural conception of sin as an indwelling tendency would have been disastrous. The error of perfectionism would inevitably have followed as a natural consequence.

Another aspect of sin, often dealt with by Keswick speakers, although for some reason not touched upon by Mr. Hopkins in his chapter on Sin in *The Law of Liberty in the Spiritual Life*, is that of *sins of ignorance*. Mr. Hopkins treats the matter rather fully in an editorial in *The Life of Faith*.[2] There are Christians, he says, who cannot see that a sin can be sin to them if they are ignorant of having committed it. It is true, he replies, that a wilful departure from rectitude is sin, but Scripture clearly teaches that any falling short of God's high standard of holiness for us is also regarded by God as sin. If only wilful transgression is to be considered as sin, then we must exclude from the category of sin all those acts of omission and commission that have been performed by us unwittingly or in ignorance. How are we then to interpret those passages of Scripture which speak expressly of sins of ignorance and the need of atonement for them, as Leviticus v. 17–19.

That ignorance does not do away with responsibility, Mr. Hopkins goes on to say, is also seen in the prayer of Christ for those who had condemned Him to death, "Father, forgive them, for they know not what they do" (Luke xxiii. 34), and in His statement, "That servant which knew his Lord's will and prepared not himself, neither did according to his will, shall be beaten with many stripes. But he that knew not, and did commit things worthy of stripes, shall be beaten with few stripes" (Luke xii. 47, 48).

"We can readily see," Mr. Hopkins concludes, "that if a man's

[1] *The Life of Faith*, February, 1885, p. 21.
[2] March 1885, pp. 41, 42.

own conscience, or a man's spiritual sense, were the guide by which he had to judge of himself everyone would have a different standard. Good and evil would depend in that case not upon God's estimate, not upon His revealed mind concerning sin, but on the creature's apprehension of it."

I think is must be said, in all fairness, that the charge sometimes made against the Keswick view of sin, that it is shallow and falls short of the scriptural definition of sin, is without substantiation. It is true that Keswick furnishes us with no formal treatise of its doctrine of sin, and no carefully prepared, weighty discourses of a theological nature such as the eighteenth-century Puritan divines were accustomed to deliver; but the addresses given at the Convention year after year for over seventy-five years—short, simple, unpretentious, and practical as they are—furnish convincing proof that the Keswick conception of sin is not defective. The impression one gets in reading the addresses is that those who give them not only have theologically correct views of sin, but that they have a spiritual awareness of sin that reminds one of the Old Testament prophets. They are not lacking in orthodoxy, but their orthodoxy is not formal and lifeless. Sin to them is not something to be theorized about; or something about which we must be very sure to hold orthodox views, and be satisfied with that; it is a terrible reality that must be reckoned with, and it is important that we know how God regards it.

B. The Sin of Christians

A fact of importance to be kept constantly in mind in a consideration of the matter of Keswick's view of sin, is that the message of Keswick is directed primarily to Christians. We find a parallel situation in ancient Israel. The messages of the Old Testament prophets were directed not to sinful mankind in general, but to contemporary apostate Israelites. The prophets were commissioned by God to declare His attitude toward sin in His own people, and to put their finger upon the particular sins of which they were guilty. The Israelites were God's chosen people; His instruments for the accomplishment of a great purpose in the world; but this purpose was being frustrated by their sinfulness. They failed to live up to God's requirements for them. The prophets saw that the situation demanded not theological discourses on the nature of sin, but a fearless pointing-out of sin in God's people and a call to repentance, so that God's plan and purpose for His people could be fulfilled.

The Keswick leaders see a similar condition in the Christian Church today. Its testimony, they say, is weak and feeble because it is itself weak and feeble. Little advancement is made against the powers of darkness because so many Christians, who should be soldiers in the van of the conflict, are laid up as spiritual casualties in some hospital in the rear. "The block in the advancement of Christ's kingdom today is not on account of the circumstances or the special difficulties of our age, but the block is found in the Church itself," said Andrew Murray.[1] And so the first thing that Keswick does is to cry out against the sin of Christians.

A large part of the Church, says Keswick, has come to the place where it takes sin for granted; indeed, where it does not call sin sin any more. Its eyes are blinded to its own sin, and it is not aware of God's uncompromising attitude towards sin. Christians need to be wakened to a sense of the awfulness of sin. They need to see sin as God sees it. Until this is done, there is little hope for a real advance of the Church in the world.

The opening address at the first Keswick Convention was given by Canon Harford-Battersby, and it was on Hosea xiv, which begins with the words, "O Israel, return unto the Lord thy God; for thou hast fallen by thine iniquity." "He taught us," wrote one who was present, "what were God's thoughts about the declines and backslidings of His people Israel in the past, and of His own Church today, and how we needed deep humiliation of soul before Him and confession of our sin, in order to obtain fuller blessing."[2] And ever since then the first day or two of the Convention has always been a time of real self-examination, when the searchlight of God's Word is turned upon His people, and they are urged humbly to cry out with the Psalmist, "Search me, O God, and know my heart: try me, and know my thoughts: And see if there be any wicked way in me, and lead me in the way everlasting" (Ps. cxxxix. 23, 24). It is understood, of course, that there are two parts to this phase of the Keswick message; the first being an uncompromising exposure of sin in all its loathsomeness and heinousness, and the second a challenge that it be confessed and put out of the life immediately. The cancer of sin eating at the vitals of the Christian is laid bare, and the Christian is urged to cut it out at once.

[1] *The Keswick Week*, 1910, p. 82.
[2] Charles F. Harford, op. cit., p. 196.

Alexander Smellie, in a little volume of addresses on Sanctification, uses an illustration from Richard Jefferies to point out how even one sin may stand between us and God.[1] "A little carelessness, a little inconsistency, a little sin, may hide from us the light, the love, and the life. Richard Jefferies relates that, one summer evening, sitting by his window, he watched for the first star to appear, knowing its position exactly in the southern sky. The dusk came on, and grew deeper; but the star did not shine. By and by, other stars less bright appeared, so that it could not be the glow of the sunset which obscured the expected one. At length he began to doubt the accuracy of his own knowledge; when, suddenly, a puff of air blew through the branch of a pear-tree, a leaf moved, and there was the star behind the leaf. A constellation, he moralizes, may be hidden by a branch; infinities may be lost through a leaf. Ah, may God make us afraid of one thought, one word, one practice, one pleasure, which conceals the Holy Ghost from our view." This illustrates the serious view of sin Keswick holds.

The inner nature of a religious movement may frequently be determined more clearly from the hymns it produces than from its formal theological works. A favourite Keswick hymn, sung on the opening days of the Convention, is the following one by the Rev. F. Bottome.

> Search me, O God! my actions try,
>   And let my life appear
> As seen by Thine all-searching eye,
>   To mine my ways make clear.

> Search all my sense, and know my heart,
>   Who only can'st make known,
> And let the deep, the hidden part
>   To me be fully shown.

> Throw light into the darkened cells,
>   Where passion reigns within;
> Quicken my conscience till it feels
>   The loathsomeness of sin.

> Search all my thoughts, the secret springs,
>   The motives that control;
> The chambers where polluted things
>   Hold empire o'er the soul.

[1] Alexander Smellie, *Lift Up Your Heart* (London, Andrew Melrose, Ltd., 1915), pp. 67, 68.

Search, till Thy fiery glance has cast
    Its holy light through all,
And I by grace am brought at last
    Before Thy face to fall.

Thus prostrate I shall learn of Thee,
    What now I feebly prove,
That God alone in Christ can be
    Unutterable love.

Let us now examine some typical Convention addresses pointing
out sin and its results in the lives of Christians.

In an address on the subject, "Carnal and Spiritual," given at the
1895 Convention, Andrew Murray says that there are, according to
Paul in 1 Corinthians iii, two kinds of Christians, carnal and
spiritual.[1] Christians live in either a carnal or spiritual state, depending upon whether the flesh or the Spirit is in control in their lives.
The carnal state has four marked characteristics:

(i) It is a state of protracted infancy. Spiritual babyhood is a
natural stage in the life of Christians, but babyhood continued too
long is a burden and a sorrow, a sign of disease. There are two
special marks of a babe—it cannot help itself, and it cannot help
others. That is the experience of some Christians who have known
the Lord for years; they are always in need of attention themselves,
and they are of no help to others.

(ii) It is a state in which sin and failure are still master. Among
the Corinthian Christians, for example, envyings, strifes, and divisions existed long after they should have been a thing of the
past.

(iii) The carnal state can co-exist with great spiritual gifts. Paul
says that the Corinthians were enriched in all utterance and in all
knowledge, and came behind in no gift, and yet they were distress-
ingly carnal. There is thus no obvious difference between spiritual
gifts and graces. A Christian may have great spiritual gifts and
still be sadly deficient in the Christian graces, which according to
Paul are of much greater value than gifts.

(iv) It is a state in which it is impossible to receive spiritual
truth. A carnal Christian may admire truth and regard it as beautiful, but he does not receive it so that his life is changed by it.

Dr. Murray then tells how one may pass from the carnal to the
spiritual state, and gives the necessary steps in the process.

[1] *The Keswick Week*, 1895, pp. 48–54.

George H. C. Macgregor, in an address given at the 1898 Convention,[1] began by saying that we sing hymns and pray prayers the meaning of which we little realize. We would be astonished beyond measure if God really took us at our word. We pray to be filled with the Holy Spirit; but we do not realize the emptying that must precede this filling.

There are two parts to the cleansing work that must go on in Christians before they can be filled with the Spirit. There is, first, a work of revelation. God's Spirit reveals to us our impurity and how terribly we need cleansing. This revealing work of God is awful and terrible, ruining our self-complacency and almost reducing us to despair.

When the Spirit comes to deal with us about our sin, He reveals, to begin with, sins of thought and feeling about God and our fellow-men. He reveals our sins of speech. Our speech about ourselves is often vain and boastful, while our speech about others is frequently calumnious, slanderous, and gossiping. We fall into speech that is unholy. We praise dissimulation and break the law of truth. Then beyond these sins of thought and feeling and speech, there lie the sins of life and character, the most fatal and numerous of all. There are sins of appetite, of avarice, meanness, temper, fretfulness, dishonesty, fickleness, laziness, and many others.

The work that the Holy Spirit comes to do is not only a work of revelation, but a work of separation. The Spirit comes both to reveal and to remove sin. The cleansing work is as thorough as His revealing work.

The first result of this work of the Spirit is that we are brought back to the position in which many of us once were; and the second result is that we are made ready for service.

At the 1929 Convention J. Stuart Holden gave an address on the subject, "Only Partially Christian."[2] He began by quoting a statement made by an American magazine, that the charge brought against the Christian Church is not that it does not take itself seriously, nor that it does not concern itself sufficiently with public and social matters, but that it is so evidently content to be only partially Christian.

Now, in a sense this humiliating description applies to us all, for there is in all of us a wide gap between what we are and what we know we ought to be, and this will be so as long as we live.

---

[1] *The Keswick Week*, 1898, pp. 43–7.
[2] *The Keswick Convention*, 1929, pp. 67–74.

Tragedy comes when we are actually satisfied to be only partially Christian, only partially controlled by Him and only partially conformed to His standard and expectation.

Dr. Holden then told of a man who said to him that he did not believe in all this talk and teaching about holiness and Christ-conformity; he was quite content to know he was saved and on his way to heaven. Dr. Holden replied, "My friend, that is hardly the proper criterion of judgment. You are satisfied to know that you are saved and going to heaven. But is God satisfied? Is that what Christ died for?" And the man was silent. The fact is that to be anything less than whole-hearted is to be something less than Christian.

Dr. Holden then gave some general features of lives that are only partially Christian:

(i) They are satisfied with partial truth, such as that God's chief interest in men is to fit them for the next world; that the Gospel has no social implications; that there is no vital connection between spiritual enrichment and ethical obligation.

(ii) They are satisfied with a partial consecration—a consecration which follows Christ's guidance only when it does not conflict with personal inclination or habit or prevent worldly advantage.

(iii) They are content with partial obedience—obedience up to a self-determined point. They regard the *status quo* as something sacred, and not to be disturbed.

(iv) They are content to give God only a partial love. None of us is willing to accept the partial when the whole is possible. We are not satisfied with partial love, or with partial health, or with partial business success. Is God to get less from us than we are willing to accept ourselves?

"The transition is fatally easy from self-persuaded satisfaction with anything less than utmost harmony with the mind of Christ to a state that is a hopeless negation of all that He stands for." A Christian content with being only partially Christian will soon become an entire worldling. "An utterly undreamed of declension is inevitable to the man who is content with merely partial Christianity when he knows it to be such."

"Hindrances to Blessing" was the subject of an address given by the Rev. W. H. Aldis on the opening day of the 1938 Convention.[1] He begins by saying that conviction of sin is often essential

[1] *The Keswick Convention*, 1938, pp. 108–11.

as a prelude to the blessing which God desires to give us. And so Monday at Keswick is not infrequently a painful day, a day when with broken hearts and penitential tears we seek for that readjustment of our lives with God, apart from which there is no fulness of blessing.

Mr. Aldis then takes two verses from Hosea, both indictments of His people Israel, and applies them to the Christians at the Conference. "Hear the Word of the Lord, ye children of Israel: for the Lord hath a controversy with the inhabitants of the land" (Hos. iv. 1). "Strangers have devoured his strength, and he knoweth it not" (Hos. vii. 9). There are Christians who come to Keswick with whom God has a controversy, though they may not know it. There is, however, in them a vague consciousness that something is wrong, and they have come to the Convention in the hope that this wrong may be put right. What is wrong? Something has come between them and God which has robbed them of their power, deprived them of their joy, and made prayer and the reading of God's Word less pleasurable than it once was. God has a controversy with them about that thing, and until it is settled there will be no real peace, no fulness of joy, and no progress of the soul.

"Strangers have devoured his strength, and he knoweth it not." There can hardly be a more tragic situation in life than to be robbed of power and not be conscious of it. Samson, who "wist not that the Lord had departed from him," is an illustration of this. Perhaps there are some of us here from whom God has, in a sense, departed. We are no longer usable by Him. This is the condition of some ministers. There was a time in their ministry when God blessed them, and souls were saved, but today it is different. The work still goes on, but there are no spiritual results. Appearances are kept up; meetings are multiplied; organizations make a fair outward show; but nothing of spiritual value is accomplished. Why? Because they have been robbed of their power and do not realize it; or perhaps, what is more likely, they refuse to see it and excuse their failure by putting the blame upon something else.

Mr. Aldis then suggests some things about which God often has a controversy with Christians. There is, first, untruthfulness. There is not the truth in the inward parts which God requires. So many of God's people have the sin of deception upon their conscience. And then there is the sin of defrauding others of what does not belong to us. In the case of Israel the controversy was about idolatry. An idol is something which usurps the place which God ought to have in our lives. Christians in whose lives some thing or person usurps the place of God are wedded to an idol. Unless that idol is dethroned and God enthroned, they are in danger of becoming what Paul feared he might become—a castaway. God cannot use us unless our idols are put from our lives. We must not try to evade the issue by making sacrifices of other things. We must come back to God at the place where we got away from Him. We must put right those things which stand between us and the blessing which God desires to give to us.

In 1944 it was planned to hold the annual Keswick Convention in London, since it was impossible, during the years of the war, to hold it in its historic setting in the Lake District; but at the last minute, owing to the flying bomb attacks on London, the Convention had to be cancelled. The speakers who had expected to take part in the meetings prepared their messages for publication in a book with the title, *The Keswick Convention in Print, 1944.* The following is a summary of an address by the Rev. W. W. Martin on the subject, "Impotent." [1]

Mr. Martin says that the words, "a great multitude of impotent folk" (John v. 3), is an all too true description of the professing Christian Church today, although according to the New Testament the Church should be on the offensive, marching on and overcoming every opposition in its path. But we must remember that the impotent Church is an aggregate of individual impotent members. Paul pictures the Christian as a soldier in an active campaign, a boxer engaged in a furious fight, a runner straining every nerve to win a prize; but how different is the description that must be applied to many a Christian today.

Mr. Martin then gives the following as some of the causes of this sad condition: a want of care in spiritual nourishment; a failure to witness to those around of the saving grace of Jesus Christ; uncleanness and impurity in the thought-life; some specific sin to which we consciously cling. The remedy for this is not gradual amelioration and amendment, but a radical, instantaneous cure. The whole question is, "Wilt thou be made whole?" Restoration of soul-health involves an unreserved surrender to Christ and the crowning of Him as King in our heart and life.

There are a number of observations to be made about the above five addresses, which are taken almost at random from the annual

[1] *The Keswick Convention in Print, 1944,* pp. 11–14.

Convention reports, and are typical of those given on its opehing days.

They do not deal with Biblical truth in an academic way. Truth is regarded existentially—as a matter of the deepest concern, a matter of life and death. They are searching, personal, and practical, and aim at a prompt response in the hearer. They are designed to bring the hearer up to a crisis that will compel an immediate decision.

Printed addresses usually lack the life and passion they had when spoken, and they often make very dull reading, but that is not true of these addresses, about which there is a prophet-like earnestness that grips and holds one's attention from the beginning to the end. They burn and glow with feeling. They manifest upon the part of the speakers a deep knowledge of God's attitude toward sin, and His requirements for His people. We cannot read them without discovering how God feels about sin—not only sin in general, but our own sin. God hates sin. He cannot tolerate it. It brings death to him who is guilty of it. It is of the greatest importance that we know that no sin stands between us and God.

There is in all of them an unsparing exposure of sin, and yet this is done not in a spirit of criticism but of love and helpfulness. There is no excusing of and no compromise with sin.

Dare we say that Keswick goes too far in this whole matter? I think not. The utter loathing with which God looks upon sin is shown from the beginning to the end of Scripture: by Achan, who brought defeat upon all Israel by one sin of disobedience; by Samson, who toyed with sin until he was robbed of his power; by Saul, who lost his kingdom because he refused to take God's commands seriously; by Ananias and Sapphira, who thought that secret sin entails no consequences; and by others too numerous to mention. In this aspect of the Keswick message we have the recovery of an almost lost emphasis that appears everywhere in Scripture: God will not tolerate sin in His people any more than He will in others.

Christians are too apt to think that only the unsaved are sinners, and that Christianity is nothing more than a kind of prudential insurance of the soul. This certainly is not Biblical. The truth is that God's Word has a great deal more to say about the sin of God's people than it does about the sin of those who do not know Him. It was the sin of God's people that delayed the entrance of Israel into Canaan for forty years. It was the sin of God's people that was responsible for the Assyrian and Babylonian captivities. It was the sin of God's people that caused the crucifixion of the Messiah. It was the sin of God's people, more than the unbelief of the heathen, that caused Paul heartache and sorrow. And it is the sin of God's people, more than anything else, that is hindering the manifestation of His saving power in the world today.

God is *shocked* at sin; Christians take it for granted. Cardinal Newman once said: "It is the one great security against sin, to be *shocked at it.*"[1] Keswick is right in putting great stress on the fact that there must be a revival among Christians of a sense of sin in themselves.

[1] J. Gregory Mantle, *The Counterfeit Christ* (New York, Fleming H. Revell Company, 1920), p. 37.

CHAPTER IV

GOD'S PROVISION FOR SIN

A. Defeat and Failure in the Christian Church

(1) GLARING DIFFERENCE BETWEEN THE NEW TESTAMENT IDEAL OF THE CHRISTIAN LIFE AND CHRISTIANITY TODAY

A person familiar with the New Testament experiences something in the nature of a shock when he notes the glaring difference between the Christian life as we are wont to live it, and the ideal of our Lord. The same staggering difference is to be observed when a comparison is made between the Church in the apostolic period and the Church today. A living person and a corpse could hardly be more unlike.

The grievous contradictions are so apparent that even those with only a superficial knowledge of the Scriptures are troubled and shocked. An illustration of this is found in a story told by Amy Carmichael, the first of the missionaries to be sent out at the charges of the Keswick Council. She says that after an afternoon meeting of a convention held in India, she noticed an Indian lady lingering in the empty hall, and thinking that she might be feeling lonely, sat down beside her. After some conversation about the Bible Reading given that afternoon, the Indian lady's face darkened and she said bitterly, "What is the use of such meetings? You missionaries say one thing, and do another!" Miss Carmichael tried to explain that the meetings were held just because they felt the need of being better than they were; but this did not satisfy the Indian lady, who in quick eager sentences went on to say that her people had noticed that when a missionary first came out to the field, he was usually warm and loving and keen to win souls, but that gradually it was noticed that he cooled. "And," she concluded, "who can say you missionaries lead specially holy lives? We Indian Christians observe. We observe you not only when you are at work, but when you are off work too. Is there anything remarkable about you? Are you burning-hot people? We look to you to show us patterns, and *you are showing us crooked patterns.*"[1]

Another illustration is found in the letter of a corporation head in Philadelphia to the director of an organization providing chaplains for industry, "I fear that our management and officers themselves need the Chaplain Councillor programme as much as our labouring men and women; but will your Chaplain's work really affect the character and conduct of enough of our personnel to show measurable improvement in morals and morale? We have not found that the present church members and so-called Christians among our employees are better men or workers than non-church members of similar education and culture."[2]

(2) GOD'S REQUIREMENTS OF CHRISTIANS CLEARLY SET FORTH

God's requirements of Christians are set forth in His Word with unmistakable clarity. We are to walk as Jesus walked. "He that saith he abideth in him ought himself also to walk, even as he walked" (1 John ii. 6). We are to love our enemies. "I say unto you, Love your enemies" (Matt. v. 44). We are to forgive as Jesus forgave—even those who blasphemed and murdered Him. "If any man have a quarrel against any: even as Christ forgave you, so also do ye" (Col. iii. 13). We are to give thanks for all things that come to us—even disappointments, sickness, and bereavements. "Giving thanks always for all things unto God and the Father in the name of our Lord Jesus Christ" (Eph. v. 20). We are to worry about nothing, but with thanksgiving let our requests be made known unto God; and then the peace of God which passeth all understanding will guard our hearts and minds. "Be careful for nothing; but in everything by prayer and supplication with thanksgiving let your requests be made known unto God. And the peace of God, which passeth all understanding, shall keep your hearts and minds through Christ Jesus" (Phil. iv. 6, 7). We are to rejoice in the Lord always. "Rejoice in the Lord always: and again I say, Rejoice" (Phil. iv. 4). We are to be blameless and without rebuke in the world of non-Christians among whom we live. "Be blameless and harmless, the sons of God, without rebuke, in the midst of a crooked and perverse nation, among whom ye shine as

---

[1] Amy Carmichael, *God's Missionary* (London, Society for Promoting Christian Knowledge, 1945), pp. 1, 2.
[2] Ernest Chase, "Chaplains for Industry," *Revelation* (May 1946), p. 206.

lights in the world" (Phil. ii. 15). We are not only to have life eternal, but to have it abundantly. "I am come that they might have life, and that they might have it more abundantly" (John x. 10). We are to be freed from the dominion of sin. "Knowing this, that our old man is crucified with him, that the body of sin might be destroyed, that henceforth we should not serve sin. For he that is dead is freed from sin" (Rom. vi. 6, 7). We are to be not only over-comers, but more than overcomers in the midst of the hardest of trials. "In all these things we are more than conquerors through him that loved us" (Rom. viii. 37).

These verses, and scores of others like them that might be cited, set forth God's standard for the Church. This standard certainly goes far beyond what human nature in itself is capable of, for it is not natural for us to love our enemies, to rejoice always, to be thankful even for the things that hurt, and to be more than conquerors in every situation in which we find ourselves. Human nature, by itself, can never attain the ideal of Christ.

Does God therefore make demands of human beings that they cannot fulfil? Does He expect of them conduct beyond their reach? Are His requirements unreasonable? Is Christianity merely a religion of lofty ideals—ideals to be striven for, but without any hope of attaining them? In the divine programme for the Church, are Christians to be like Tantalus, who was in water up to his neck, yet could never quench his burning thirst, and who saw trees laden with fruit waving their branches directly over his head, yet could never reach them to satisfy his gnawing hunger; or like Sisyphus who had to roll a huge stone up a steep mountainside, and found that when-ever he partially succeeded, the stone always rolled down again?

There is no suggestion anywhere in Scripture that God's require-ments of Christians are unattainable, or that He overlooks and condones their failure to meet them. Nothing is more clear than that God expects a consistent, and not merely a spasmodic and inter-mittent, walk in the Spirit, with all that that connotes of unbroken fellowship with Him, victory over sin, and steady growth in Christ-likeness. God's requirements cannot be greater than His enable-ments. If they were, man would be mocked.

(3) TYPICAL EXPERIENCES OF EARNEST YET DEFEATED CHRISTIANS

But earnest Christians, aware, on the one hand, of the uncom-promising nature of God's standard, and, on the other, of their pathetically futile attempts to reach it, are faced with a dilemma. Let us consider the testimonies of a few well-known Christians closely identified with the Keswick movement who at one time faced this dilemma in all its crushing force, but later found a way out.

(A) T. D. HARFORD-BATTERSBY

In 1852, during the first year of his incumbency as curate of St. John's, Keswick, Mr. Harford-Battersby made the following entry in his journal,

"I am just in the condition of the person described in Romans vii. This is my habitual state, however much I may realise at times the blessedness of peace and justification; and thus being anxious about myself, not being whole within, it is impossible that I can have leisure or abstraction of mind enough to treat the diseases of others, or to enter upon my work heartily." [1]

A year later he writes to the same effect—"*30th October (1853), Sunday evening*—I feel again how very far I am from enjoying that peace and love and joy habitually which Christ promises. I must needs confess that I have it not; and that very ungentle and un-christian tempers often strive within me for the mastery. . . . What, then, is the remedy but deep humiliation before God, prayer, self-denial, and repentance?" [2]

Almost twenty years later, in 1873, he still writes in the same vein, and says that he is utterly dissatisfied with himself and his state. "I feel that I am dishonouring God and am wretched myself by living as I do; and that I *must* either go backwards or forwards reaching out toward the light and the glory which my blessed Saviour holds out to me, or falling back more and more into worldliness and sin. Yesterday I preached in the afternoon on Psalm lxxx. 7, 8, and pleaded with others to *hope* for better things—redemption from *all* iniquities. Shall I not seek after these things? A great prize is set before me: shall I not seek after it? Is it not worth every possible effort to attain to? God reveal to me the secret of this 'more excellent way,' and enable me to walk in it now and always. Amen." [3]

(B) THEODORE MONOD

Theodore Monod was born in France of an English mother, and after being brought up and educated in the United States he returned

---

[1] *Memoir of T. D. Harford-Battersby*, by Two of His Sons (London, Seeley and Company, Limited, 1890), p. 146.
[2] Ibid., p. 146.
[3] Ibid., pp. 151, 152.

to France where he became one of the best-known clergymen of the day. In a letter written from Paris to Robert Pearsall Smith, he says that after his conversion in 1858 he gave up the study of law for preparation for the ministry. In the next fifteen years he achieved some prominence as a minister. He also wrote two little books, *Looking unto Jesus* (1862) and *The Secret of Strength* (1865), showing it to be our duty, our privilege, and our only resource, to look away from all else to Christ, and find in Him, through simple faith, our peace, strength, joy, and life.

"Some will conclude," he goes on, "that my experience must have been a holy and happy one. But, alas! it was one that I cannot look back upon without deep shame and sorrow: full of coldness, of levity, of selfishness, of neglected duties, and oftentimes of downright and wilful disobedience. Periods of comparative nearness to God and circumspect walking were followed by far longer periods of half-hearted service, with innumerable and conscious failures, very little prayer, and hardly any reading of God's Word beyond what the immediate necessity of family and public worship imperatively demanded. In short, my heart condemned me, and I could find real rest neither in God nor yet at a distance from Him. All the time I passed for a child of God, which I was, and perhaps for a faithful child of God, which I was not. That there existed a truer Christian life, one at once more devoted to God and more happy in Him, I well knew; but how was I to enter it?"[1]

(c) HUDSON TAYLOR

In a letter to his sister written in 1869, three years after he had founded the China Inland Mission, Hudson Taylor wrote as follows: "Well, dearie, my mind has been greatly exercised for six or eight months past, feeling the need personally and for our Mission of more holiness, life, power in our souls. But personal need stood first and was the greatest. I felt the ingratitude, the danger, the sin of not living nearer to God. I prayed, agonized, fasted, strove, made resolutions, read the Word more diligently, sought more time for meditation—but all without avail. Every day, almost every hour, the consciousness of sin oppressed me.

"I knew that if only I could abide in Christ all would be well, but I could not. I would begin the day with prayer, determined not to take my eyes off Him for a moment, but pressure of duties, some-

---

[1] *The Christian's Pathway of Power*, Sept. 1st, 1874, p. 157.

E.

times very trying, and constant interruptions apt to be so wearing, caused me to forget Him. Then one's nerves get so fretted in this climate that temptations to irritability, hard thoughts and sometimes unkind words are all the more difficult to control. Each day brought its register of sin and failure, of lack of power. To will was indeed 'present with me,' but how to perform I found not.

"Then came the question, Is there no rescue? Must it be thus to the end—constant conflict, and too often defeat? How could I preach with sincerity that, to those who receive Jesus, 'to them gave he power to become the sons of God' (i.e. Godlike) when it was not so in my own experience? Instead of growing stronger, I seemed to be getting weaker and to have less power against sin; and no wonder, for faith and even hope were getting low. I hated myself, I hated my sin, yet gained no strength against it. I felt I *was* a child of God. His Spirit in my heart would cry, in spite of all, 'Abba, Father.' But to rise to my privileges as a child, I was utterly powerless.

"I thought that holiness, practical holiness, was to be gradually attained by a diligent use of the means of grace. There was nothing I so much desired as holiness, nothing I so much needed; but far from in any measure attaining it, the more I strove after it, the more it eluded my grasp, until hope itself almost died out, and I began to think that—perhaps to make heaven the sweeter—God would not give it down here. I do not think that I was striving to attain it in my own strength. I knew I was powerless. I told the Lord so, and asked Him to give me help and strength. Sometimes I almost believed that He would keep and uphold me; but on looking back in the evening—alas! there was but sin and failure to confess and mourn before God.

"I would not give you the impression that this was the only experience of those long, weary months. It was a too frequent state of soul, and that towards which I was tending, which almost ended in despair. And yet, never did Christ seem more precious; a Saviour who could and would save such a sinner! . . . And sometimes there were seasons not only of peace but of joy in the Lord; but they were transitory, and at best there was a sad lack of power. . . .

"All the time I felt assured that there was in Christ all I needed, but the practical question was—how to get it *out*. He was rich truly, but I was poor; He was strong, but I was weak. I knew full well that there was in the root, the stem, abundant fatness, but how to get it into my puny little branch was the question. As gradually light dawned, I saw that faith was the only requisite—was the hand to lay hold on His fulness and make it mine. But I had not this faith.

"I strove for faith, but it would not come; I tried to exercise it, but in vain. Seeing more and more the wondrous supply of grace laid up in Jesus, the fulness of our precious Saviour, my guilt and helplessness seemed to increase. Sins committed appeared but as trifles compared with the sin of unbelief which was their cause, which could not or would not take God at His word, but rather made Him a liar! Unbelief was I felt *the* damning sin of the world; yet I indulged in it. I prayed for faith, but it came not. What was I to do." [1]

(4) Such Defeat and Failure the Usual Experience of Many Christians

No one will deny that the experience of these well-known Christians was not only pathetic but tragic in the extreme. One cannot accuse them of being careless or indifferent about their responsibilities to God. They were all Christian workers, striving with all their might to serve their Lord. They were intelligent Christians of the highest type. Consciously at least, they clung to no sin that would hinder their spiritual progress. They were familiar with God's standard for them as Christians. They had, moreover, been Christians for years. Yet they confess that their usual experience was one of defeat and failure rather than of victory, and that their fellowship with God was often broken.

The experience that they describe, however, cannot be regarded as unique; it was in their generation almost universal in the Church, and is widely prevalent even today. In an address given at Keswick in 1896, J. Elder Cumming described this situation in these words: "What is the process of sanctification? To many Christians there is no process whatever, because there is no advance. It is an appalling thing—I hardly know if there be any more appalling thing in the Christian Church than the fact that many Christians are not advancing in holiness at all. Is it not true that some are rather going back, and that the best days they have spent before God were the early days after their conversion? Others seem to be standing still where they were a few years ago. If they examine

---

[1] Dr. and Mrs. Howard Taylor, *Hudson Taylor's Spiritual Secret* (Philadelphia, China Inland Mission, 1935), pp. 113, 114.

themselves with regard to any one of their ordinary habits, with regard to any one of their accustomed *sins*, shall I say? they can hardly tell any difference between five years ago and today. And there are many who never seem to expect any special growth in holiness until, perchance, they come to the shadow of death. Is it not an appalling thing that there should be divine life within the soul of God's people, and that divine life should apparently be making no advance or increase at all?" [1]

The American Higher Life writer, Miss Ruth Paxson, who addressed the women's meetings at Keswick on a number of occasions, compares, as Keswick speakers have often done, the defeat and failure of such Christians to the wilderness wanderings of the children of Israel. "The vast majority of Christians stop short in their experience of the blessings of salvation with the joy of forgiveness of past sins and with the hope of Heaven in the future. But the present is a forty-year wilderness experience full of futile wanderings, never enjoying peace and rest, never arriving in the promised land." [2] This I believe, is a legitimate comparison. The writer of the Epistle to the Hebrews draws such an analogy. "Let us therefore fear, lest, a promise being left us of entering into his rest, any of you should seem to come short of it. . . . Let us labour therefore to enter into that rest, lest any man fall after the same example of unbelief" (Heb. iv. 1, 11).

J. East Harrison, another American writer—though not connected with English Keswick—says that although the Christian course is intended by God to be one of continued triumph and constant progress, "Notwithstanding all this, we are compelled to recognize that there are numbers of Christians who sorrowfully own that their spiritual condition is absolutely unsatisfactory. They turn with a sigh from the perusal of the Bible, feeling that their experience in no way answers to the expectations which so many passages of the Scripture warrant." [3] And then the writer goes on to say that this situation would be sad enough, even if the only result were the loss of joy and triumph that might be theirs; but the situation is positively tragic when the disastrous effects upon the cause of Christ are realized. How, he asks, can those who find the Christian life unsatisfactory be zealous about leading others into the enjoyment

---

[1] *The Keswick Week*, 1896, p. 38.
[2] Ruth Paxson, *Life on the Highest Plane* (Chicago, Moody Press, 1943), Vol. II, p. 66.
[3] East Harrison, *Reigning in Life* (Philadelphia, The Sunday School Times Company, 1922), pp. 13–15.

of it; or how can non-Christians who observe them be drawn into it?

B. Wrong Ways of Seeking Sanctification

Keswick tells us that one of the principal reasons for this failure and defeat on the part of earnest Christians is found in wrong, unscriptural ways of seeking sanctification. There are many such ways, of course—too many even to refer to them all, but the following are regarded as the principal ones.

(1) REGARDING SANCTIFICATION AS A MATTER OF COURSE

It is a grievous mistake, says J. Elder Cumming,[1] to suppose that the sanctification of the believer is a matter of course, and that he need not trouble himself about it. For one thing, he says, this position ignores the whole question of backsliding, which is not only possible but quite common among Christians. Moreover, it fosters carelessness of Christian living, for if sanctification will proceed automatically without our doing anything about it, then why be concerned about it? "So far from encouraging us to think that the new life of the soul in us will go on of itself, and of necessity, the New Testament continually warns Christians to 'give all diligence' to 'make their calling and election sure,' to 'watch and pray,' 'to give earnest heed' to the things they have heard, to 'hold fast that which they have, that no man take their crown'; and to 'fear lest haply a promise being left of entering into His rest, any one should seem to have come short of it.' Let every Christian beware of the folly of sitting down in unconcern and leaving his renewed soul to take care of itself! The lusting of the flesh 'will in that case soon assert itself to his downfall'."[2]

Dr. Cumming might have added that if sanctification in the divine plan takes place automatically, then the hortatory parts of the New Testament would be superfluous. In that case, moreover, God would have no right to be disappointed in the development of Christians; and yet we read that He was grieved by the meagre growth of those to whom the Epistle to the Hebrews was addressed, "For when for the time ye ought to be teachers, ye have need that one teach you again which be the first principles of the oracles of

---

[1] J. Elder Cumming, *Through the Eternal Spirit* (Stirling, Stirling Tract Enterprise, 1937), pp. 112, 113.
[2] Ibid., p. 113.

God; and are become such as have need of milk, and not of strong meat" (Heb. v. 12). In that case, too, there would be no point to Paul's statement about himself, "I *press* toward the mark for the prize of the high calling of God in Christ Jesus" (Phil. iii. 14).

(2) Regarding Sanctification as a Matter of Gradual Growth

There are many people who regard sanctification as merely a matter of *gradual* growth, not to be stopped or hindered or accelerated by anything the Christian may do. This notion, Dr. Cumming tells us,[1] leads to two harmful effects: it leads Christians to expect no positive holiness for a long period of years; and it prevents them from taking any definite steps toward holiness that would lead to an improvement in their condition.

If this view were correct, says Dr. Cumming, no young Christian could be holy, and what is to be said of the painful fact that there is no growth in holiness in many men who have long been Christians, and who have to confess that they have either been standing still or going back? There are many whom the Lord must address as He did the Church at Ephesus. "I have this against thee, that thou didst leave thy first love. Remember therefore from whence thou art fallen, and repent, and do the first works" (Rev. ii. 4, 5).

As to gradual growth, he says, there are two things to be said. For one thing, spiritual growth is not to be compared with growth in the vegetable and animal kingdoms, which, those who hold this view say, is gradual and slow. Growth in the vegetable and animal kingdoms is not as slow and as gradual as is often supposed. A tree, for example, has periods when there is practically no growth; and some years it grows faster than others, as the rings of the tree trunk show. The growth is broken into quite recognizable stages, and the causes of the varying growth are quite well known. External factors like rain and sunshine have much to do in determining growth. This is even more true in the Christian life.

Again, growth depends largely upon health. Sickness stops it. Growth arrested by ill-health is to be restored only by the cure of the disease which is afflicting the system. So, too, it is with the soul. When the soul is making no progress in holiness, or very little, the cause of the arrest must be removed if growth is to be resumed.

Evan Hopkins, writing of Christians who believe that deliverance

---

[1] J. Elder Cumming, *Through the Eternal Spirit*, (Stirling, Stirling Tract Enterprise, 1937), pp. 113, 114.

from conscious sinning can come only by growth and is just a question of time, says that they inevitably make excuses for themselves. "Being only young believers," they say, "they are, of course, very weak, but the evil nature is strong within them. The new nature must have time to grow and become strengthened. In the meantime, as the old nature is so strong, victory over sin cannot be expected. Failure is regarded as inevitable, and as a consequence a sad and dark experience follows." [1]

It must not be thought that Keswick denies that sanctification is progressive and a matter of growth. It denies only that growth is necessarily imperceptibly slow and that it cannot be retarded or hastened by anything the believer may do. In this it is plainly on scriptural ground.

(3) ERADICATION OF THE SIN PRINCIPLE

There is a theory held by some Christians that it is possible in this life, either at regeneration or at some subsequent crisis of religious experience, to reach a point in spiritual development where the sin nature is eradicated and therefore no longer operative. This theory is so obviously contrary to the plain teachings of the Bible and to human experience that it is not seriously advanced by many thinking Christians.

A theory of *gradual* eradication is held by others—notably by B. B. Warfield. In his examination of the Victorious Life movement in America, which stems from the Keswick movement in England, he says, "It is a fatally inadequate conception of salvation which so focuses attention on deliverance from the penalty of sin and from continued acts of sin, as to permit to fall out of sight deliverance from sin itself—that corruption of heart which makes us sinners. . . . To keep a sinner, remaining a sinner, free from actually sinning, would be but a poor salvation; and in point of fact that is not the way the Holy Spirit operates in saving the soul. . . . He cures our sinning precisely by curing our sinful nature; He makes the tree good that the fruit may be good. It is, in other words, precisely by eradicating our sinfulness—'the corruption of our hearts'—that He delivers us from sinning. . . . To imagine that we can be saved from the power of sin without the eradication of the corruption in which the power of sin has its seat, is to imagine that an evil tree

[1] Evan H. Hopkins, *The Walk That Pleases God* (London, Marshall Bros., 1887), p. 15.

can be compelled to bring forth good fruit. . . . It surely would be better to be freed from the 'principle of sin' in us than merely from its effects on our actions. And this is in fact what the Scriptures provide for. What they teach, indeed, is just 'eradication.' They propose to free us from sinning by freeing us from the 'principle of sin.' Of course, they teach that the Spirit dwells within us. But they teach that the Spirit dwells within us in order to affect us, not merely our acts; in order to eradicate our sinfulness and not merely to counteract its effects." [1] He goes on to say that grace is progressively extirpating the old nature now, "and that is the fundamental fact in supernatural sanctification." [2]

Keswick has from the beginning regarded all theories of eradication as being both unscriptural and dangerous. In one of his first editorials for *The Christian's Pathway of Power*, Evan Hopkins wrote, " 'If we say that we have no sin, we deceive ourselves, and the truth is not in us.' That declaration, we believe, is applicable to the saint as long as he is in the body. . . . The word of God does not teach us to expect, in this life, either the *eradication* or *improvement* of the 'flesh.' God's provision in Christ for us, in order that we may walk so as to please Him, supposes the existence, the incurableness, and the continuance of the sinful nature within us up to the very end of our earthly course." [3]

Again and again in his books and addresses Mr. Hopkins insisted upon the necessity of distinguishing between a *state* of purity and a *maintained condition* of purity. To emphasize the difference between the two principles, he sometimes used the following illustration. When a light is introduced into a dark chamber, the darkness disappears at once. But the tendency to darkness persists; it has not been eradicated; and the room is kept illuminated simply because, and just so long as, the light counteracts the tendency. If it were possible for the room to continue in a state of illumination by passing the candle through it once, the room would not be dependent on the continued presence of the lighted candle for its light. Holiness, Mr. Hopkins would say, is a condition of life which must be maintained, moment by moment, through living fellowship with Christ. It is a *maintained condition*, never a *state*.

If Dr. Warfield is right in holding that sanctification is the progressive extirpation of the old nature, then the longer a person lived

[1] B. B. Warfield, *Perfectionism* (New York, Oxford University Press, 1931), Vol. II, 579–83.
[2] Ibid., p. 584.
[3] *The Christian's Pathway of Power*, March 1876, p. 41.

the Christian life the less possible it should be for him to sin, and toward the end of his life it should be practically, if not entirely, impossible to sin.

But everyone knows that this condition does not prevail at all. A Christian's spiritual growth is not determined by the length of time he has been a Christian. There are Christians who have known the Lord a long time who sin more than some who have known him for only a short time, and there are Christians who live a holy life over a long period of time and then, through yielding to some temptation, suddenly collapse spiritually and sin in a most frightful way. An example of this is Demas, for years a fellow-worker of the apostle Paul, of whom Paul wrote from his prison in Rome, "Demas hath forsaken me, having loved this present world" (2 Tim. iv. 10). Moreover, years after his conversion on the Damascus road, Paul himself declared that he dared not be careless, "lest that by any means, when I have preached to others, I myself should be a castaway" (1 Cor. ix. 27).

Still another thing would be true if Dr. Warfield were right that gradual eradication is the means God uses to deliver us from sin. If we lived long enough, then conceivably we must reach a stage of spiritual development where the old nature was completely eradicated, and the statement of the apostle John would no longer apply to us, "If we say that we have no sin, we deceive ourselves, and the truth is not in us" (1 John i. 8), and such injunctions as "reckon," "yield," "let not," "put off," "mortify," "abide," would no longer have any meaning for us. And when we reached this state of purity we would no longer have to depend upon Christ and the Holy Spirit to enable us to live a holy life. We would become ethically self-sufficient.

Keswick is plainly right in rejecting the theory of eradication, whether instantaneous or gradual, as the divine way of sanctification. Any theory of eradication carries with it great dangers. It tempts the Christian to negligence in watchfulness and in continued reliance upon the keeping power of God. The Word of God teaches us to "watch and pray" and to "walk in the Spirit," and should there be any carelessness about these things—easily fostered by a belief that sin was eradicated from one's nature—there would be an immediate return to the lusts of the flesh. Jesus said, "Apart from me ye can do nothing" (John xv. 5). There would, moreover, be no need to abide in Christ and rely upon Him for victory over temptation if sin were no longer in us.

(4) SUPPRESSION OF THE OLD NATURE

Perhaps the most widely-held view of sanctification is that it is to be gained through our own personal efforts by trying to suppress the flesh in us. Justification, it is believed, is by faith, but sanctification is by works—at least to a large extent. "Great is the bondage into which many fall," says J. Elder Cumming, "and in which they continue for years, by this unceasing effort to become godly, and by its fruitlessness. No amount of anxiety spent upon the question of growth will enable us to grow. And no anxiety about it is needful, if we will only fulfil the conditions and remove the hindrances. . . . Neither a tree nor a man grows by effort."[1]

Evan Hopkins often spoke and wrote on the futility of seeking freedom from the dominion of sin by trying to conquer the old nature. In one of his addresses he said that Christians who do this are endeavouring to *tame* the old life. By bringing themselves under spiritual discipline "they hope so to subdue, so to curb, so to change the old life, that they will have very little trouble with it after a while. . . . Are there not many who have been doing this for years? It is a kind of sanctification of the flesh. . . . They think it is a question of discipline and culture and training, that by-and-by they will have very little difficulty with the old life."[2]

In another address, on "Self-Conquest,"[3] he distinguishes between the conquest of self by self, and the conquest of self by Christ. He says that the first is impossible. He quotes our Lord's saying, "How can Satan cast out Satan," and says that the inference is that it is impossible. And yet there are a great many people who are trying to do this. They go to God and earnestly seek for grace to get the victory over themselves. But self trying to conquer self is full of disappointment, a hopeless battle, a painful struggle.

Again in another address, on "Self-Conquest and Self-Control,"[4] he says that there are a great many notions about self-control that we must get rid of. "I cannot help thinking that a good deal of what the heathen philosophers taught of old has been grafted upon the teaching of Christianity in connection with this subject." They taught that to conquer self man must conquer his own evil propensities; and this could be attained only by long, hard training and severe discipline. Man is enthroned, so to speak, as his own

[1] J. Elder Cumming, *Through the Eternal Spirit*, p. 114.
[2] *The Keswick Week*, 1897, p. 51.
[3] Ibid., 1907, pp. 55-8.
[4] Ibid., 1904, p. 95.

conqueror. Christianity, however, teaches that self is to be controlled by another power greater and higher than itself. "By the teaching of philosophy you can make a man a Stoic; but you cannot make him a Christian."

Canon Hay Aitken likewise says that to fall back upon mere moral processes to overcome sin is not Christianity, but pagan philosophy, which offers nothing better than self-effort as the only way of improvement. If a Greek philosopher were asked, "Can you tell me how I am to improve myself?" he would very likely answer, "Well, you cannot do it all at once; it will have to be by the formation of habit. It will be slow work, hard, difficult work; and, probably, to a great extent disappointing work. But you must go on trying, and still trying; and, if you keep on, the probability is that you will make some sort of progress at any rate." [1] A good many Christians, he says, regard the possibilities of deliverance from the power of sin in very much the same way. They go on struggling, striving, working, hoping that God will help them to master their sins, but without any real expectation that He will do so.

"The supreme danger of the Christian life is that of legalism," says W. H. Griffith Thomas, "for there is an inevitable tendency to assume that although justification is by faith, sanctification is somehow by struggle; that although the sinner is powerless in regard to salvation, he is not so in the matter of holiness. He thinks that he cannot be sanctified unless largely aided by his own efforts." [2]

THE STRUGGLE OF ROMANS VII. 7–25

This famous passage, about which there has been so much controversy, describing a man who is trying to be good and holy by his own efforts and is defeated every time by the power of indwelling sin, is important in Keswick teaching. It has been interpreted in various ways, of which the following are the most generally accepted.

(1) Paul is describing the experiences of an unregenerate Jew—very likely himself—as he tries to keep the law. He strives in real earnest to become holy by his own efforts, and apart from grace, but is beaten back every time, so that he seems to himself a double self—the one wanting unavailingly to be good, the other being intractably bad. The passage thus is thought to teach the powerlessness of law and the need of grace to lead a holy life.

[1] *The Keswick Week*, 1903, p. 58.
[2] W. H. Griffith Thomas, *Principles of Theology* (London, Church Book Room, 1945), pp. 208, 209.

(2) Paul is describing the *normal* experience of every Christian in his struggle with sin. In support of this view, we are referred to verse 22, "I delight in the law of God after the inward man".—a statement, it is said, which an unconverted man could not truly make of himself. It is contended by those who hold this view that Christians who do not moan with Paul, "O wretched man that I am," are in an abnormal and unhealthy state spiritually, deceived about the condition of their hearts, and full of pride and conceit about their imagined spiritual condition. Nor is it only backslidden Christians who are convicted of sin that mourn thus: all those who are truly in communion with Christ emit this groan daily and hourly. It is true that to the cry, "Who shall deliver me from the body of this death," the answer is given in the next verse, "I thank God through Jesus Christ our Lord," but according to those who hold this view the deliverance referred to is not present but future—in the life to come, when we shall all be transformed into the likeness of Christ.[1]

Dr. Alexander Whyte held to this view. His biographer says that for a time in his ministry his whole interpretation of the New Testament was coloured by the account of the divided self in this passage. He used to tell his people, "You'll never get out of the seventh of Romans while I'm your minister," meaning that he would always maintain that no Christian could ever emerge from the experience of heart-breaking defeat which Paul describes here.[2]

(3) Paul is describing the experiences of a Christian in his unsuccessful conflict with sin before he has learned the secret of deliverance. According to this view, Romans vii and viii picture successive stages in the experience of the same person. Some Christians never emerge out of the experience of struggle and defeat of Romans vii, while others, who have discovered the secret of victory (usually through a second work of grace) enter into the experience of "no condemnation" described in Romans viii. The struggle ceases in very few Christians; for the majority the conflict and the defeat are lifelong.

Writing of those who claim that they have left the experience of Romans vii far behind, and look upon it as Israel's wilderness life, never more to be returned to, and that they have passed from the bondage of the law to the liberty of the Spirit. Andrew Murray, who expresses the Keswick view, says that however large the

[1] See for an expression of this widely-held view, Arthur W. Pink, *The Christian in Romans 7* (Swengel, Pa., Bible Truth Depot, n.d.) pp. 3–18.
[2] C. F. Barbour, *The Life of Alexander Whyte* (London, Hodder and Stoughton 1925), p. 305.

measure of truth there is in this view, it does not fully satisfy. "The believer feels that there is not a day that he gets beyond the words, 'In me, that is, in my flesh, dwelleth no good thing.' Even when kept most joyously in the will of God, and strengthened not only to will but also to do, he knows that it is not he, but the grace of God: 'in me dwelleth no good.' And so the believer comes to see that, not the two experiences, but the two states are simultaneous, and that even when his experience is most fully that of the law of the Spirit of life in Christ Jesus making him free, he still bears about him the body of sin and death. . . .

"If there is one lesson the believer needs to learn, who would enjoy the full indwelling of the Spirit, it is the one taught in this passage with such force: that the law, the flesh, that self-effort are all utterly impotent in enabling us to serve God. It is the Spirit within, taking the place of the law without, that leads us into the liberty wherewith Christ hath made us free. 'Where the Spirit of the Lord is, there is liberty.' " [1]

(4) There is no official Keswick view, but the second and third views given above are rejected by all Keswick leaders I know. W. H. Griffith Thomas held to the first,[2] but not many other Keswick leaders have done so. He, however, saw in the passage an important lesson for the regenerate, too: it shows what God provides by His grace for the Christian in the matter of sanctification. The contrast between Romans vii and viii—a life of defeat in the one chapter and of victory in the other—is intended to teach us what God purposes for the believer. Union with Christ by God's Spirit makes possible real holiness of life—a life in which God's requirements find their fulfilment.

The view of this chapter generally held by Keswick teachers is most clearly stated in the addresses of Evan Hopkins. It is that the experience of struggle and defeat here described is not the God-intended normal experience of Christians, but shows what happens when any person, regenerate or unregenerate, tries to conquer the old nature by self-effort. In an address on "Deliverance from the Law of Sin,"[3] based on Romans vii. 18, "For to will is present with me; but how to perform that which is good I find not," he begins by saying that too often this chapter is used by Christians as an

[1] Andrew Murray, *The Spirit of Christ* (London, Nisbet & Co. Ltd., 1888), pp. 171–3.
[2] See W. H. Griffith Thomas, *St. Paul's Epistle to the Romans. A Devotional Commentary* (Grand Rapids, W. B. Eerdman's Publishing Company, 1946), 190–9.
[3] *The Story of Keswick, 19th Convention*, 1893, pp. 89–93.

excuse for sinning. Satan uses it as a warrant for expecting defeat. It is full of encouragement, however, not to those who regard defeat as inevitable, but to those who sincerely desire to know the secret of overcoming sin.

The chapter, he says, is descriptive of a Christian *regarded in himself,* apart from active faith in Christ. The *standing* of every Christian without exception is "in Christ," but there is such a thing as not abiding in Him. When our Lord commands His disciples to abide in Him, He implies that it is possible for them not to abide in Him. Again He says, "Without Me"—that is, apart from Me, not abiding in Me—"ye can do nothing." There are multitudes of Christians who fall into this category—in Christ in *position* and *standing,* not in Christ in regard to present experience and condition.

Paul shows in this chapter what happens to a Christian as he tries to overcome his sinful nature apart from the Divine remedy. In the whole story of the inward struggle there is not a single mention of God the Father, the Son, or the Holy Spirit as a source of help, but over thirty references to the personal pronoun "I." In spite of all our good intentions and our desire to do good, the law of sin in us is too stong for us. We are helpless in ourselves, even though we be Christians.

Mr. Hopkins then illustrates the up-and-down life so often experienced by Christians. "Suppose that I take a rod and attach to it a piece of lead. I drop it into a tank of water. By the law of sinking bodies it descends; that illustrates the law of sin. Now I get a piece of cork, and fasten that also to the rod, and placing it in the water I see that by the law of floating bodies, it has a tendency to ascend. But the lifting power of the cork is not strong enough to overcome the downward tendency of the lead, so that it may be kept from sinking. It rises and sinks alternately." [1] The "law of the mind" is not strong enough to counteract the "law of sin and death" in our members.

The remedy for this unsatisfactory situation is given by Paul in the second verse of the following chapter, "For the law of the Spirit of life in Christ Jesus hath made me free from the law of sin and death." Then continuing his illustration Mr. Hopkins says, "Let us suppose that I place my rod with the lead and the cork into a little life-belt, and I put them into the tank of water. The rod now does not sink. Why? Because it is in the life-belt. There is suffi-

---

[1] *The Story of Keswick, 19th Convention,* 1893, p. 92.

cient lifting power in it to keep it from sinking, but it is only as it is in the life-belt that it has the benefit of that law. It is the power of a superior law counteracting the other law. The lead is not taken away, but the rod has the benefit of a stronger power so long as it abides in the life-belt." [1]

The main point to be borne in mind is that abiding in Christ we are made "free from the law of sin and death." This is not an attainment—something that takes place in us so that we no longer have the tendency to sin, any more than that the law of gravitation is suspended when, instead of sinking, we float on the water within the life-belt. All we have is the counteraction of one law by another which is superior or stronger. "Hence we see we must not only know what it is to be in Christ in the sense of standing for our acceptance and justification, but also in the sense of *abiding*, that is, of fellowship with Him, if we would live in the power of His victorious life." [2]

In another address on this chapter, [3] Mr. Hopkins says that Paul here describes "the nature of the forces within him, and the results of their working, as apart from Christ. . . . He is here considering himself a regenerate man apart from the indwelling Christ, apart from the Holy Ghost, and this in order to show that even though he was converted and renewed, he was not sufficient himself, apart from Christ, to overcome the forces of evil. . . . It is a description, then, of the nature and tendency of the forces present within us, considered apart from Christ." [4]

Again Mr. Hopkins uses one of his famous illustrations—one used by him in many of his addresses. Mr. Hopkins had an unusual gift for clarifying theological truths of an abstruse nature with homely, easily-understood illustrations, and this one he used repeatedly when teaching the essential truths of counteraction. If a piece of iron could speak, he asks, how would it describe its nature? It would say, "I am black; I am cold; I am hard." But put the iron into a glowing furnace, and what a change takes place! It has not ceased to be iron; but the blackness and the coldness and the hardness are gone! It has not lost its nature; it is still black and cold and hard; but as long as it remains in the fire it is red and hot and malleable. The fire and the iron are still distinct, and yet how complete is the union—they are one. If the iron could speak,

[1] *The Story of Keswick, 19th Convention,* 1893, p. 92.
[2] Ibid., p. 93.
[3] *The Keswick Week,* 1906, pp. 178–81.
[4] Ibid., p. 179.

it would not glory in itself, but in the fire that makes and keeps it a bright and glowing mass. Take it out of the fire, and it again becomes black and cold and hard. So it is with the believer. Ask him what he is in himself, and he will answer, "I am carnal, sold under sin." By nature he is lacking in zeal for God; he is defiled with sin; and his heart is hard; but it is his privilege to enter into fellowship with Christ, and in Him to abide; and as long as he abides in Christ—and only so long as he does so—these natural tendencies in him are counteracted. The Holy Spirit penetrates every part of his being, and he is no longer carnal but spiritual; no longer overcome by sin and brought into captivity to it, but set free from the law of sin and death and preserved in a condition of deliverance. This blessed experience of freedom from sin's service and power implies a momentary and continuous act of abiding in Christ.

From this he learns two things, he says. "First of all, I learn that conversion or regeneration does not secure or ensure victory over sin. The power of the 'new man' is not sufficient to overcome the power of the evil nature. . . . The next thing is this: that deliverance does not come by the removal of the tendency to evil within us, but by the counteracting influence of another power, a divine power." [1]

And to shed light on the verse, "The law of the Spirit of life in Christ Jesus hath made me free from the law of sin and death" (Rom. viii. 2), he uses another illustration. "You throw me into the sea, and by the law of gravitation I go to the bottom. But there is another law; it is the law of floating bodies. I get into a life-belt, and I do not sink. By the law of gravitation I sink. By the law of floating bodies I am now kept from sinking. But there is one condition. *Abide in the life-belt.* Now this is a grand thing to see. I may be floating about in the life-belt for twenty-four hours, but I am just as heavy at the end of that time as when I got into the life-belt. The very moment I get out of the life-belt, down I go." [2]

What Evan Hopkins says on the meaning of Romans vii is echoed by other Keswick speakers who deal with this chapter. There is no need to set forth what they say except possibly to refer to Bishop Handley Moule's comment in his well-known book, *Outlines of Christian Doctrine*, that Paul here describes a real element in every

[1] *The Keswick Week*, 1906, p. 180.
[2] Ibid., p. 181.

regenerate life, one that it is liable to be experienced at any stage or moment. Paul, he says, contemplates the regenerate man at his very best—eager and anxious to do the will of God, "but isolated (as it were) from the activity of the divine Indweller." [1]

Now, is Keswick right in maintaining so strongly that the experience of ineffectual struggle and defeat described in Romans vii does not set forth the God-intended normal experience of Christians? The question is very important, as the answer to it determines our opinion of what God expects of us as Christians, and also our opinion of what provision God has made for sin. The earnest non-Christian struggling to be good must indeed confess, "The good that I would I do not: but the evil which I would not, that I do" (Rom. vii. 19), and "O wretched man that I am! who shall deliver me from the body of this death?" (Rom. vii. 24); but is such a confession consistent with such statements by Paul as, "they which receive abundance of grace and of the gift of righteousness shall reign in life" (Rom. v. 17) and "My grace is sufficient for thee" (2 Cor. xii. 9)? Someone has suggested that if normal Christian experience does not rise any higher than that, then we must change our Lord's invitation to read, "Come unto me all ye that labour and are heavy laden, and I will tell you how to be wretched, by presenting the requirements of the law and revealing that you cannot keep them!" [2]

I believe that Prof. John Laidlaw is right when he says that this passage "has been too often read as if it described the ordinary and normal state of a child of God; as if nature and grace were so exactly balanced in believers that 'they cannot do the things that they would'; as if the sum and substance of sanctification were this death in life, or this living death expressed by the perpetual cry, 'O wretched man that I am!' Now it has been well said, that if this were all that grace did for its votaries, St. Paul would only have proved that it was as futile and insufficient as the law. If all that regeneration could accomplish were only to awaken a sense of inward discord without being able to do it away, this 'would certainly destroy the influence of spiritual Christianity and disgrace its character.' But the mistake lies in not perceiving that chapter vii gives us only one side of the picture. The delineation is progressive, and the full account of the conflict is not before us till we

---

[1] H. C. G. Moule, *Outlines of Christian Doctrine* (London, Hodder and Stoughton, 1889), p. 197.

[2] Robert C. McQuilkin, *The Message of Romans. An Exposition* (Grand Rapids, Zondervan Publishing House, 1947), p. 80.

F

pass on to chapter viii, and see how the victory is secured for believers." [1]

If we have here the normal Christian life, then grace offers us at best nothing more than a spiritual stalemate. One half of the New Testament, one may almost say, would be rendered nugatory. What would then be the meaning of such joyously triumphant descriptions of Christian living as these, "We are more than conquerors through him that loved us" (Rom viii. 37); "I can do all things through Christ which strengtheneth me" (Phil. iv. 13)? The truth is that whether we regard the experience depicted here as that of an unregenerate Jew or a Christian, the lesson intended is the same —that holiness of life is possible, but only in Christ; while apart from Christ there is only defeat and failure. If the experience is that of an unregenerate man, then we find him confessing it impossible to be holy by self-effort, and finally discovering that this is possible in Christ. If the experience, however, is that of a Christian, then we observe him seeking holiness of life by self-effort, and likewise failing; finally discovering that there *is* victory in Christ. It is wrong to place the emphasis on the negative message of sin and defeat, as if that is all the Christian has a right to expect. Paul exultingly says that there *is* deliverance "through Jesus Christ our Lord" (Rom. vii. 25).

The key to the interpretation of the passage, as Keswick leaders rightly point out, is found in the frequent repetition of "I," while there is not a single mention of the Holy Spirit. We see what the "I" is struggling to do by unremitting effort, but failing utterly to accomplish. In chapter viii, however, where there are at least twenty references to the Holy Spirit and the "I" drops out, there is a triumphant note throughout. We are therefore not to regard Romans vii as expressive of the normal conflict of the Christian, inevitable to the end of his earthly life. The normal Christian life is in Romans viii, and is experienced as the Holy Spirit by His counteractive power is permitted to have His way.

Keswick is also on scriptural ground, I believe, in holding that Romans vii and viii are not intended to describe successive stages in the experience of Christians. All Christians do not live either in Romans vii or viii. The normal Christian life should indeed be lived in Romans viii, and there is no good reason why any Christian should remain in Romans vii, but as long as a Christian lives it

[1] John Laidlaw, *The Bible Doctrine of Man* (Edinburgh, T. & T. Clark, 1879), p. 204.

will always be possible for him to lapse into the defeat of Romans ·ii, and he will do so if he depends for victory upon his own strength rather than upon Christ. There is a distinction here that is not often considered, but it is a very important one. Sanctification is never a *state*; it is always an *experience*—an *experience* that is the fruit of abiding in Christ. It is not a state, but a maintained condition of purity—a condition of life maintained moment by moment through living fellowship with Christ. As the branch must abide in the vine if it is to bear fruit, so must the believer abide in Christ if he is to bear fruit for Christ. We can never attain to a state where holiness of life can be taken for granted; or to a state where the tendency to sin, and therefore the possibility of sinning, will be absent. That is the plain teaching of Scripture.

It is the teaching of Keswick that an important reason for the defeat and failure of so many Christians is that they try to *suppress* the old nature, like the "wretched man" of Romans vii; but there is a way of deliverance—through Jesus Christ, by the counteracting power of the Holy Spirit of God. Sanctification is therefore not by works but by faith. Victory comes by accepting the method of divine provision. That is the distinctive message of Keswick.

(5) OTHER ERRONEOUS METHODS

Keswick leaders often refer to other erroneous methods of seeking deliverance from the defeat and failure that Christians so commonly experience. There are those who endeavour to attain to a state of holiness by a ceaseless round of Christian service; but they find that this is followed sooner or later by a feeling of spiritual reaction and exhaustion. There can indeed be no true sanctification without service, and lack of service is bound to hinder sanctification; but service is not the divine means of sanctification. Then there are those, Evan Hopkins points out, who make the mistake of "beginning with the work of the Spirit in them, rather than the work of Christ for them. They recognize that Christ is the Author and the Source of pardon and acceptance, but they look to the Holy Spirit to set them free from the tyranny and service of sin. They believe there can be no freedom for them until it is wrought in them by the Holy Ghost."[1] They overlook the fact that while the Holy Spirit carries out His work *in us*, he

---

[1] Evan H. Hopkins, *Talks with Beginners in the Divine Life* (London, Marshall Brothers, Ltd., n.d.), p. 40.

always works, not apart from, but in connection with, Christ's work on the cross *for us*. The Holy Spirit only imparts to us what Christ has purchased for us at Calvary. Others, again, trust for their sanctification to a diligent use of the means of grace, to watchfulness over their own heart and life, taking themselves to task ever and again for the coldness of their heart. The result of all these unscriptural ways of pursuing holiness, as W. Graham Scroggie rightly says, is that "the experience of Christians is, too often, one of dispeace, of joylessness, of prayerlessness, of worldliness, and of defeat." And, he exclaims, "Can anyone imagine that such an experience as that is Christianity!" [1]

In the very first issue of *The Christian's Pathway of Power* the editor stated what he conceived to be the practical possibilities of faith. "We believe the Word of God teaches that the *normal* Christian life is one of uniform sustained victory over known sin; and that no temptation is permitted to happen to us without a way of escape being provided by God, so that we may be able to bear it." [2] Keswick has never departed from this faith. From the beginning until the present it has taught that a life of faith and victory, of peace and rest, are the rightful heritage of every child of God, and that he may step into it "not by the laborious ascent of some *Scala Sancta*, not by long prayers and laborious effort, but by a deliberate and decisive act of faith." [3] It teaches that "the normal experience of the child of God should be one of victory instead of constant defeat, one of liberty instead of grinding bondage, one of 'perfect peace' instead of restless worry. It shows that in Christ there is provided for every believer victory, liberty, and rest, and that this may be obtained not by a life-long struggle after an impossible ideal but by the surrender of the individual to God, and the indwelling of the Holy Spirit." [4]

C. The Keswick Solution—Sanctification by Faith

(1) ASPECTS OF SANCTIFICATION

Keswick leaders, when considering the subject of sanctification, often make the conventional threefold division—positional sancti-

---

[1] *The Keswick Convention*, 1933, p. 81.
[2] *The Christian's Pathway of Power*, February, 1874 p. 1.
[3] Harford, *The Keswick Convention*, p. 6.
[4] Ibid., p. 6.

fication, experimental sanctification, and ultimate sanctification. Positional sanctification is that sanctification which was wrought by Christ on the cross of Calvary for every believer, and is the possession of every Christian from the moment of his regeneration. There is a reference to it in 1 Corinthians i. 30, "But of him are ye in Christ Jesus, who of God is made unto us wisdom, and righteousness, and sanctification, and redemption." Experimental sanctification is the day-by-day transformation of the believer into the image of Christ, and is progressive in nature. Beginning at regeneration, it continues all through life, but is never complete. Ultimate sanctification is that perfect sanctification which will be the portion of all believers in the life to come. The apostle John refers to it in the words, "Beloved, now are we the sons of God, and it doth not yet appear what we shall be: but we know that, when he shall appear, we shall be like him; for we shall see him as he is" (1 John iii. 2).

More often, however, another division, more characteristic of Keswick, is made—sanctification as a process, as a crisis, and as a gift.

(A) PROCESS

Sanctification as a process is experimental or progressive sanctification—that gradual transformation, by the Holy Spirit, of the believer into the likeness of Christ. It begins at regeneration, but is not the same thing as regeneration. Regeneration is not capable of degrees; no one is more or less regenerate than another. Sanctification, on the other hand, does admit of degrees.

The gradual and progressive nature of sanctification as a process may be seen from such passages of Scripture as 2 Corinthians iii. 18, "We are changed (or, are being changed) into the same image from glory to glory, as by the Spirit of the Lord." The change here described is something more than mere reformation of character by moral culture and discipline, but a gradual transformation by the Holy Spirit who works within—a change like that of a bud into a flower, or a caterpillar into a butterfly.

In this sense, of course, our sanctification can never reach a point beyond which there can be no further progress; it can tnerefore never be said to be complete in this life.[1]

---

[1] Evan Hopkins, *The Law of Liberty in the Spiritual Life*, pp. 92–102.

(B) CRISIS

Much is made by Keswick of sanctification as a crisis. It is true, Keswick says, that sanctification invariably begins at regeneration. There can be no question about this. On the other hand, many Christians do not make the progress in sanctification that they should. Instead of growing into spiritual maturity, for various reasons their development is hindered or even halted.

For this reason real progress is often not made until they come to a spiritual crisis, which may arise as a result of an enlargement of vision of their spiritual resources in Christ, or a more adequate realization of God's requirements of them as Christians, or a willingness to surrender some sin that stands between them and God. After such a crisis they may often make more progress in sanctification in a week than they had previously made in a year.

This aspect of sanctification will be considered more fully in the next chapter, as it is of primary importance in Keswick teaching.

(c) GIFT

This is the same as positional sanctification, and, as was said above, is that sanctification which was wrought by Christ on the cross for every believer. According to Keswick, we are not sanctified by self-effort or by works, but by faith in what Christ has done for us at Calvary. Sanctification, like justification, is by grace alone. Sanctification as a gift is so central in Keswick teaching that Keswick cannot be understood without knowing exactly what is meant by it.

(2) SANCTIFICATION AS A GIFT

(A) GOD'S PROVISION FOR SIN

Evan Hopkins once received a letter in which the writer disagreed with the Keswick position on sanctification. "We are asked," he said, "to accept holiness by faith in the same way that we accept justification by faith. Now that presents a real difficulty to my mind. Is not holiness a growth, a process, the result of the work of the Holy Spirit in the heart? Justification is something already complete; to accept it therefore by faith, is clear and intelligible to me. But sanctification being a process that can never be absolutely completed in this life, I cannot see how it can be received by faith in the same way that justification is received by faith." [1]

---

[1] *The Keswick Week*, 1899, pp. 79, 80.

Mr. Hopkins replied that before we can experience sanctification as a process, we must know what it is to receive it as a gift. Holiness is a process, but that is not the only or even the chief aspect in which it is presented in Scripture. Salvation in its fullest sense is a gift. Everyone acknowledges that. "The gift of God is eternal life through Jesus Christ our Lord" (Rom. vi. 23). But somehow not everyone realizes that sanctification, which is only a part of salvation, is in its fullest sense a gift too—one of the benefits for the believer of the death of Christ on Calvary. Multitudes of Christians know justification as a gift, but regard holiness only as a process. They have got one way by which they obtain pardon, and another way by which to get victory over sin. The first is by simple faith, the second is by painful effort—by works. They are under grace as to justification, but under law as to holiness. We must realize that holiness is a gift before sanctification can be worked out in our lives.

The Word of God tells us that Christ "is made unto us wisdom, and righteousness, and sanctification, and redemption" (1 Cor. i. 30). Christ must be definitely accepted as our sanctification; and as we had to give up our own self-righteousness when we were regenerated, so, if we wish to make any progress in holiness, we have to give up belief in the value of self-effort in holiness. The gift of holiness must be worked out in our daily life, but we work *from* holiness, not *to* holiness.

To illustrate this point Mr. Hopkins often quoted some words by Alfred Edersheim, from his life of Christ: "Every moral system is a road by which, through self-denial, discipline, and effort, men seek to reach the goal. Christ begins with the goal, and places His disciples at once in a position to which all other teachers point as the end. They work up to the goal of becoming children of the kingdom. He makes men such freely of His grace, and this is the kingdom. What the others labour for, Christ gives. They begin by demanding, He by bestowing." [1]

Bishop Taylor Smith, for many years a speaker at Keswick, in an address on "The Meaning of Keswick" makes a similar statement. "Does some one ask, How can I become the happy possessor of this abundant, victorious life? My answer is, Not by a fresh resolution, but by a fresh revelation. Not by a human effort, but by a divine gift. Not by turning over a new leaf, but by the reception of a new life. . . . And so, just as the new spiritual life

[1] *The Keswick Week*, 1899, p. 80.

is the gift of God, so the abundance of life is ours by reception also." [1]

Again and again Keswick speakers emphasize that sanctification is a gift of God's love, in the same way that salvation itself is. It is not something for which we have to struggle or strive; it is something that we are to receive as a free gift of God's grace. God does require holiness of His creatures, but what He requires He first provides. Sanctification is primarily and fundamentally "neither an achievement nor a process, but a gift, a divine bestowal of a position in Christ." [2] Sanctification is thus the rightful inheritance of every child of God. Whether or not he enters into the enjoyment of that inheritance depends upon several factors, but principally upon a clear knowledge that by the death of Christ he as a believer is a legal beneficiary of sanctification, and a willingness to meet God's conditions for the reception of this gift.

(i) *The Believer's Identification with Christ in His Death to Sin the Ground of His Sanctification*

One great aim of Keswick is to teach Christians what are their possessions in Christ, and to show them how to possess those possessions. It is amazing, according to Keswick, how little Christians know of the extent of their inheritance in Christ. They have at their disposal the "unsearchable riches of Christ" (Eph. iii. 8), yet many live like paupers. Often their knowledge of the extent of salvation does not reach beyond the fact that it includes the forgiveness of sins, and eternity in heaven when this life is over. These privileges, they know, are theirs through the cross; but somehow they do not see that at Calvary God dealt with the whole problem of sin, in all its aspects.

Calvary, Keswick informs us, is God's answer to the problem of man's *sin* as well as his *sins*. Christ died *for* us, it is true. By the shed blood of God's own Son the guilty sinner is reconciled to God and justified in His sight. God remembers his sins against him no more. But this, while exceedingly important—so important, indeed, that its importance cannot be over-emphasized—is only one aspect of the significance of Christ's death. Another aspect is that when Christ died on the cross to sin, we were identified with Him in that death to sin. That is, we died *with* Him. By our union with Him in His death we were freed from the penalty of sin and

[1] *The Keswick Convention*, 1934, p. 88.
[2] Ruth Paxson, *Life on the Highest Plane*, Vol. II, p. 107.

emancipated from the power of sin. All our sanctification therefore must be traced to, and rests upon, the atoning sacrifice of our
Lord Jesus Christ. The cross of Christ is the efficient cause of
deliverance from the power of sin. Freedom from the dominion
of sin is a blessing we may claim by faith, just as we accept pardon.
Sanctification is thus one of the benefits of the cross, and is just as
much our inheritance as is the forgiveness of sins. F. B. Meyer calls
this "the heart and essence" of Keswick teaching.[1]

   (a) *Locus Classicus on this—Romans vi.* The most important
passage in the New Testament on this aspect of Keswick teaching
is Romans vi. Evan Hopkins once said that in the early days of
Keswick there was no passage of Scripture that was more frequently
to the front than this chapter.[2] That is true, but it is just as frequently used today. It is doubtful whether a Keswick Convention
has ever been held in which one or more speakers did not deal with
this chapter. Because of its extreme importance, more than once it
has been called the Magna Charta of the Christian. There is no
understanding of Keswick without an appreciation of the place
accorded by it to this chapter in its whole scheme of sanctification.
One of the key verses in the chapter is the sixth: "Knowing this,
that our old man is crucified with him, that the body of sin might
be destroyed, that henceforth we should not serve sin." Let us see
how this verse is interpreted in two typical addresses.

   In an address on "Our Old Man Crucified"[3] Evan Hopkins first
defines the terms the "old man" and the "body of sin." The "old
man," he says, is our old unregenerate self—the man we were before
our regeneration. The "body of sin" is not the totality of sin, nor
the substance or essence of sin, but our natural body as used and
claimed by sin.

   Turning then to an exposition of the verse, he says that it states
a fact—that we as sinners died with Christ. It is judicially true of
all believers without exception that they were identified with Christ
in His death to sin. The *result* of this fact is that our bodies are
now free from sin's claim, and we need no longer serve sin.

   But it is not enough to know that historically all believers died
with Christ; we must appropriate that truth if it is to be real in our
experience. God reckons us dead to sin because of our union with
Christ in His death to sin. Now by faith we must enter into God's

[1] Harford, op. cit., p. 162.
[2] *The Keswick Week*, 1906, p. 94.
[3] Ibid., pp 94–8.

reckoning. This is not a matter of feeling but of faith. We must claim by faith the freedom from sin's authority which has been secured for us in virtue of Christ's death and our identification with that death. Experimental freedom should follow legal deliverance.

Mr. Hopkins then illustrates this point with one of his unique illustrations.[1] "In America the Deed of Emancipation which set free millions of slaves was first executed before a single slave could know practically what freedom meant. We come to the Cross and see that we are free, that, in virtue of our identification with Christ, the body of sin, as such, is emancipated,—'being now made free from sin.' Go and claim it; this is faith's function. It is done. It is just what a slave had to do in America. The news comes to him that the Deed of Emancipation has been executed. But he is still in bondage, he is under the power of a cruel master. It is not a question of struggling out of his power, but of simply claiming his right. He is legally set free. By faith he claims that privilege. Then comes the practical experience."

"Your old master, sin," he continues, "has no legal claim upon you; it may assert its power, but it has no authority. Sin may put its hand upon you and overcome you, but it has no right to do so. Legally you are set free. Claim your legal freedom and you will know experimental freedom. 'Being now made free from sin.' That is true of all Christians. And yet they may be in terrible bondage, they may be under the power of sin. Like it was with many a slave in America, emancipated under the Act of Emancipation, they might still be in bondage. And yet they could claim their freedom. They had a legal right to be free."

We begin by seeing in Scripture what is judicially true of all Christians, that we died with Christ and were identified with Him to this very purpose—that sin should have no legal claim upon us. Then by the reckoning of faith we must claim our freedom and present our bodies to God for His service. In proportion as we fix our eye upon God's fact, and enter into God's reckoning, and act upon it, just in that proportion are we brought into the blessed experience of deliverance. Deliverance from the power of sin is not an attainment, any more than the pardon of sins is. It is a gift of God's grace. Deliverance is not attained by struggle and painful effort, by earnest resolutions and self-denial, but through the cross. It is stepped into by simple faith.

Mr. Hopkins then again makes use of an illustration—one he used

[1] *The Keswick Week*, 1906, p. 97.

over and over again. "Do not wait for feeling," he says. "I used to put it before my working-men, in Richmond, in this way. Here are three men walking in procession—Mr. Fact goes first, Mr. Faith follows him, and Mr. Feeling follows Mr. Faith. Supposing the middle man turns around and looks at Mr. Feeling, everything goes wrong. His business is to fix his eye upon Mr. Fact, and Mr. Feeling follows him. Get hold of the fact, first of all—*free* in Christ, *free* on the cross. There is the fact. Do not reverse the order.

"Satan says three capital things. 'Listen to me. Look at your heart; how cold it is! Look at your life, which is given up to sin. There is no fact yet; you have got to wait until you have got the fact until you realise your freedom. That is to be your fact. *Feeling, faith, fact,*' he says. But if you work upon these lines, you will make no progress. You have to put it in God's order, not waiting to realise, but *believing,* what God says. Enter into His reckoning. I was nailed to the Cross with Christ, that this body, which has been the instrument of sin, that which sin has usurped and laid hold of, might be set free. Now I go to claim the privilege that I should no longer serve sin. At once, from this moment, I take this body and hand it over to Christ, my new Master, and enter into the new service. And when He takes the body He will keep it."

In an address on "The Power That Overcomes"[1] the Rev. E. L. Hamilton said that the cross of Christ is not only the ground of our justification, but the ground of our sanctification. When Jesus Christ died at Calvary "He not only made a full and complete atonement for all our sins, but He delivered us from the power and dominion of sin. By His death He 'delivered us out of the hand of all our enemies, that we should serve him without fear in holiness and righteousness all the days of our life.'"[2]

Mr. Hamilton draws three lessons from the text:

First, he says, we have here a certain fact—our old man has been crucified with Christ. The "old man" is the old sinful life which we inherited from Adam; all that we were before we were born again. It is the old corrupt nature with which we were all born, and which is the cause of all our sinning, that was crucified with Christ. Christ thus not only deals with our sins, which are the effect of our sinful nature, but with the very cause of sinning. This is not a matter of feeling, but of fact. It is just as much a fact as that Jesus Christ was crucified.

[1] *The Keswick Week,* 1920, pp. 155–60.
[2] Ibid., p. 155.

Second, he says that our old man was crucified with Christ for a certain purpose—"that the body of sin might be destroyed." Like Mr. Hopkins, he interprets "the body of sin" as meaning this human body of ours as the servant of sin, the body through which sin expresses itself. The body is not sinful in itself; it is the servant of sin. The word "destroyed" here does not mean to annihilate, but to render inoperative. "Jesus Christ by His death has emancipated us from sin as a master, so that these bodies of ours, being freed from sin as a master, are now freed so that they can serve God."[1]

Third, the crucifixion of our "old man" with Christ should have a certain result: henceforth we should not serve sin. We read in Romans vi. 12, "Let not sin therefore reign in your mortal body, that ye should obey it in the lusts thereof. Neither yield ye your members as instruments of unrighteousness unto sin: but yield yourselves unto God, as those that are alive from the dead, and your members as instruments of righteousness unto God." Now that we have been emancipated from sin as a master, we are free to serve God with the members of our body. It is possible to serve sin again, but not necessary, for Christ has freed us. "That," he says, "is the special message we have to deliver at Keswick."[2]

"The enemy," he goes on to say, "tries to keep us in ignorance of this glorious fact, that Jesus Christ by His death has emancipated us from sin and that we are free."[3] He then tells the story of a slave whose master deliberately kept the news of Abraham Lincoln's Emancipation Proclamation from her, and who, when she heard that she was legally free by an act of the U.S government, immediately left his service, saying that she would serve him no more. In the same way we have got to reckon on our freedom. "God would never tell us to reckon a thing which was not a fact, and it is when we really do reckon on it, when we lay hold of it by faith—it is then that the Spirit of God makes it true in our experience."[4]

To people who say that they do reckon their "old man" crucified with Christ but do not find it true experimentally, he answers that they are not reckoning with a living but with a dead faith. A dead faith is an intellectual assent to the truth; a living faith, a heart grasp of it. If we have trouble with faith in this matter, let us remember that there is almost always a moral cause for unbelief. Some sin is in the way, but directly we repent we find it becomes easy to believe.

[1] *The Keswick Week*, 1920, p. 157.
[2] Ibid., p. 158.
[3] Ibid., p. 158.
[4] Ibid., p. 158.

(b) *Other Passages in the New Testament on the Believer's Identification with Christ.* "For the love of Christ constraineth us; because we thus judge, that if one died for all, then were all dead: And that he died for all, that they which live should not henceforth live unto themselves, but unto him which died for them, and rose again" (2 Cor. v. 14, 15).

"I am crucified with Christ: nevertheless I live; yet not I, but Christ liveth in me: and the life which I now live in the flesh I live by the faith of the Son of God, who loved me, and gave himself for me" (Gal. ii. 20).

"Set your affection on things above, not on things on the earth. For ye are dead, and your life is hid with Christ in God" (Col. iii. 2, 3).

"Who his own self bare our sins in his own body on the tree, that we, being dead to sins, should live unto righteousness: by whose stripes ye were healed" (1 Pet. ii. 24).

From these verses we learn that the crucifixion of the "old man" is an already accomplished fact, and that it is a co-crucifixion with Christ. It is plainly according to the plan of God that everything that pertains to the old corrupt nature of man should terminate its sinful course at Calvary. The cross is God's place of deliverance. God declares to all who cry out for deliverance from the tyranny of self that this self was crucified with Christ.

It is a fact of great importance for the believer's sanctification that not only was he crucified with Christ, but that he was identified with Christ in His resurrection and ascension. Co-crucifixion opens the door into co-resurrection and co-ascension. "For if we have been planted together in the likeness of his death, we shall be also in the likeness of his resurrection. . . . Now if we be dead with Christ, we believe that we shall also live with him" (Rom. vi. 5, 8). "But God, who is rich in mercy, for his great love wherewith he loved us, Even when we were dead in sins, hath quickened us together with Christ, (by grace ye are saved;) And hath raised us up together, and made us sit together in heavenly places in Christ Jesus" (Eph. ii. 4–6). These are Scriptures often used by Keswick leaders.

(ii) *The Holy Spirit*

Calvary, Keswick tells us, is God's answer to the whole problem of sin. Christ's purpose in going to the cross was to deal drastically and decisively with sin in all of its aspects. In the whole matter of man's salvation everything begins at the cross. This is true of sanctification as well as justification. Man cannot become holy without the cross. The ground of the believer's sanctification is his identification with Christ in His death to sin.

But the Scriptures also make clear, Keswick declares, that the Holy Spirit has a part in sanctification so important that it cannot be over-estimated. If the cross is the ground, the Holy Spirit is the Agent of our sanctification. It is the office and work of the Holy Spirit to make true in our experience that for which Christ died for us upon the cross. It is not enough for us just to *know* that by our union with Christ in His death upon the cross we have been freed from the dominion of sin. That freedom is only potential. It must be progressively realized in daily experience, and this is done by walking in the Spirit. Christ is our sanctification (1 Cor. i. 30), and all sanctification is dependent primarily upon His work. The Holy Spirit is our sanctifier. He renders real and operative our death to sin and our life to God.[1] Unless the Holy Spirit is given His rightful place in the life of the Christian, then even though historically and judicially he was crucified with Christ, the experience of the "wretched man" in Romans vii will be the result.

In the process of sanctification the Holy Spirit never works apart from the cross. He brings us into the path of freedom by beginning at the cross. He does not obtain our freedom from sin's dominion in the sense in which Christ has secured it for us, but by bringing us into it as something already obtained. He takes the blessings that Christ died on Calvary to secure for us as benefits already obtained and provided, and He teaches us to work and strive *from* freedom rather than *to* it. In carrying out His work *in* us the Holy Spirit always works in connection with Christ's work *for* us. What Christ purchased for us the Spirit imparts to us.

(*a*) *Counteraction.* Keswick leaders often say that God's method of sanctification is not *suppression* or *eradication,* but *counteraction.* Romans vii describes what happens when anyone tries to suppress the "law of sin" in his members. We learn there that the bias to sin in human nature is too great to be dealt with apart from Christ, even by regenerate souls. But, it may be asked, as not even the Christian will ever be free from the drive to sin, how can it be kept in subjection? Only, answers Keswick, by the counteracting influence of the Holy Spirit as He is permitted to work out in us the death of the cross to sin.

[1] Alexander Smellie, *Lift Up Your Heart,* pp. 36, 37.

A text frequently used in this connection is Romans viii. 2, "The law of the Spirit of life in Christ Jesus hath made me free from the law of sin and death." It is fatal, we are told, to think that directly we get under the sway of the Spirit of God, that that moment the law of sin and death is eradicated. The law of sin and death is operating all the time. It is something fixed and permanent, and will remain in us as long as we live. Like the law of gravitation, it is a continuous downward tendency—present even when counteracted by another and stronger law.

But from this law, the law of sin and death in our bodies, there is deliverance. That deliverance is by a new law, a mightier force, which counteracts the power of the law of sin. As real as is the energy of sin working in our members, and more mighty, is the energy of the Holy Spirit dwelling in our bodies.

The principle of counteraction is so basic in Keswick teaching that many attempts are made to make it clear with illustrations. Some have already been given. One not yet given, but frequently used, is the story of Peter walking on the water. We are told that he was able to walk on the water not in virtue of anything that Christ had wrought in him, or because his tendency to sink had been eradicated by the power of Christ, but because through faith-contact with Christ he was perpetually receiving a supply of divine power which completely counteracted his weight. He was kept from sinking, moment by moment, as long as he was in contact by faith with the source of all power. He sank just as soon as he got his eyes of faith off Christ and on to circumstances.

(b) *The "Rest of Faith" and Conflict.* When the believer realizes and accepts by faith God's provision for sin—the identification of believers with Christ in His death to sin, and the gift of the Holy Spirit as the indwelling Agent of sanctification—he ceases from his own struggles to live a holy life, and enters the "rest of faith." This, however, Keswick teaches, is not rest from spiritual conflict and temptation, but rest *in* temptation, the heart rest of those who have learned the secret of perfect and constant victory over temptation.

It is of the utmost importance, we are told, "that we should understand clearly the principles on which the warfare with sin is to be waged, and what are the essential conditions to be maintained in order that there should not only be conflict, but victorious conflict." [1]

---

[1] Evan H. Hopkins, *The Law of Liberty in the Spiritual Life*, p. 181.

It is necessary that the Christian prepare himself for the conflict. He must "be strong in the Lord, and in the power of His might" (Eph. vi. 10). For this he must first clearly see the nature of the victory Christ has obtained for His people: at Calvary He vanquished all our spiritual adversaries. The next step is to identify himself with Christ in His victory. He must by faith plant his feet on the victorious position which Christ has obtained for him. To do this is not a question of progressive attainment, but a matter of immediate acceptance by faith. It is a position superior to all his enemies. So long as he retains that ground by faith, his position is impregnable. This at once shows the nature of the fight; he fights not in order to reach the place of victory, but, occupying the position already obtained for him by Christ, he fights from it. The third step is to put on the whole armour of God.

We must distinguish carefully between rebellion and true Christian conflict. A Christian who refuses to let God have His way with him, and sets up his will in opposition to God's will, is in a state of rebellion against God, not engaged in Christian conflict.

A Scripture passage bearing on the subject of conflict often dealt with by Keswick leaders is Galatians v. 16–18: "This I say then, Walk in the Spirit, and ye shall not fulfil the lust of the flesh. For the flesh lusteth against the Spirit, and the Spirit against the flesh; and these are contrary the one to the other: so that ye cannot do the things that ye would. But if ye be led of the Spirit, ye are not under the law." The conflict here, it is pointed out, is not between the two natures, flesh and spirit, as is so often thought, but between the flesh and the Holy Spirit. The apostle declares that walking in the Spirit is the means of living in continual triumph over the lust of the flesh. The believer often makes the mistake of thinking that he can overcome the flesh by his own struggles. Really he has no power to conquer the flesh; but he is free to yield either to the flesh or the Spirit; and by the constant surrender of his will to the Holy Spirit he finds a power in God that completely conquers the flesh and brings deliverance from its lusts. It is in, and through, and by the Spirit, that the mortifying or putting to death of the flesh is to be accomplished, and this only by means of the cross.

"What therefore this chapter of the Epistle to the Galatians puts before us, is not a description of that struggling between the two natures which so many Christians mistake for true Christian warfare, but the way of deliverance from one of our most serious hindrances to victorious conflict. It shows us how by the power of the Holy Ghost we may stand in a position of freedom from the harassing influences of the 'lust of the flesh'—a freedom which is essential in order that we may engage in the conflict, run in the race, labour in the work, and abide in the fellowship to which by God's grace we may have been called." [1]

After the Brighton Convention the Rev. J. B. Figgis—later one of the Keswick leaders—made a statement about the Brighton position on conflict which applies just as well to Keswick, and indeed was often echoed by many of the Keswick men, "The difference between the old teaching and the new, if we must classify them so . . . seems to be this: That in former times it was conflict with the expectation of defeat, and now it is conflict with the expectation of victory." [2]

(B) THE PLACE OF FAITH IN SANCTIFICATION

God's provision for sin is a twofold one—our identification with Christ in His death to sin, and the gift of the Holy Spirit through whose counteracting influence we are freed from the dominion of sin. Sanctification is thus, first and foremost, the gift of God's grace—not the result of self-effort—and is available to all believers.

The Keswick position is that in Scripture sanctification comes by faith, and not in another way. Knowing what was accomplished on the cross—that our old man was crucified with Christ, that the body of sin might be destroyed, in order that henceforth we should not serve sin, we are by faith to reckon ourselves dead unto sin and alive to God. We have seen how Mr. Hopkins said that the order is fact, faith, feeling—or, he might have said, experience. The Christian begins with certain divine facts; he believes and acts upon those facts; and then those facts become realities in his everyday experience.

Keswick is very careful to point out that its doctrine of sanctification by faith is not the same thing as Quietism. In the words of Bishop Handley Moule, "The Scripture doctrine of Sanctification teaches no effortless passivity. No will is so fully constituted for work as the regenerate and surrendered will. And in this matter of inner sanctification . . . the will has abundant work to do, in watching and prayer, in self-examination and confession of

---

[1] Evan H. Hopkins, *The Law of Liberty in the Spiritual Life*, p. 199.
[2] *Record of the Convention for the Promotion of Scriptural Holiness held at Brighton*, 1875, p. 448.

G

sin, in diligent study of the divine Word, in the spiritual use of sacred ordinances, in holy contemplation of Christ, in attention to every whisper through the conscience. But these works will all be done with a view to maintaining and deepening that sacred practical contact with Christ by faith which is the one ultimate secret of spiritual success. They will be helps and guides to faith, not substitutes for its divine simplicity. The temptation of the hour will be met less by direct efforts of the will than by indirect; through, and 'in, Him who enableth.' " [1]

(c) THE LIMITS OF SANCTIFICATION

In 1875 R. W. Dale of Birmingham spoke in defence of the Oxford and Brighton Conventions at the autumn meeting of the Congregational Union. Evangelical leaders everywhere were then discussing—and many were criticizing—the teaching of the Conventions. Dale himself had not attended either of the Conventions, but, he said, contact with the leaders of the Conventions, and with many of those who had attended, had made it perfectly clear to him that a new life and a new strength had come to many as a result of the new teaching. "The people tell us they have come to see a larger power in God for the sanctification of the soul than they had ever imagined before . . . they say that power is larger, and can be more completely trusted than they have before suspected."

Then he continues that in practice the Church has divided sins into two classes—gross sins like drunkenness and profanity, and genteel sins like temper, selfishness, and envy. Those guilty of the first are taught to trust God perfectly for strength to overcome; they trust and do overcome; while those guilty of the second are told to fight and struggle, but are given no hope that power will be given them by God to get rid of them, and it is not thought strange if even after fifteen and twenty years they are still under the power of these sins. He says that his impression is that the substance of the teaching of the conference is that God is able to save men from one set of sins as from another. What Dale said of the Oxford and Brighton Conventions applies as well to Keswick, for, as Harford points out, "a continuity of teaching has been maintained which, in spite of many variations, is the same as that given at the Oxford Conference." [2]

[1] H. C. G. Moule, *Outlines of Christian Doctrine*, pp. 193, 194.
[2] *Record of the Convention for the Promotion of Scriptural Holiness held at Brighton*, 1875, pp. 450, 451.
[3] C. F. Harford, *The Keswick Convention*, p. 20.

Fundamental in Keswick teaching is the declaration that a life of victory over conscious sin is the rightful heritage of every child of God. The normal experience of every Christian should be one of victory instead of constant defeat. At one of the meetings of the 1890 Convention, H. W. Webb-Peploe put the difference between the ordinary teaching and this in a crisp sentence. "Before I expected failure, and was astonished at deliverance; now I expect deliverance, and am astonished at failure."[1]

"How far may a believer go in holiness in the present life?" Dr. Andrew Bonar once asked. Dr. Alexander Smellie replied, "Our answer to the query must be, Never so far as absolute sinlessness, till evil in us is eradicated and destroyed, till within and without we wear only the spotless glory of the Son of God; never to that ultimate end beyond which nothing remains to be coveted. . . . As they said of the medieval statue which depicted His figure, He is always taller than the tallest man who approaches Him. Ah, but with most of us, the danger is not of falling into the delusion that we are sinless, or may soon be sinless; it is of being content with something miserably short of sinlessness, and of holiness which may and should be ours."[2]

In a discussion of the limits of sanctification, Bishop Handley Moule says that the question arises whether a Christian may actually attain "such a deliverance here from sinfulness in his constitution and from sinning in his acts (inward and outward) as to entitle him to say, 'I am devoid, in all respects, of sin'."[3] The promises and offers of Scripture, he avers, are indeed magnificently large, and the New Testament obviously contemplates the Christian's life *"not intermittently, but normally,* a 'walk with God' in the deep peace of a loving obedience of motive and act, pleasing to Him in Christ." The lives of many Christians fall far below this divinely intended realization.

But, he continues, Scripture presents another side, of limit and caution. From the side of God's grace and gift, all is perfect, but from the human side, because of the effects of the Fall, there will be imperfect receptivity, and therefore imperfect holiness, to the end of life. So to the very last the Christian is to pray with profound sincerity, "Forgive us our trespasses," and to reflect on his need of cleansing from all sin by the propitiatory blood of Jesus Christ. He

[1] J. B. Figgis, *Keswick from Within* (London, Marshall Brothers, Ltd., 1914), p. 105.
[2] Alexander Smellie, *Lift Up Your Heart,* pp. 90, 91.
[3] H. C. G. Moule, *Outlines of Christian Doctrine,* pp. 194, 195.

is divinely entitled to, and enabled for, a continuous spiritual emancipation from the dominion of sin, for by the cross he has become
dead to sin; but he is not yet exempted from sin's presence, and he
has still to reckon with the flesh. He no longer lives in the sphere
of the flesh, but the flesh is in him, and just so far as its "infection"
is there, he needs every moment the conquering counteraction of the
Holy Spirit.

The teaching of Keswick regarding the limits of sanctification
clearly is not open to the charge of being perfectionist. It is not
taught that the believer is ever beyond the reach of temptation, or
the possibility or ability to sin. It is not taught that the believer's
crucifixion with Christ implies that sin is dead or that it is eradicated. It *is* taught that in Christ he is brought positionally into such
a relationship to sin that he is beyond the reach of sin's dominion
and lordship, and that if he walks in the Spirit that which is
positional may be made experimental. If he continues to remain
under the dominion of sin, it is because he wants to sin and does
not claim his privileges in Christ.

D. A Consideration of the Problem of God's Provision for Sin

The heart and core of Keswick teaching is its doctrine of sanctification by faith. "The Keswick position," says one of its speakers,
"is that in Scripture sanctification comes by faith, and not in any
other way." [1]

There are Christians who think otherwise, and so from the very
beginning there have been those who have attacked this doctrine
as unscriptural. Especially in the first years of the movement,
critics were very numerous. Writing of those early days when
Keswick was so unpopular, one of its leaders said, "In those days
we went to Keswick more or less with the feeling that we were
losing our reputation in doing so, especially if it happened to be a
ministerial reputation. We were speckled birds. We were associated with those who were looked down upon, and frowned upon,
to a considerable extent; and our doctrines were much criticized,
as well as ourselves." [2]

Prebendary Webb-Peploe, writing of the way Keswick was regarded in its early years, says that once he was asked to set forth

[1] Norman C. Macfarlane, *Scotland's Keswick*, p. 13.
[2] *The Keswick Week*, 1903, p. 2.

"Keswick teaching" before some fifty or sixty Evangelical clergy, and after he had done so the chairman of the meeting, who was perhaps the very centre of Evangelical Churchmanship in those days, arose and said: "Heresy! Heresy!! Damnable Heresy! I hold that it is for the glory of God that we should fall into sin, that He may get honour to Himself by drawing us out of it!" [1]

No one will question the truth of Arnold Toynbee's statement that "the answer to the problem of history is the answer to the problem of evil." [2] The one great problem in the world is the problem of sin, and this is true of Christians as well as non-Christians. The value of a system of thought or of a doctrine therefore depends upon the manner in which it proposes to deal with the problem of sin. Any failure here means failure all along the line. Let us see what the Word of God has to say about the problem and God's solution of the problem.

(1) The Statement of the Problem

The Word of God declares that man's first estate, before the Fall, was one of *life*, because of unhindered communion with God; of *righteousness*—the logical result of that life and communion; and *dominion* over God's creation on earth. As a result of disobedience, he fell from that first estate, bringing about disastrous changes in himself and in the world outside that have continued ever since. Ever since then his estate has been one of *death, sin,* and *subjection.* Rebellion against God brought death—the death of the soul (that is, separation from the life of God), the death of the body, and the death of soul and body eternally. Separation from God brought the fruit of sin. When fellowship with God was broken, the harmony of man's entire being was disrupted; and being at odds with God he became an immoral being, and his acts could therefore be only sinful. By refusing to submit to the will of God he brought himself under subjection to Satan. As a result of the Fall, man therefore labours under the tyranny of death, sin, and Satan.

That is the situation in which man finds himself. Any minimizing of the awful seriousness of the problem is bound to lead to attempted solutions that are inadequate. The problem is so radical in nature, that only a remedy of the most drastic kind can be effective. All sorts of human solutions have been proposed, but none

[1] Charles F. Harford, *The Keswick Convention*, pp. 39, 40.
[2] Quoted in *The Presbyterian*, June 21st, 1947.

have succeeded. It is this situation that called forth out of God's love the coming of Christ.

(2) The Divine Solution of the Problem Centred in Christ

The Scriptures are clear in teaching that Adam was constituted by God the representative of the entire human race. When he sinned, the entire race is considered to have sinned, and in him receives the results of sin. The results of his disobedience—death, sin and subjection—have been passed on to all of Adam's posterity.

In the same way, Christ was constituted by God the representative of the entire human race. He represented all that race in His death at Calvary, and through its relationship to Him the race is considered to have rendered satisfaction and obedience to God, and in Him receives the results of that satisfaction and obedience. By virtue of Christ's capacity as man's representative, He therefore became the focal point of the entire problem of sin. Somehow the problem of mankind's sin became His personal problem at Calvary. Through the death of His Son, God undertook to deal with sin in such a way as to free sinners from the dominion of sin. The foundation of God's dealing with sin in man is the death of Christ on the cross. The cross is therefore the central event in history. There is no solution of the problem of sin apart from it.

(3) Christ's Triumph over Death, Sin, and Satan first of all a Personal One

The death of Christ at Calvary was first of all a great personal triumph for Him. His three great enemies—death, sin, and Satan —poured out all their wrath upon Him and attempted to destroy Him, but He defeated them all decisively. He triumphed over death and established life; He triumphed over sin and established righteousness; He triumphed over the kingdom of Satan and established His own realm. We read that "Christ being raised from the dead dieth no more; death hath no more dominion over him" (Rom. vi. 9); that "he died unto sin once" (Rom. vi. 10), and therefore sin can touch Him no more; and that "having spoiled principalities and powers, he made a show of them openly, triumphing over them in it" (the cross) (Col. ii. 15). The completeness of His triumph is shown by His resurrection and ascension.

(4) UNION WITH CHRIST

Immediately upon His resurrection Christ received the full benefits of that triumph in Himself. But His sacrifice was also a *representative* sacrifice, the whole human race being represented in Him. In Him therefore all mankind likewise conquered, and finds release from, its enemies. The question, however, is, How is Christ's experience of release and triumph at Calvary to be passed on to a world of sinners still under the dominion of its enemies?

The answer is that when a sinner comes to Christ, abandoning all ground for salvation other than Him, and by faith accepts Him as his Saviour, he is thereupon joined to Christ, in a spiritual union, and sealed by the Holy Spirit. It is this union with Christ which provides the basis for a duplication of Christ's triumph within the believer's own experience. By virtue of this union he is forever considered by God to be one with Christ, and the beneficiary of all of Christ's triumph.

Union with Christ, as theologians have been discovering only in comparatively recent years,[1] really is the heart of Paul's theology, more so than justification. Protestant theologians had for long concentrated on the thought of justification, and had regarded it as more typically Pauline than anything else. The death of Christ came to be made a mere refuge-house for pardon, a mere release from the penal consequences of sin. Redemption became something that operates mechanically and almost magically. Sanctification, since it was not organically related to the rest of redemption, was left, as it were, hanging in the air. As a result, a man like Lord Beaconsfield cast aspersions upon the doctrine of the atonement and said that it is positively immoral.

But what theologians have been only recently discovering, that the heart of Pauline theology is the doctrine of union with Christ, Keswick called to the attention of the world seventy-five years ago, and has been stressing ever since.

When the Holy Spirit, on the condition of faith, baptizes a man into Christ and joins him permanently and eternally to Him, he becomes a man "in Christ," in union both with the person and the work of Christ. God considers him to be joined to Christ in all of Christ's atoning work. He is identified with Christ in His death

[1] For some books that point this out, see the following: A. H. Strong, *Systematic Theology* (Philadelphia, Judson Press, 1907), pp. 793–809; James S. Stewart, *A Man in Christ* (New York and London, Harper & Brothers, n.d.), p. 147; F. J. Huegel. *Bone of His Bone* (Grand Rapids, Zondervan Publishing House, n.d.).

(Rom. vi. 3), in His resurrection unto new life in God (Rom. vi. 4, 5), and in His ascension (Eph. ii. 4–6). This threefold identification with Christ now forms a solid basis for the duplication of Christ's triumph in him.

The place in the New Testament where the truth of the believer's identification with Christ in His death and resurrection is most clearly set forth is the sixth chapter of Romans. It would not be possible, I think, to exaggerate the importance of this chapter for the doctrine of sanctification. It has rightly been called the Magna Charta of the soul and the Emancipation Proclamation of the Christian. Failure on the part of a child of God to realize that it is intensely practical and entirely applicable to our present circumstances, and that it is God's answer to the whole problem of sinful human nature, means failure at the very first step of the Christian life and walk. It is astonishing that theologians have not seen this, and have passed by the chapter almost as though it did not exist. One has only to examine the sections on "Sanctification" in the systematic theologies of such standard theologians as Charles Hodge, William Shedd, Henry B. Smith, J. J. Van Oosterzee, and Louis Berkhof to see that they make scarcely any reference to it. This is really astonishing! Only since Keswick first called attention to the vital significance of this chapter to the whole question of sin and sanctification have theologians even begun to give it its proper place.[1]

Until theologians see the centrality of the cross and of our identification with Christ as the basis and ground of sanctification, there is bound to be confused thinking on the subject. There can be no true ethics, no valid doctrine of sanctification, unless it is seen that they have their basis in the teaching of this chapter, that the believer is identified with Christ in His death to sin and in His resurrection to new life and power. Keswick sees this, and very rightly puts great stress upon it. It is hardly possible to over-emphasize it.

(5) The Mediation of Christ's Triumph in the Believer's Life

It is good to know that Calvary is God's answer to the problem of sin. It is good to know, too, that the believer is joined to Christ by

---

[1] In 1875 R. W. Dale, in his book, *The Atonement*, called attention in a memorable passage to the importance of Romans vi for the doctrine of sanctification; and in 1879 John Laidlaw, professor of Systematic Theology at New College, Edinburgh, and later to become one of Keswick's enthusiastic supporters, in his well-known book, *The Bible Doctrine of Man*, pointed out that the teaching of Romans vi is that the death of Christ, besides being an expiatory death for cancelling guilt and bringing in everlasting righteousness, is the ground of our sanctification. Our union with Christ in His death and resurrection, he says, secures moral renovation as well as justifying grace (pp. 483–8).

the Holy Spirit, and that this union forms the basis for his participation in the triumph of Christ over sin. For sanctification a knowledge of these spiritual facts is not only good, but indispensable.

The problem still remains, however, as to how that which is practical for the believer becomes actual, and how imputed sanctification becomes experimental sanctification. For it must not be forgotten that when a person is regenerated he continues to have his old nature, and that this old nature will continue to want its way as it did before. This old nature, called in the New Testament by various names—usually the "old man" and the "flesh"—stands squarely athwart God's will for the believer that he live a holy life. D. L. Moody used to say that he had more trouble with himself than with any other man, and what he said of himself must be echoed by every honest Christian.

The New Testament gives no promise that in this life the Christian will ever be free from the flesh. The Corinthian Christians are called "carnal" by Paul because they allowed the flesh in them to manifest itself by envy, jealousy, and strife. The Galatian Christians, Paul says, were called unto liberty, but some were using their liberty for an occasion to the flesh (Gal. v. 13). If God desires that positional sanctification become experimental, then He must have made some provision to this end. Somehow our inherited sinful nature, in which, says Paul, there is no good thing, must be kept in the place of subjection, so that it will not be able to rule over the personality.

Keswick tells us that the Holy Spirit, who indwells every believer from the moment of his regeneration, is the counteracting agent of the flesh, and the divine means of making the victory of Calvary a reality in his experience. Because of the Spirit's personality, and His intimate relationship to the believer, the process of sanctification of necessity must involve personal contact between believer and Spirit—intelligent co-operation of two persons, rather than blind resignation to an unknown force. There is no lack of power or of ability on the part of the Holy Spirit to bring Christ's victory into the realm of human experience. Whatever failure there may be in the Christian's life is sure testimony of a lack of co-operation with the Spirit.

Scripture nowhere teaches that sanctification proceeds automatically in the believer's life, but everywhere there is emphasis on the grave responsibilities resting upon Christians. It is possible for them to walk after the flesh, or after the Spirit. There are

Christians who almost habitually walk after the flesh, as there are those who almost consistently walk after the Spirit. And it is quite possible for the believer to be at one moment walking in the Spirit, and at the next moment walking in the flesh. We are told that God through Christ condemned sin in the flesh, "that the righteousness of the law *might be* fulfilled in us," but the condition of such fulfilment is that we "walk not after the flesh, but after the Spirit" (Rom. viii. 3, 4). The good news of the Gospel in the matter of sanctification is that we may walk in accordance with the new creation rather than with the old, if certain conditions are met.

The conditions of consistent progress in sanctification are three-fold. The first condition is proper knowledge of the truth. There is liberating power in divine truth. "Ye shall know the truth, and the truth shall make you free" (John viii. 32). "For their sakes I sanctify myself, that they also might be sanctified through the truth" (John xvii. 19). The believer must have a sufficient understanding of the triumph of Calvary, the union of the believer and Christ, and the scriptural method of progressive sanctification. A Christian with vague and undefined ideas about the divine basis and method of sanctification will inevitably try to wrestle with his sins, although with scarcely any hope of overcoming them. The truth of God's plan for victory over sin must be clearly understood before any real progress may be made in sanctification.

But mere apprehension of the truth is not sufficient. There must also be proper faith—and faith is not a mere mental assent to the truth of the Gospel, but is a resting on the truth of God. When a believer comes to an understanding of the truth that he has been joined to a triumphant Christ and is positionally in possession of that triumph, it is incumbent upon him to rest upon that truth in faith. He is to reckon himself to be dead unto sin and alive unto God (Rom. vi. 11).

The third condition of consistent progress in sanctification is the believer's consent to die to every fleshly desire in him. Before Christ could rise in newness of life, triumphant over all His foes, He must die; and so before we can enter experimentally into the fruit of His resurrection, we too must enter experimentally into His death. The believer has a definite responsibility in sanctification. He is to hand over the fleshly deeds of the body to the Spirit for mortification. "If ye through the Spirit do mortify the deeds of the body, ye shall live" (Rom. viii. 13). He is then to stand by faith in the knowledge that he died to sin in Christ at Calvary. It is the Holy Spirit's responsibility to do the rest.

Sanctification is thus the result, not of attempts at suppression of the flesh, but of faith in the finished work of Calvary. It is not self-mortification, but mortification through the Spirit. It is the place of the Holy Spirit to accomplish sanctification in the believer's life; it is His function to put to death the deeds of the body in the believer. It is the believer's responsibility to consent to die; but this is by no means an easy thing. It means that in all things I choose not to do the thing *I* want to do, but the thing *God* wants. It means that God shall be all-in-all in my life, and that the Holy Spirit shall be obeyed in every particular.

It must be granted that in its doctrine of sanctification by faith Keswick has restored to the Church an emphasis that is strictly Biblical. It is not something new. There have always been saints who have seen it clearly. For centuries the doctrine of justification by faith only was not known and preached in Christendom. There were but few who in the prevailing ignorance of the Middle Ages knew and declared this great truth. At the Reformation there was a return to this Scriptural and apostolic doctrine. In the same way, the doctrine of sanctification by faith was allowed to lie dormant for centuries, unknown and unappreciated except by a few isolated Christians. It remained for Keswick to call the attention of the Church to it.

CHAPTER V

CONSECRATION

The message of Keswick, says Charles F. Harford, a son of the founder of the Convention, "is perhaps best expressed in the terms of its original title, in which it is described as a "Convention for the Promotion of Practical Holiness.' This is the one reason for its existence. The Keswick Convention has set up no new school of theology, it has instituted no new sect, it has not even formed a society, but exists for the sole purpose of helping men to be holy." [1]

The Convention is not interested in academic discussions of theology and ethics, or even in adding to the store of Bible knowledge of those who attend, but simply and only in helping men to be holy. Holiness as understood by Keswick, it must be remembered, however, is not an ascetic withdrawal from the world; not a subjective pietism, interested in its own whiteness; not striving after a vague, mystical oneness with God; but spiritual wholeness and health that will issue in a practical walk in the Spirit and the daily doing of God's will.

This practical aim of the Convention is illustrated in the annual Letters of Invitation that are sent out before each Convention, in which are usually also set forth in a few words the object and purpose of Keswick. In one such Letter, for example, it is said that Keswick "is a fresh call to a deeper consecration, a clearer vision, and a more thorough appropriation—a call to the fulfilment of those conditions in which lies the secret of the truest and fullest manifestation of the Christ life, both in the inner experience and in the outer walk of the followers of Christ." [2] In another Letter the Trustees of the Convention say, "It is unnecessary to say that spiritual enjoyment is by no means the end we have in view at such meetings. We come in order to be brought into more complete harmony with the mind of God, to be more thoroughly separated in heart and practice from everything that is alien to Him, and be more fully yielded to His will for His service and glory. Hindrances

[1] Charles F. Harford, op. cit., p. 4.
[2] *The Keswick Week*, 1907, ix.

to our progress—still existing—as well as failures in the past, have to be discovered, confessed and renounced." [1]

We have seen that for the attainment of Keswick's purpose a certain progression of teaching is followed at every Convention. The leaders assume that many of the Christians who come to the Convention—especially some of those who come for the first time—are not in a state of spiritual health, and therefore are not growing and developing normally into Christian maturity. In some way, perhaps unknown to them, they are afflicted with the disease of sin, so that their spiritual vitality is sapped and their usefulness and effectiveness as Christians crippled. The first day or so of the Convention is therefore spent in spiritual diagnosis. Sore spots of sin are unsparingly exposed. God's requirements of His people, and the way He regards sin, are set forth with honest yet loving boldness, and in such a way that the Christian knows how he stands before God.

The Keswick leaders realize, however, that to tell a man he is sick, and just where the source of his illness is, without telling him how he may be cured, is of no help to him, but only adds to his despair. On the second day of the Convention, therefore, there is a setting forth of God's wonderful provision for the whole problem of sin—not only of sin as guilt, but of sin as moral defilement, as a ruling principle, as a spiritual disease, as a habit, and as an indwelling tendency. The Christian is told that the cross of Calvary and the Holy Spirit are the divine solution for every aspect of sin, and that all attempts to deal with it apart from the divine provision are bound to end in disappointment and failure. Sanctification as well as justification is by grace through faith.

But even a knowledge of God's requirements and of His provision for the meeting of those requirements, while indispensable to Christian growth, are not sufficient. It is true, as Jesus said, that the truth shall make us free; but for the bringing of freedom where there is bondage to sin of any kind, there is need of something more than mere knowledge of the truth of God, more even than assent of a mental kind to the truth. It is true also, as the Scriptures point out, that sanctification is by faith, but faith is considerably more than agreement that certain divine realities are really so. God's blessing of deliverance from the power of sin is not to be had merely for the asking, but is conditional upon our willingness to meet His terms—and His terms, Keswick says, are a complete

[1] *The Keswick Week*, 1910, ix.

personal consecration. All God's provision is conditioned upon human acceptance for full realization and enjoyment. This is so at every stage of the Christian life. In Keswick's programme of teaching, Wednesday is the day when an effort is made to bring Christians to the point of making such a consecration.

A. The Nature of Consecration

The subject of consecration—sometimes also referred to as dedication and full surrender—a branch of the wider and larger matter of holiness, faces us with a number of disturbing questions, the very mention of which suggests how widely divergent are the opinions of various schools of thought upon this subject. Is it a single act, or a continual process? Is it absolute and complete by one decisive step of the soul, or is it a gradual and progressive development, lifelong and ever incomplete? Is it a reality that exists as a matter of course in all Christians alike; or are some Christians consecrated and other Christians not? Must the experience of consecration be separated from that of regeneration by a length of time, or may it be included in it? Does it always involve a real crisis in the life, or may the reality exist without such a crisis ever having taken place? When once existing in the soul, is it necessarily permanent, or may it vary in its reality and power?

(1) CRISIS AND PROCESS

Statements frequently heard at Keswick are: "Sanctification is a process beginning with a crisis," and "Sanctification is a crisis with a view to a process." They are very characteristic of Keswick, and set forth in a few words some of its basic teachings.

In order to understand what they mean it is necessary to know first what, according to Keswick, sin basically is. "What is sin?" asks F. B. Meyer, and then answers his question, "Isn't it me-ism? . . . In its ultimate analysis, sin is the assertion of self: 'I want that; I'll do this; I'll have my way; I think God is hard to block me.'"[1]

Evan Hopkins writes in the same vein. "Man was never made to be his own centre. And yet it is this that sin has brought about. As originally created, God was the object of his affections. His whole being revolved round *Him*. And so long as this was so there

[1] *The Keswick Week*, 1902, p. 56.

was perfect harmony and peace between God and man. But sin entered, and man's moral being at once became uncentred, and the result was chaos, confusion, and discord. It threw man out of his original orbit. It changed his centre. The place once occupied by God was now taken up by self. Man continued to love, to serve, and to trust—but it was no longer God who was the object of his affections, of his service, or of his faith. It was himself. And so the great characteristics of fallen man are *self*-love, *self*-pleasing, and *self*-confidence. He has become essentially selfish. He thinks first of himself, judges of things in relation to himself, and prefers his own interests above everything else. He lives for himself—seeks his own glory and reputation and ease. He trusts to himself—believes in his own worthiness and sincerity and ability.

"Here we have the secret of all the selfishness and pride and unrest we see in the world. It is because man has lost his true centre. He is *eccentric*." [1]

The essence of sin then, according to Keswick, is for man to live independently of his Maker, and to make self the centre of his life. From the very first, he was faced by the terrible alternative of making God or self the centre of his life. Everything in his make-up and experience told him that true happiness lay only in a life directed to his Creator, but the time came when he thought he could still be happy and blessed—indeed, more so—if he became the director of his own life. He wanted to be on his own and take care of his own future; to have something of which God might perhaps have a reasonable part, but which, nevertheless, was *his,* not God's, something of which he could say, "This is mine, not yours; and I want to dispose of it as I like."

This act of self-will constituted the Fall. When man became an autonomous being, with self, not God, as the centre of his life and the director of his actions, he cut himself off from the source of his peace and of his moral power.

Man became a sinner when he insisted on his right to himself. For man to get back into right relations with God involves not merely, as is so often thought, an acceptance of Christ as a propitiation for sin, but a surrender of his right to himself. An assertion of his independence was his primal sin. At the Fall, God was forced to abdicate the throne of man's heart. Union with God is re-established when self is dethroned, and He is again permitted to assume His rightful place as Sovereign.

[1] *The Christian's Pathway of Power*, September 1878, p. 161.

Sanctification, or the formation of Christ-like character, says Keswick, begins at regeneration, when man is justified of his sins and reconciled to God, and when too he becomes a son of God. A man cannot be born again by the Spirit of God and be entirely destitute of even the first beginnings of sanctification. "No one," Evan Hopkins tells us, "can be really trusting Christ to save him from the penalty of sin who is not as sincerely desiring to be saved from its power. . . . The essence of conversion is the turning away from sin unto God. The soul that truly receives forgiveness is set also upon holiness. . . . When the soul comes to Christ in conversion, he is practically consecrated up to the light that he has." [1]

But although a soul may be practically consecrated up to the light that he has at conversion, nevertheless it is true that many a soul at conversion has very little light. Indeed, Andrew Murray points out, [2] very many Christians at conversion know almost nothing of taking Christ to be their Master. They take Jesus to take away their sin; to bring them to heaven; to help them when they pray; but they never think of saying that they are no more going to have their own will, and that Jesus must have their will every hour. And there is real need, he says, to put one's whole life under the management of Jesus.

Where there has not been a thorough and whole-hearted dedication and committal of the whole being to God, even though it be from ignorance that God demands it, progress in sanctification is bound to be halting and growth in conformity to Christ impeded. God's conditions for growth and progress in holiness are immutable and inescapable. As the divine Potter He cannot shape the human vessel unless it is committed into His hands and remains unresistingly and quietly there. If we are to be used by Him in the performance of His will, the supreme and undivided Lordship of Jesus Christ must be a fact in our lives.

Let us see what the Keswick leaders have to say regarding the nature of consecration.

The act of consecration, says Hubert Brooke, [1] one of the early speakers at the Convention, "implies that the powers of the body, the affections of the heart, and the possessions of the offerer, are put in the hands" and held out before God as an offering to Him.

[1] *The Life of Faith*, August 1890, p. 141.
[2] Andrew Murray, *What Full Surrender Means* (Zondervan Publishing House, Grand Rapids, 1942), p. 9.
[3] Hubert Brooke, *Personal Consecration* (London, James Nisbet & Co., Ltd., 1897), p. 10.

Where it is done with real sincerity, he adds, "the effect must be enormous in the life. It goes as deep as the heart's affections, spreads as wide as the whole being, rises as high as the mind can reach, lasts as long as life itself. It is a tremendous upheaval in the existence where it is first consciously and thoroughly carried out; for it means the entire transference of rule, choice, decision and selection in life from self to God. It means the enrolment of the soldier, who will henceforth obey only one voice; the engagement of the servant to recognize only the master's will; the marriage of the bride, who leaves her own in order to share her husband's home."

W. H. Aldis, in an address on "An Absolute Surrender"[1] says that consecration means being devoted to Christ as a slave to a master, recognizing His absolute authority. It means being separate from every rival, and being separated unto Him alone for His service. A person who makes a full and unreserved consecration will be able to say, "This business is under entirely new management."

The nature of consecration as conceived by Keswick is succinctly expressed in the following poem by one of its leaders, Theodore Monod.

> Oh, the bitter shame and sorrow,
>   That a time could ever be,
> When I let the Saviour's pity
> Plead in vain, and proudly answered,
>   "All of self and none of Thee."
>
> Yet He found me; I beheld Him
>   Bleeding on the accursèd tree;
> Heard Him pray, "Forgive them, Father,"
> And my wistful heart said faintly,
>   "Some of self, and some of Thee."
>
> Day by day His tender mercy,
>   Healing, helping, full and free,
> Sweet and strong, and ah! so patient,
> Brought me lower while I whispered,
>   "Less of self, and more of Thee."
>
> Higher than the highest heavens,
>   Deeper than the deepest sea,
> Lord, Thy love at last hath conquered:
> Grant me now my soul's petition,
>   "None of self, and all of Thee."

[1] *The Keswick Convention*, 1937, p. 190.

H

Such an experience, involving the once-for-all presentation of oneself to God, for His use alone, so that we can in all honesty say we are no longer our own but His who created us and bought us, is a definite step, usually involving a crisis. "In some cases, as in conversion," says Charles F. Harford, "it is impossible to tell the exact moment in which the surrender has taken place, but at the same time there is the definite assurance that this step has been taken, that the Spirit of God is ruling in the heart, and that all is at rest." [1]

Speaking on the subject, "Crisis and Process," at the Keswick Convention in 1907, Evan Hopkins said, "Sanctification in the sense of conformity to the life and character of Christ is a process, a gradual process, a continuous process, an endless process. But sanctification, in the sense of a definite decision for holiness, a thorough and whole-hearted dedication to God, the committal of the whole being to Him is a crisis, and the crisis must take place before we really know the process. Before you can draw a line you must begin with a point. The line is the process, the point is the crisis.

"Two men were arguing upon this subject. One had been brought to understand it not only theoretically but practically, experimentally, and the other one was fairly puzzled—he could not see it. The first man said, 'How did you come from London to Keswick?' 'I came by train.' 'Was it by one sudden jump into Keswick?' 'Oh, no, I came along more and more.' 'Yes, I see, but first you got into the train. How did you get into the carriage? Was it more and more?' 'No, I just stepped in.' 'Exactly; that was the crisis, and as you journeyed along, it was more and more. There is the crisis; there is the process.' " [2]

Dr. J. Stuart Holden, in an address given at the Convention the year before, spoke in similar terms. "That is what consecration is —acceptance, on my part, of the righteous claims of God upon me, 'the acknowledgement,' as Bishop Moule once said on this platform, 'that because I believe, therefore I belong'; the recognition, the glad recognition, on my part, that the great purchase, unspeakable as it is, and, thus, transaction, has taken place, and I am no longer my own. And I make this covenant in my Lord in response to His call to me to be holy, even as He is holy, and I yield to Him gladly and delightedly the life that He claims, and has a right to claim— all I am, and, hence, all I have. That is the work of a moment. That

[1] Charles F. Harford, op. cit., p. 7.
[2] *The Keswick Week*, 1907, p. 132.

is the crisis. It does not take more than a moment. It may take me a long time before it dawns upon me, it may take a long time before I really see my duty and responsibility, my reasonable service, but, once I do, it takes me but one moment to enter into the covenant with my Lord which makes this life possible to me. Have you made the covenant? Have I? Have we really laid upon the altar of God our whole life because we have no right to possess ourselves? 'Called to be saints'—possessed absolutely and entirely by God.

". . . It is a definite transaction—the yielding of myself to God, the incoming of God in all His power into my life, which I have been hearing and to which I am called today.

". . . But what about the process? The process succeeds the crisis. When Jesus cómes He comes to be Master of His own house, He comes by the Holy Ghost to sanctify us wholly. The process will go on every day, but the process cannot begin, apart from Christ Jesus. You cannot be a student in the university until you have matriculated. Matriculation is the crisis; instruction is the process. Let me give you an illustration. This morning I was in a photographer's studio. It is one of the things that we have to do here just to keep us humble, and it did not take very long. I was put into position. That took a little time. But when I was in position, and the lens was there, and the sun was striking at right angles upon the lens and on the sensitized plate, it just took one moment. But it will take some time before the photograph is developed. The likeness is imprinted on the sensitized plate, but there are the acid bath, and the dark room, and various other processes to be gone through, and then the image which was imprinted in one moment of time will be developed and seen, for better or for worse. The crisis may take place in this tent. God grant that it may today. But the process will be carried out perhaps in dark rooms, and, maybe, in acid baths—God alone knows. But the image will be developed. 'Changed into the same image, from glory to glory, as by the Lord the Spirit.' " [1]

We will seriously misunderstand what Keswick means by the word "crisis" unless we realize that it refers to the decision by which a believer commits himself wholly to his Lord, pledging himself henceforth to be obedient unto Him in all things; a decision which initiates, not the process of sanctification, for that began at regeneration, but sanctification in real earnest. It is the removal of the

[1] *The Keswick Week*, 1906, pp. 92, 93.

impediments to sanctification as a normal process, like the removal of boulders in a stream which hinder a free flow of water. Whenever it takes place, it necessarily marks a turning-point in Christian experience. The surrender of the will to God puts one into a position where spiritual progress is possible. Sometimes it is a climax in the life of the believer comparable to the crisis of regeneration. On the other hand, it is possible so gradually to recognize God's claim upon us, that only one by one are the different parts of life yielded to His rule and command.

There is no need, according to Keswick, for the experience of consecration to be separated from that of regeneration by a length of time, more or less extended. It is possible that at regeneration a person may instantly recognize Christ's claim to the soul's consecration, and then and there make a loyal surrender to His claim. There is no logical and inherent necessity for a separation between the two. As we have before noted, every truly born-again soul at regeneration has made an act of consecration, up to the light he has. But both Scripture and experience teach that, due to inadequate instruction, many acts of consecration made at regeneration are very incomplete, and that the consecration of some Christians is an inconstant thing. W. H. Aldis tells of a man who at one time had been a devoted servant of God, and greatly used, who in a moment of confidence said to a friend, "My consecration today is just like smouldering embers." [1] "The crucial point," Hubert Brooke points out, "the urgent need for every true Christian is this: Whether gradually or suddenly, whether in a moment or after years, it matters not; but is your life now yielded to God?" [2]

Consecration, according to Keswick, is neither only a single act nor only a continual process; it is a continual process that has its beginning in a single act. It begins with a big "YES" to God, and is maintained with a lifelong series of yes's to Him. It is both a crisis and a process. Consecration is only the starting-point of the sanctification process, but the process will be hindered and even halted unless the response made to God at consecration is continued.

(2) DENYING SELF AND CONSECRATION

The surrender or the committal of oneself to Christ and the pledge to be eternally loyal to Him as Lord and Master, is only one

---

[1] *The Keswick Convention*, 1937, p. 191.
[2] Hubert Brooke, *Personal Consecration*, pp. 16, 17.

of the two sides of consecration, the positive side. There is another side to it, a negative side.

Saying "Yes" to Christ inevitably and inescapably involves saying "No" to self. The implication of separation unto Christ is separation from self. If we are to present our members unto Christ for His use, then it means that we must decide no longer to use them for the expression of the desires of the flesh. To decide to identify ourselves henceforth only with Christ's interests implies the decision entirely to give up one's own interests. If Christ is to be invited to occupy the throne of the heart, then there must first be a dethronement of self.

Consecration is God's door into fulness of blessing; on one side of the door there are the words, "dedication to God"; on the other side, the words, "denial of self." All through the Christian life entrance into blessing is through this door, and the door is swung open only through the twofold act of dedication to God and denial of self.

We must be careful, says Keswick, not to confuse the denial of self with the prevailing conception of self-denial—involving, for example, the doing without certain desirable things during the season of Lent. J. Russell Howden, in one of his addresses, puts it in this way. "Self-denial in the common usage of to-day means going without something for a time, that later on you may be able to indulge your desires. To deny self means nothing less than that you have definitely and for ever chosen the will of the Lord Jesus Christ as your Guide and Director through life, in place of your own will. To deny self will frequently include self-denial. But a great deal of self-denial may be quite consonant with a life that has never learned to deny self at all."[1]

Referring to the kind of self-denial practised by some religiously-minded people during the Lenten season, Hubert Brooke[2] says that although it may possibly be good for them, mentally, physically, or spiritually, it ought to be understood that it is not what the Scriptures mean by self-denial. Self-denial does not consist of saying "No" to something we like, but in saying "No" to ourselves.

We must turn to Christ for our example of what denying self really means. His life shows that it means the substitution of the divine will for the will of self in all the motives and conduct of life. In such statements as the following, typical of Him, He reveals the inner motives of His conduct and life: "I seek not mine own will,

[1] *The Keswick Week*, 1924, p. 240.
[2] Hubert Brooke, *Personal Consecration*, p. 99.

but the will of the Father which hath sent me" (John v. 30); "I do always those things that please Him" (John viii. 29). They show that His actions, aims, and words were not His own, but His Father's.

On three different occasions Christ gave, in slightly varying terms, the stringent and unvarying conditions upon which alone the principles of discipleship can be carried into practice.

The first occasion upon which these terms are unfolded occurs in the tenth chapter of the Gospel of Matthew. Christ's words are spoken to His disciples as He sends them on their first mission journey. He tells them of the hatred and persecution they will meet with, and then states the conditions which must underlie all service for Him in these words: "He that loveth father or mother more than me is not worthy of me: and he that loveth son or daughter more than me is not worthy of me. And he that taketh not his cross, and followeth after me, is not worthy of me. He that findeth his life shall lose it: and he that loseth his life for my sake shall find it" (Matt. x. 37–39).

The Lord's demand here, as the first condition of consecration, is that the first place in the heart's affections be given to Him. All human relationships are to be taken to the cross, and there we are to die to them. We are to permit no ties of natural affection to side-track us from the doing of God's will in our lives.

The second statement of Christ's in which these conditions of discipleship are given is found in three of the Gospels—Matthew xvi. 21–6; Mark viii. 31–7; and Luke ix. 22–5. He has just told the disciples for the first time of the suffering and death He must undergo at the hands of the Jews, and Peter, amazed and shocked at such an end to their good Master, rebukes Him, saying, "Be it far from thee, Lord: this shall not be unto thee." Jesus then rebukes Peter, declaring that his thoughts were earthly and not divine, and says that God expects the same surrender to His will and the same obedient walking in His path, even though it mean reproach, suffering, and death, of all Christ's disciples. "If any man will come after me, let him deny himself, take up his cross and follow me. For whosoever will save his life shall lose it; and whosoever will lose his life for my sake shall find it. For what is a man profited, if he shall gain the whole world and lose his own soul? or what shall a man give in exchange for his soul?" (Matt. xvi. 21–6.)

The third place where these conditions of discipleship are given is found in the fourteenth chapter of Luke's Gospel. They are preceded by the parable of the great supper, and are followed, in the next chapter, by those marvellous parables of love and grace—the lost sheep, the lost coin, and the lost son. The context, Hubert Brooke says with penetrating insight, lends special force to these conditions. "It is as though the boundless freeness of the Gospel, as shown in the parable of the supper, and the infinite love of God unfolded in the following three parables, required to be guarded from misuse. Nothing may be detracted from the grace and goodness of God therein revealed, but care must be taken to show what effect they must have in the recipients. No one must be allowed to deceive himself, and say, 'I have received the Gospel, I believe in God's love, it is all right with my soul, and now my life does not matter much.' Between these parables, with all their grandeur of divine fulness and grace, there comes this sharp, solemn, incisive statement of what it means to have received the Gospel; of what God intends to result from its reception; of what fruit in discipleship must follow real coming to Christ, being found of Him, returning to God." [1]

Here, then, is Christ's third statement of the conditions of discipleship, "If any man come to me, and hate not his father, and mother, and wife, and children, and brethren, and sisters, yea, and his own life also, he cannot be my disciple. And whosoever doth not bear his cross, and come after me, cannot be my disciple. . . . So likewise, whosoever he be of you that forsaketh not all that he hath, he cannot be my disciple" (Luke xiv. 26, 27, 33).

Discipleship costs so much, Jesus says, that it is well to weigh, coolly and calmly, what is involved in it; and He enforces His words with two parables about counting the cost. "For which of you, intending to build a tower, sitteth not down first, and counteth the cost, whether he have sufficient to finish it? Lest haply, after he hath laid the foundation, and is not able to finish it, all that behold it begin to mock him, saying, This man began to build, and was not able to finish" (verses 28–30). Jesus says in effect, that disciples of His are building a life—a life patterned after His—and unless they know the cost of such a life, they will ere long cease to build and end in miserable failure. When they discover that becoming a Christian involves more than they had bargained for, they will give up, and worldlings will mockingly say, "This man began to build, and was not able to finish."

"Or what king," He goes on, "going to make war against another king, sitteth not down first, and consulteth whether he be able with

[1] Hubert Brooke, *Personal Consecration*, p. 62.

ten thousand to meet him that cometh against him with twenty thousand? Or else, while the other is yet a great way off, he sendeth an ambassage, and desireth conditions of peace." Christians are engaged in a warfare against a mighty foe, and they should not underestimate the wiliness and destructive power of that foe. Unless they know what it costs to be equipped to meet and defeat him, they had better not engage him in conflict at all, as the battle would be lost almost as soon as it was begun.

In these three statements by our Lord of the conditions of discipleship He says, as strongly as He can in words, that He must have the first place in the heart's affections; that in personal conduct self must be denied, the cross must be borne, and the life be lost for His sake; and that all possessions must be forsaken for His sake.

Hubert Brooke puts it in this way: "So, then, here is a call to a life's decision, by which the conduct is henceforth to be ruled. Once and for all, from the moment that discipleship is entered upon and consecration becomes a reality, self is to be dethroned and Christ enthroned, as Ruler and Decider in all life's business and conduct. A position is to be assumed, and a relationship to Christ entered upon, by which the whole life is henceforth affected: no other rule but His, no other Lordship but Christ's, may be known: 'Other lords beside Thee have had dominion over us: but by Thee only will we make mention of Thy name' (Isa. xxvi. 13)." [1]

The denial of self therefore means the rejection of authority or rule by man's self, and the substitution of the will of God in the life, in all relationships. True self-denial exists only where Christ takes the place of self in all of life's decisions. It implies a definite act and decision, though not necessarily a great conscious climax in the life, and is the door to normally progressive sanctification.

Such a decision, Keswick is careful to point out, often involves considerable suffering. Frequently it is necessary, for example, for a letter to be written to some person who has been wronged; for a sacrifice to be made; for an idol to be broken; for a plan of life to be altered. It is a very practical act. It is not real unless everything that stands between the believer and God is put out of the way, and the believer can say, in the words of the well-known Keswick hymn, written by Evan Hopkins. "Nothing between, Lord, nothing between".

On more than one occasion Dr. F. B. Meyer recalled his own experience of consecration. His early life was marred and his

[1] Hubert Brooke, *Personal Consecration*, p. 101.

ministry paralysed just because he had kept back one thing from the Lord. The key of one room was kept for personal use, and the Lord was shut out. The effect of that incomplete consecration was found in lack of power with God, lack of assurance, lack of joy and peace. It was only after a fierce struggle at one of the Keswick Conventions that this last key was handed over to God, and He was made sole and only Ruler of his life and possessions.

But such an act and life of consecration, Keswick leaders tell us, do not involve the merger of the personality of the believer with that of God; nor do they involve the destruction of the personality. The true personality, the new man in Christ, can emerge only as Christ is allowed to rule. It is the self-life that is to be terminated, not the personality.[1]

B. The Effect of Consecration

The effect of a thorough and whole-hearted consecration is that the ground is cleared for sanctification as a process. Through consecration we get into the position where progress becomes possible, in a degree in which it has never been possible heretofore. Speaking of consecration E. W. Moore says, "It is a definite experience. If I were asked to state it theologically, I should say it is the restoration of the normal relationship between the soul and Christ·"[2] Holiness, he goes on, is not some transcendental thing, so that no man can get near it, but spiritual wholeness; and consecration brings about the restoration of the soul to health. In consecration there is an adjustment of the will that ensures sanctity.

Sometimes Keswick leaders describe consecration as the adjustment of spiritual dislocations that are responsible for hindering growth and progress. A man may be an excellent runner, but if a bone is out of joint or if he is out of condition, he can never win a race. So if a Christian's will is out of adjustment with the will of God, he will be so crippled that he cannot make any spiritual progress. Consecration is adjustment of spiritual condition. It is instantaneous—just as the setting of a bone is an instantaneous thing. But the result is progressive sanctification.

In an editorial in *The Life of Faith*, on the subject of "Health and Maturity,"[3] Evan Hopkins says, "The question is frequently

---

[1] *The Keswick Week*, 1907, p. 56.
[2] Ibid., 1901, p. 192.
[3] November 1880, pp. 225, 226.

asked: 'How are we to understand the testimony of those who speak of having received sudden or immediate blessing, as marked and definite as that experienced at conversion? If our knowledge of Christ is gradual, and the reception of His grace progressive, how can it be sudden? Growth cannot be immediate. Development must be gradual. What then is the blessing which so many bear witness to having received in connection with conferences for the deepening of the spiritual life?'

"The answer is plain. It is this: first, the hindrances, which for so long, perhaps years, have retarded the growth and stunted the life, have been seen, confessed and renounced. The removal of these hindrances has not been gradual, but as sudden as it has been thorough. The will, which perhaps for a time rose up in opposition, has given way, and has been brought not to a gradual, but to an immediate decision in the matter. All has been yielded to the Lord.

"Then, second, as a result, faith, which before was weak and fettered, being suddenly liberated, bounds forth in simple and unwavering confidence toward God, and takes its stand in a new and restful attitude, on the promises of His word.

"Blessing must of necessity be at once realized. But what *is* the blessing? Is it that the believer at one bound has reached the goal? Is it that he will now no longer need to grow? Not at all. Just the contrary is nearer the truth.

"It is that the true *conditions* to growth having been brought about, life in new vigour and fulness begins to put forth its power. Health of soul having been established, progress and growth are manifested as never before. The barrier that obstructed the stream being removed, the channel is no longer dry, but is filled at once with the living waters. The massive stone that crushed the plant and buried it in darkness being rolled aside, the life begins immediately to revive, and growth henceforth follows.

"The sudden blessing, therefore, is the result of a full and immediate surrender of the whole heart to God. This sweeps away the obstacles to progressive sanctification.

"The great hindrance to our progress is want of faith. And the great hindrance to our faith is want of thoroughness.

"Let the child of God who would live in the fulness of the Spirit seek by earnest, solemn waiting upon God, this thoroughness of heart, this full consecration of himself to the will of God, and assuredly blessing, rich, full, and definite, will be his. He will be brought into harmony with the mind of God. His spiritual health will immediately revive. And the effect will be, his 'faith will 'grow exceedingly.' He will at once see fresh beauty in the Lord, and such a fulness and richness in the promises, that they will become altogether new to him. There will open out to him possibilities of faith in this life that will fill him with joy and courage. No wonder that his heart is glad, for God's word becomes a new book to him. No marvel that his mouth is filled with praise, for Christ has become unspeakably precious to him.

"Yet with all this he can thoroughly enter into the words of the apostle, and adopt them as expressive of his own experience: 'Not as though I had already attained, either were already perfect: but I follow after, if that I may apprehend that for which also I am apprehended of Christ Jesus.'

"He does not rest on *attainment*. But he rejoices, not only because he sees the possibility, but finds the reality of *attaining*. In other words, because he learns that growth and progress are not merely blessings to be aimed at, but blessings to be known and exemplified.

"As fresh hindrances present themselves in our progress, the same course of action must be pursued. For it is only as this thoroughness of heart is maintained that spiritual health continues.

"A will that is always yielded, and a heart that is ever trustful, is a soul that is continually increasing in the knowledge of God, and abounding in the fruits of righteousness."

Consecration sweeps away all barriers between the believer and God, and clears the ground for the Spirit's control of the personality. As long as the barrier of an active self-life stands between him and God, he is not in a position to claim the power of the Holy Spirit, for God will not allow the Spirit to fill an unconsecrated heart; but with self put out of the way and the Holy Spirit given His rightful place at the seat of controls in every phase of personality, there can be a consistent walk in the Spirit and continued progress in the development of Christ-like character. There is an irreconcilable enmity between self and the Spirit of Christ, and it is when self gives way that the Spirit can work.

C. A Final Appraisal of This Aspect of Keswick Teaching

A primary reason, Keswick tells us, why so little progress in sanctification is made by Christians, is that so many of them have never really faced and yielded to the conditions of Christian discipleship our Lord lays down. They have never faced a crisis in their lives— a crisis involving who will be the master of their lives: they themselves, or Christ. They have never decided, with a full consciousness of what they were doing, whether Christ would be King and Lord of all they are and all they possess.

Not that such a crisis and decision is always subsequent to regeneration, for Keswick tells us that the normal experience is for Christians to have it at regeneration, and God means that it be made then. Nor that some do not enter it without realizing it, as some are regenerated without knowing when; for Keswick informs us that it is inconsequential whether we remember when we made it, the important thing being that we know we have made it.

Is Keswick right, according to the New Testament, that progress in sanctification will be intermittent and halting unless such a decision has been made and maintained? Let us see what the New Testament has to say about it.

Our first parents, created in the image of God and with a will free to choose, were faced with this supreme question, Who will be master of our lives, God or we? When they decided to be master themselves, they brought death and ruin upon themselves and their posterity. Scripture is clear that when a man chooses to live his own life, the consequences are ruinous not only to himself but to others.

Life's greatest decision for us is the same, Who will be the master of my life, God or I? Will I consent to God's verdict upon the flesh, that there is no good in it; will I say "No" to myself; will I direct my own life; or will I choose, voluntarily, that what God made true of me positionally at Calvary—that my old man died with Christ —will become true in my everyday experience?

This decision marks the greatest crisis in a person's life. To cease directing one's own life; to cease going one's own way; to cease being one's own master; to say to God, "Lord, I abdicate the throne of my life in order that Thou mayest rule in every detail of my life"—this is life's greatest decision. It is the major, the supreme decision of life, and it cannot but be a crisis, a turning point in life. Anyone who goes through this experience with a full realization of all that it means, will very likely go through an agonizing crisis. For many people the crisis is prolonged—perhaps even over years— and the decision is made piecemeal; for some there are stages in the crisis and in the decision; and then for a few, of course, there is hardly any struggle in making the decision because their trust in God is so absolute and their love for Him so wholehearted. Such a decision should normally be made at regeneration, but frequently it is not, because we were not told of its necessity; but if it does not come then, it must come later. The decision is the inescapable condition of progressive sanctification.

Even non-Christians recognize the need of self-renunciation, as for example, Goethe, who said, "It is only with renunciation that life, properly speaking, can be said to begin." One of the great themes of the New Testament is the necessity of coming to the place where we are willing, as it were, to go to our own funeral. The words Jesus spoke on the three occasions when He set forth the conditions of discipleship are examples of this. A man is to "hate" not only all those dearest to him, but "his own life also" (Luke xiv. 26), and his possessions are to mean nothing to him.

The great principle of death to self is taught all through the Epistles, as in such apostolic precepts as the following: "they which live should not henceforth live unto themselves, but unto Him which died for them and rose again" (2 Cor. v. 15); "he no longer should live the rest of his time in the flesh to the lusts of men, but to the will of God" (1 Pet. iv. 2); "I am crucified with Christ: nevertheless I live; yet not I, but Christ liveth in me: and the life which I now live in the flesh I live by the faith of the Son of God, who loved me, and gave himself for me" (Gal. ii. 20).

"The carnal mind," Paul tells us, "is enmity against God" (Rom. viii. 7); and there is no good, he says, in the "flesh" (Rom. vii. 18). The flesh wants to assert itself; it wants to be independent of God; to think its own thoughts, make its own decisions, go its own way. God and the flesh cannot at the same time rule in the heart; one must give way to the other. This is true of the flesh in Christians as well as in non-Christians. And so Paul constantly urges Christians to make instantaneous decisions (as the aorist of his verbs shows) to yield their members unto God (Rom. vi. 13), to present themselves unto God (Rom. xii. 1), to mortify the deeds of the body (Rom. viii. 13). Justification, he tells them, involves a complete reversal of all relationships to the old life, and they are therefore to live as dead unto sin and alive unto God. The old life and the new are irreconcilably antagonistic.

It is important to observe that Paul does not take for granted that because those to whom he writes are Christians, that therefore

Christ is ruling supreme in their lives. Quite the contrary; he knows that many of them are carnal, when they have no business being so, and he repeatedly exhorts them to come to an end of themselves and to decide to live wholly for God.

Keswick is right in putting so much emphasis upon the negative side of consecration—the matter of dying to self. To ask a Christian to live unto God without telling him that it implies death to self, will surely lead to an experience of frustration and disappointment. Not enough of this is said in the Church today. The teaching of Scripture is clear, that there must be a Good Friday if there is to be an Easter; death must precede the manifestation of eternal, resurrection life. In the Christian walk, life issues out of death.

The distinction Keswick makes between denying self and what is usually thought of as self-denial is a crucial one, and is thoroughly Biblical. True denial of self is not sometimes, or even always, doing the thing we do not like to do or the thing it is hard for us to do, but the thing God wants us to do. It is not withdrawing from society into a monastery or a nunnery; it is not leaving home and country and going into a foreign land as a missionary; it is not doing without things we like, like candy or meat; it is not getting up on a cold night and spending hours in prayer. It is just doing the will of God, even though the flesh rebels against it. The true Christian does not have to look for suffering; suffering will come his way as he walks with God. Many Christians have fallen into the error of imagining that when they are faced by a decision involving, on the one hand, something easy to do, and, on the other, something hard to do, that the right thing to do is the thing that is hard. That is not Scriptural at all. The hard thing may very well be the wrong thing to do, and the easy thing may quite likely be the right thing. The denial of self means that in all our decisions and acts, self does not enter into the picture at all, and that the will of God will be followed regardless of the consequences to ourselves. It reaches right down to the core of personality, the very centre of the heart.

Keswick is undoubtedly right that an act of consecration, if intelligently and sincerely made, brings about a restoration of soul-health that is the only sure condition of progressive sanctification. The need and the possibility of soul-health is an aspect of Biblical teaching that is sadly missing, and greatly needs emphasis in the Church today. An unscriptural complacency with spiritual ill-health, very often the result of unconsecrated members, prevails in the Church. The Word of God, however, provides no excuse for sickness of soul for which there is a cure.

Keswick is often criticized for teaching that real progress in sanctification is largely a matter of the adjustment of the will to the will of God. There is no doubt in my mind that Keswick is strictly Pauline in this. There would be absolutely no point to Paul's frequent exhortations to Christians to yield and present themselves unto God and to walk in the Spirit, unless they had wills free to do or not to do these things. In the background of all these exhortations there is the implication that if only the wills of God's people were divinely adjusted, phenomenal spiritual progress would be made by them. An indispensable condition to growth and progress is that spiritual dislocations be adjusted, and such dislocations invariably have their centre in a maladjusted will, a will in conflict with the will of God. When we can say, "Thy will be done," then God is able to work in the matter of sanctification, and we will function normally as Christians. God's conditions will then be met for growth into Christ-like character, and without a doubt we shall grow.

Keswick's teaching on consecration is a return to a badly neglected aspect of New Testament teaching on practical holiness. There is nothing unscriptural about it. It correctly describes the human response that must be made to the divine provision for sin.

CHAPTER VI

THE SPIRIT-FILLED LIFE

Jesus meant very much to the Twelve during the three years He was with them. Whenever they were faced with a problem to which they could find no solution, they turned to Him for help, certain that He would give them the right answer. Whenever they were troubled and sad, they had only to go to Him, and He would unfailingly give them comfort. He helped them when they appealed to Him regarding decisions they had to make. There was no trial, no trouble through which they went, but they shared it with Him. They could call upon Him in every emergency, for He was their Comforter, the one who would come to their assistance in every time of need. He was more than an ordinary friend. As man, He could share their every trouble; as God, He could meet their every need.

When, therefore, on the evening before His crucifixion, He told them that they were not to be grieved at His imminent departure, for He would send them another Comforter, His promise meant that the Holy Spirit would mean to them all that He had meant during those three years of intimate fellowship with them. As the Spirit of truth, the Holy Spirit would lead and guide them into all truth, answering their questions and solving their problems according to the mind of God, just as He had done. As their Comforter, the Holy Spirit would be available at every time of trial, at every emergency, at every need. As their Teacher, the Holy Spirit would make real to them and show them how to appropriate the salvation that Christ came into the world to bring.

At the time, it must have been hard for them to see the truth of His words. It must have seemed incredible that anyone could ever fill His place. But Jesus spoke the truth. The time came, after Pentecost, when they realized that He did speak the truth, for the Holy Spirit did become their intimate friend and companion, one to whom they could go for help in every time of need.

The Acts of the Apostles abounds in illustrations of the truth of Christ's words. When the Church was faced with the crucial question as to whether Gentile Christians would be compelled to observe the Jewish law, the apostles and elders who were met in council appealed to their Teacher, the Holy Spirit, who, Jesus had promised, would lead and guide them into all the truth. The decision made, they said in the letter announcing it to the Churches, "seemed good to the Holy Ghost, and to us" (Acts xv. 28). Apparently it should be the normal thing for Christians to say that their decisions are made in consultation with the Holy Spirit and have His full approval.

In the midst of a fruitful ministry in Samaria the deacon Philip was instructed by the Lord to leave his work there and journey on the road from Jerusalem to Gaza, which went through desert country. He obeyed, and found an Ethiopian eunuch in a chariot absorbed in reading a book. Philip did not know what he was reading, but the Holy Spirit did, and more than that, knew the very state of his heart—that it was a heart hungry for the truth of the Gospel. We are told that Philip was a man "full of the Holy Ghost" (Acts. vi. 3), so it is not surprising that he recognized the Spirit's voice when He spoke to him. There is no doubt that the teaching of Scripture is that the Holy Spirit is meant by God to be to us the Guide that He was to Philip.

The Holy Spirit was recognized as the Administrator and Director of the whole work of the Church. It was He who determined the place and the duty of each person in the army of Christ. It was He, too, who planned the strategy of the war against the hosts of darkness. It is therefore not strange to read that, as the Christian leaders of the Church at Antioch waited in prayer before the Lord, "the Holy Ghost said, Separate me Barnabas and Saul for the work whereunto I have called them" (Acts xiii. 2). Let us observe that the call to Barnabas and Saul came from the Holy Spirit, and that He had a definite work for them to do. Barnabas and Saul, we read later, were "sent forth by the Holy Ghost" (Acts xiii. 4)—as soldiers are sent forth on a mission by their commander.

On his second missionary journey the apostle Paul, in company with the young disciple Timothy, travelled throughout Phrygia and the region of Galatia preaching the Gospel, but we read that they "were forbidden of the Holy Ghost to preach the word in Asia" (Acts xvi. 6), although some time later the Holy Spirit saw fit to permit Paul to spend considerable time preaching the Gospel in Asia; and when, after going through Mysia, they tried to enter Bithynia to preach the Gospel, "the Spirit suffered them not" (Acts xvi. 7). Paul knew in experience the meaning of the "fellowship of the Spirit" (Phil. ii. 1) and the "communion of the Holy Ghost"

I!

(2 Cor. xiii. 14). That is apparently the principal reason why his ministry was so fruitful.

No one can read the New Testament without realizing that, in the intention of God, the Holy Spirit is meant to have a predominant place in the life of the Church as a whole and in the lives of individual Christians. Christians are to be "filled with the Spirit" (Eph. v. 18). They are commanded to "walk in the Spirit" (Gal. v. 16). They are to "mortify the deeds of the body" through the Spirit (Rom. viii. 13). God commands them, "grieve not the Holy Spirit of God" (Eph. iv. 30), and "quench not the Spirit" (1 Thess. v. 19). They are to be "led by the Spirit of God" (Rom. viii. 14). In the words of Jesus, those who believe in Him are not to have a modicum of the Spirit, but "rivers of living water" (John vii. 38) are to issue forth from their inward being, so that through the Spirit they will carry life and blessing to others. The Holy Spirit is everywhere set forth as the power for holiness, enabling the Christian to *be* what he ought to be, and the power for service, enabling the Christian to *do* what he ought to do.

In spite of the plain teaching of Scripture regarding the important place that the Holy Spirit is to have in the life of the Church, there is on the part of its members a woeful ignorance and consequently a failure to come up to God's standard in this respect. G. H. C. Macgregor,[1] in one of his Keswick addresses, tells of a Scottish minister who said that he believed in God the Father and he believed in God the Son, but, he confessed, "I don't really see where the Holy Ghost comes in." The writer once heard a minister say to a group of ministers and lay leaders of the Church, that a girl in his parish took instructions in Catholicism from a priest after she had become engaged to a Roman Catholic. Before long, however, she discontinued the lessons because she realized that Catholicism offered her nothing spiritually satisfying. She told her minister that the priest had asked her whether Protestants believed in the Holy Spirit, but she did not know what to reply. "Do we?" she pathetically asked. The writer remembers the Dean of a seminary telling of an elder in a Church who thought the Holy Spirit is a man's conscience. For multitudes of Christians the Holy Spirit is an impersonal divine influence. The Holy Spirit as a Person, as a member of the Godhead, simply is not real to them.

It is these two facts—God's provision of the Holy Spirit for the Church, and the failure of the Church to avail itself of this provision

[1] *The Keswick Week*, 1897, p. 100.

—that are responsible for the emphasis that Keswick puts on this subject—the Spirit-filled life. It is the climax toward which the teaching of the first three days of the Convention leads. In an address given at Keswick in 1947, Montague Goodman said that the message of the Spirit-filled life is "the central dominating theme of Keswick" and "the very *raison d'être* of the Convention." [1] Harford says that the Keswick Convention exists to make the article of the Creed, "I believe in the Holy Ghost," not merely a theological formula to be believed in, but a living reality to each Christian soul; [2] and in another place in the same book he says that one of the key-notes of Keswick is the teaching on the fulness of the Spirit, and that while it is everywhere acknowledged that it is a great privilege to be filled with the Spirit, at Keswick it is earnestly proclaimed that it is a great sin not to be filled with the Spirit. [3] Again and again Keswick speakers stress the fact that to be filled with the Spirit is not presented in Scripture as an optional matter, but as a holy obligation that rests upon all Christians.

A. The Nature of the Blessing

(1) ALL CHRISTIANS HAVE THE HOLY SPIRIT

It is the teaching of Keswick that the Holy Spirit dwells in every child of God. There are Christians who hold that the "baptism of the Spirit" is a spiritual experience in addition to, and subsequent to, regeneration, which they speak of as "a second blessing," to be asked for and waited for as the disciples did on the day of Pentecost. This view, Keswick says, is utterly unauthorized by Scripture. In the words of one of its speakers, "The baptism of the Spirit is the primary blessing; it is, in short, the blessing of regeneration. When a man is baptized with the Spirit, he is born again." [4] The gift of the Spirit, or the baptism of the Spirit, is not, therefore, a blessing which the believer is to seek and receive subsequent to his experience of conversion.

Evan Hopkins puts it in this way, "The first point to be recognized, as clearly set forth in the Scriptures, is the fact that all Christians have the Holy Spirit. They have not only been brought

---

[1] *The Keswick Week*, 1947, p. 199.
[2] Harford, op. cit., p. vii.
[3] Harford, op. cit., pp. 218, 219.
[4] G. Campbell Morgan, *The Spirit of God* (New York, Fleming H. Revell Company, 1900), p. 169.

under His influence, they have received the Holy Spirit Himself.
'If any man have not the Spirit of Christ, he is none of His' (Rom.
viii. 9)." [1]

(2) Not all Christians Have the Fulness of the Holy Spirit

We must recognize the fact, Keswick tells us, that to have the
Spirit is one thing, but to be *filled* with the Spirit is quite another
thing.[2] There is a distinct possibility, says J. Stuart Holden, of a
believer being genuinely regenerated, and having no doubt whatsoever about his salvation, and yet never to have received in His
fulness the Holy Spirit.[3] And Clarence H. M. Foster says that while
every true believer, without exception, is in very deed a temple of
God, the fulness of the Holy Spirit is not experienced by every child
of God. He goes on to say, "It is largely true to say that it was a
recognition of this fact on the part of Christian people that brought
the Keswick Convention into being so many years ago."[4]

Keswick is undoubtedly right in teaching that while every Christian has the Spirit and has been baptized by the Spirit, not every
Christian is filled with the Spirit or has the fulness of the Spirit.
There would be no point to the command of the apostle Paul, "be
filled with the Spirit" (Eph. v. 18), if it were *ipso facto* true that
every Christian is filled with the Spirit. To be filled with the Spirit
means the complete possession and guidance of the believer by the
Spirit. If this were true of all Christians, the Church would advance
irresistibly against the hosts of darkness in the world, as it did in
its early days.

(3) The Significance of the Fulness of the Spirit

The sum of New Testament teaching is that a Spirit-filled life is
the normal condition of the believer.[5] In the Acts of the Apostles
there are constant references to a state of spiritual fulness as the
state of certain Christians. It means that they were controlled by
the Spirit and guided by the Spirit, so that He was able to use them
as His instruments.

According to the teaching of the New Testament, it is the Spirit
who makes Christ real to us and mediates Christ's gifts to us.

[1] Hopkins, *The Law of Liberty in the Spiritual Life*, p. 204.
[2] Ibid., p. 205.
[3] *The Keswick Week*, 1902, p. 123.
[4] *The Keswick Convention in Print*, 1941, p. 57.
[5] G. Campbell Morgan, *The Spirit of God*, p. 185.

Where the Spirit dwells in full and undisputed possession, He brings freedom into the soul, and this He does not by obtaining our freedom in the sense in which Christ has secured it for us, but by bringing us into it as something already obtained. He does nothing *in* us apart from what Christ has done *for* us.[1]

"The fulness of the Spirit," says Andrew Murray, "is simply the full preparation for living and working as a child of God."[2] It is for holiness and service, which are impossible without it. The power of the Holy Spirit is needed for living a consistent Christian life. A Spirit-filled Christian will not necessarily be used of God to perform miracles in the realm of nature or to do spectacular things in the realm of the Spirit, but he will lead a normal, consistent Christian life; and without the Spirit that would be impossible. In such a life God is in full control, and is thus able to work out His purposes.

Evan Hopkins distinguishes between being "full" and being "filled." "The first indicates an abiding or habitual condition, the latter a special inspiration or illapse—a momentary action or impulse of the Spirit for service, at particular occasions."[3] In the Book of Acts Stephen and Barnabas are described as men full of the Holy Ghost, the word "full" denoting an abiding characteristic. They were habitually full of the Holy Ghost. But for special service, to those who were full there came additional supplies, causing them to overflow. What Christians should seek is the habitual condition—always to be full of the Spirit, and then they will find that as special difficulties arise there will always be that filling, or momentary supply, which will enable them to triumph, to serve, to witness, or to bring forth fruit, as the case may be, according to the will of God.

Bishop Handley Moule likewise points out the difference between full and being filled. The former, he says, refers to a habitual condition, the latter to a special gift or manifestation at special moments, for special ends. "Fillings" are never for the sake of spiritual luxuries, but spiritual supplies for special need, for special service, and are not to be looked for otherwise.[4]

"What is needed for life," says G. Campbell Morgan, "is the

---

[1] Evan Hopkins, *Talks with Beginners in the Divine Life*, p. 43.
[2] Andrew Murray, *The Full Blessing of Pentecost* (New York, Fleming H. Revell Company, 1908), p. 110.
[3] Evan Hopkins, *The Law of Liberty in the Spiritual Life*, p. 206.
[4] H. C. G. Moule, *Need and Fulness* (London, Marshall, Morgan & Scott, 1946), pp. 52, 53.

perpetual filling of the Spirit which is the normal condition of those who are living in the way of God, and the specific fillings to overflowing which may always be counted on when special service demands." [1]

W. H. Aldis once said in an address that the fulness of the Spirit is not in order to work miracles, but to make Christians a living miracle.[2] It may be in the purpose of God to use them to do great things and to work wonders, but Christians are not to expect that because they have received the filling of the Holy Spirit, this will necessarily be so. The fulness of the Spirit is not something which will make an easy pathway. There are no short cuts to holiness, or easy pathways in the Christian life. To be filled with the Spirit may be the beginning of the fiercest conflict they have ever known. Nor will the fulness of the Spirit mean the destruction of the Christian's personality. It will simply give God a chance to take hold of the personality, breathe through it, and work through it. The Holy Spirit wants to free and liberate the personality, so that it can fulfil the purposes of God. The fulness of the Spirit is not necessarily or merely some emotional experience. The reception of the Spirit to empower and direct the life may bring with it a great rush of emotion, but this happens only occasionally. The experience that lasts is often a quiet transaction of faith, without any confirmatory emotion at the time, though that may come later.

(4) It is a Definite Experience

Keswick tells us that the reception of the fulness of the Spirit is by a definite act of faith separable from regeneration, but not necessarily separated from it. There is no need for a lapse of any time between the reception of Christ for salvation and the baptism of the Spirit which takes place at regeneration, on the one hand, and the reception of the fulness of the Spirit for sanctification of life and power in service, on the other, but, as a matter of fact, in the experience of the great majority of Christians, a personal knowledge of the power of God comes only at varying intervals after regeneration.

There are Christians who believe and teach that the fulness of the Spirit is not merely a *second blessing* in the experience of many Christians, but in the purpose of God. Keswick, however, teaches

---

[1] G Campbell Morgan, *The Spirit of God*, p. 194.
[2] *The Keswick Week*, 1928, pp. 75, 76.

that in the economy of God the filling of the Spirit is coincident with regeneration. God intends that when a man is born of the Spirit and baptized with the Spirit, he shall also be filled with the Spirit and lead a Spirit-filled life. "It follows, therefore," G. Campbell Morgan tells us, "that the will of God for His people is that they should be filled at once; that God does not give a man the Spirit today, and then make him, as a necessity, wait for perhaps a number of years before he is filled with the Spirit." [1] And J. Stuart Holden likewise says, "There is no reason why a newly converted soul, from the very moment of his acceptance of Christ, should not likewise accept and receive the great gift of the Holy Ghost." [2]

Dr. Stuart Holden gives two reasons why the fulness of the Spirit is usually experienced by Christians only at varying intervals after regeneration. [3] First, there is a lack of knowledge of what the Word of God teaches about the place of the Spirit in the believer's life. When souls are brought to Christ, usually the only blessing of which they are taught is the gift of forgiveness and justification. They are not told about the gift of the Holy Spirit and His relationship to the Christian. "They live in post-Pentecostal days but have a pre-Pentecostal experience." [4]

The second reason is that there is in Christians frequently a lack of knowledge of personal need. Up to regeneration the soul sees the need of certainty of forgiveness, and is satisfied when forgiveness comes. But often the need of a new power—the power of God the Spirit—by which to live the Christian life is unrecognized, and is only discovered later through repeated failure. A soul will not seek the fulness of the Spirit until it realizes that no man can live the Christian life save as he is filled with the Spirit.

The reception of the Spirit's fulness is, however, not regarded as a once-for-all experience. The blessing may be lost by disobedience, disloyalty, and rebellion. The Spirit can use us only as we permit Him to do so. To say "No" to Him immediately cuts us off from the only source of divine power. But if there has been loss in this respect, the blessing may be restored by getting right with God and by a new yielding of the life to the Spirit. To be filled once, moreover, does not exclude at all the possibility of succeeding needs arising,

[1] G. Campbell organ, *The Spirit of God*, p. 187.
[2] *The Keswick Week*, 1902, p. 123.
[3] J. Stuart Holden, *The Price of Power* (New York, Fleming H. Revell Company, 1908), pp. 24–7.
[4] Ibid., p. 24.

and, therefore, of succeeding infillings. The fulness of the Spirit must be a continuous experience, and new fillings may be had time and time again as new needs arise. Not only is there a second blessing, but a third, and a fourth, and so on, as long as life shall last.

Bishop Handley Moule, who is one of the most lucid Keswick exponents of the Scriptures upon this subject, carefully and cautiously sets forth the whole Keswick position. The subject sometimes suffers by unwise treatment, he says. "Things which outrun Scripture may be said about *the way to receive* spiritual fulness, as if it must always come as a definite experience which can be separately recorded and described, and always as a sudden experience, and always later than the period of conversion, and always after a time of distinct and intentional waiting and expectation.

"Every one of these mistakes of teaching about spiritual fulness has a connexion with great and precious truths. *It is true* that spiritual fulness tends to produce an experience so different in degree from what went before it that the whole matter may sometimes seem like a thing really different from the grace that went before. *It is true* that spiritual fulness tends to make the man thus filled a means of blessing to others very much more than he otherwise was. *It is true* that it tends to make a calm within so deep and blessed that conflict and failure become comparatively and practically the exception, not the rule; and sad disappointment, rather than the sad expectation. *It is true* that an entrance into it is often a definite event in Christian life, and the man knows that at such a time, 'whereas he was blind, now he sees' what the blessed Spirit can do for him, filling his inner world with Christ, and with 'peace and joy in believing' in the indwelling Lord. *It is true* that such experiences very often indeed come later than conversion, even when conversion has been a marked and memorable event. *It is true* that an experience of spiritual fulness is not seldom given after a time of definite and particular watching and prayer. The mistake is when what is frequent is laid down as universal and necessary. There is always a risk of mischief and trouble when Christians make their personal experiences standards of truth for others. True experiences are sacred, precious things. But false inferences are often drawn from true experiences, especially when I say to you, 'You must feel, you must go through, what I have felt, or you cannot be right.' Eternal truth is the same for all; the way in which it is realized is not so." [1]

[1] H. C. G. Moule, *Need and Fulness*, pp. 50, 51.

I include this quotation from Bishop Handley Moule to show that while Keswick regards the fulness of the Spirit as a definite experience, so that every Christian either is or is not "full," nevertheless no pattern is laid down to which it is expected that all Christians must conform. Isolated statements may be taken from addresses and books by Keswick speakers that seem to "outrun Scripture," but a careful reading of Keswick literature as a whole on this subject reveals that the Convention is very cautious in its teaching.

The New Testament offers to Christians the wonderful possibility of a life taught, empowered, and guided by the Holy Spirit of God. More than that, such a life is not optional with them; God demands it. There is no real Christian life without it. A Christian cannot know the things of God except as he is taught by the Spirit; he cannot live victoriously over sin except as he walks in the Spirit; he cannot know God's will for him except as he looks to the Spirit for guidance. All this is possible, however, only when it is realized that the Holy Spirit is a Person, and that in the purpose of God the relationship between the Holy Spirit and the Christian must be a personal one. If it is asked, Cannot there be a close relationship between the Holy Spirit and a believer, and the believer not be aware of it? the answer is decidedly No.

The Christian is expected to live in communion with the Spirit and in fellowship with the Spirit. Can there be communion and fellowship between two personalities, and one of them be unaware of it? The answer is obvious. If a Christian lives a life in which the Holy Spirit plays no conscious part, we may be certain that there is not in that life the relationship between him and the Spirit that the Scriptures set forth as the standard of the normal Christian life. The Acts of the Apostles make it abundantly clear that the early Church was at all times consciously dependent upon the Holy Spirit. The relationship between them was close and intimate. Such an intimate relationship is of course a growing thing; it is not acquired overnight. But a growing thing must have a beginning, and a beginning is always a definite thing. A Spirit-filled life has its beginning when a person, at his regeneration or later, deliberately and consciously gives up the reins of his life to God the Holy Spirit and asks Him henceforth to have full control. There is always, of course, the possibility that the Christian will act or walk according to the flesh rather than according to the Spirit, and when this is so he will at once walk in darkness, become spiritually powerless, and be misguided; and this will continue to be true of him until things are made right with God, and the Holy Spirit is again given His rightful place. A Spirit-filled life, Keswick rightly points out, is not a once-for-all experience. It must be maintained with diligence, by watchfulness, prayer, and obedience.

B. The Subjects of the Blessing

The fulness of the Spirit, we are told, is for every child of God. It is not for ministers only, or Christian workers, but for all believers. All Christians need the Spirit in all His fulness. They cannot become what God desires them to be, or accomplish what God desires them to do, unless the Holy Spirit is allowed unhindered control in their lives. No real Christian life is possible unless this is so.

Christians not filled with the Spirit sin against their own spiritual life, against the Church, against the world, against God. It is therefore obligatory upon every Christian to permit God to fill him with the Spirit. The Spirit is present, waiting to fill every child of God; and if He does not fill the whole life with His own power and light, it is because there is something in the life which prevents Him. The fulness of the Spirit can become a reality only if certain conditions are met. The ground must be cleared for Him, and He must be allowed full right of way.

C. How This Blessing is to be Made Experimental

It has been said before that Keswick is a Convention for the promotion of practical holiness. We may therefore expect that much is said by its leaders about how a Christian may be filled with the Spirit and lead a Spirit-filled life. It is not enough to know that God commands all Christians to be filled with the Spirit. The problem is, How is this to be accomplished? What are the divine conditions of the filling?

Andrew Murray,[1] who has written very fully on the subject, says that there is only one great hindrance in the way of the full blessing of Pentecost. "It lies in the fact that two diverse things cannot at one and the same time occupy the very same place. Your own life and the life of God cannot fill the heart at the same time. Your life hinders the entrance of the life of God. When your own life is cast out, the life of God will fill you. So long as *I myself* am still

[1] Andrew Murray, *The Full Blessing of Pentecost* (New York, Fleming H. Revell Company, 1908), pp. 65–73.

something, *Jesus Himself* cannot be everything. My life must be expelled; then the Spirit of Jesus will flow in."

In order that this may be done, he continues, it must be realized that our individual self is entirely and completely under the power of sin. At the Fall man's whole life and individuality were perverted and withdrawn from the control of God, that he might seek and serve *himself*. That is why we must hate and utterly lose that life, before the Spirit of God can be ours. Unless always and in everything, to the minutest details, we deny that self-life, the life of God cannot possibly fill us. A primary condition of the fulness of the Spirit is a deep conviction of the entire corruption of our nature, manifesting itself in the fact that even the Christian still pleases himself in many things and is not dependent upon the Spirit in all things.

Then our own life must be utterly cast aside, to make full room for the life of God. "So long as a Christian imagines that in some things—for example, in his eating and drinking, in the spending of his time or money, in his thinking and speaking about others—he has still the right and the liberty to follow his own wishes, to please himself, to maintain his own life, he cannot possibly attain to the full blessing of Pentecost." [1] For a man to be filled with the Spirit of God is so unspeakably holy and glorious a thing, that it requires inevitably that "the present occupant and governor of the heart, our individual self, shall himself be cast out, and that everything within us, everything wholly and entirely, shall be surrendered into the hands of the New Inhabitant, the Spirit of God." [2]

There must then be a realization upon the part of the Christian of his helplessness and impotence in bringing about this great transformation in himself; and this must be followed by a surrender of faith to Christ for the death of the cross of all of the self-life. The self-life sets itself in the place of God; pleases and honours itself more than God. It must be hated as our worst foe and as the foe of God.

In the same book Dr. Murray lists some steps the taking of which will result in obtaining the blessing of the Spirit-filled life, once the decision has been made to dethrone self and enthrone Christ. [3] (i) It must be firmly believed that the full blessing of Pentecost is the inheritance of all children of God. (ii) There must be an honest and frank admission that we do not as yet have this blessing—not

---

[1] Andrew Murray, *The Full Blessing of Pentecost* (New York, Fleming H. Revell Company, 1908). pp. 68, 69.
[2] Ibid., p. 69.
[3] Ibid., pp. 74–85.

that we do not have the Spirit, but that we do not have Him in His fulness. (iii) We must realize that the blessing is for us. There is no spiritual health without it. The body of Christ, the Church, cannot be healthy unless all the members of it, even to the very least, are in a state of health. (iv) We must confess that we cannot grasp this blessing in our own power. It is a supernatural gift. We can as little by our own efforts obtain the fulness of the Spirit as we could bring about the first manifestation of the Spirit's work in our soul. (v) We must determine to have this blessing at any cost. Like the merchantman in our Lord's parable, we must be willing to sell all that we have to get possession of the pearl of great price. (vi) Then, in faith that God accepts our surrender and bestows this blessing upon us, we must appropriate it for ourselves. Even though at this crisis no marked change in experience may be noted, we must persevere in faith that God is true to His Word—not that He will bestow the blessing at some future time, but that He has bestowed it from the very moment of our appropriation of it for ourselves by faith. (vii) Lastly, we must wait upon God to lead us to the actual inheritance of the blessing He has bestowed upon us, and which we have appropriated by faith. We must not rest content with a belief that does not lead to experience.

J. Elder Cumming, who has also written fully on the subject, asks why it is that very few Christians have received the fulness of the Spirit.[1] One reason, he answers, is that many are not prepared to receive it. Either they do not know what they are asking for, or "they have not submitted themselves to that preliminary dealing by God, which is needful before so great a gift can be bestowed by Him."[2] The Holy Spirit would not be a good gift to them as they are. So there must be a work of emptying and of self-abasement, showing their need and helplessness without the Holy Spirit. A second reason why God withholds this gift of the Spirit is that men so often desire it for their own purpose. Self mingles in a subtle way in their prayer for fulness. "Ye ask, and receive not, because ye ask amiss, that ye may consume it upon your lusts" (Jas. iv. 3). Christians ask for the Holy Spirit and do not receive Him, because they are not willing to receive Him in His fulness upon God's own terms.

Dr. Cumming then suggests some positive steps for receiving this

[1] J. Elder Cumming, *After the Spirit* (Stirling, Drummond Tract Depot, n.d.), pp. 181–94.
[2] Ibid., p. 182.

blessing. (i) We must subject ourselves to a searching inquiry as to whether we are right with God—not whether we are born again and justified in God's sight, but whether there is anything in our lives that is not in line with God's will for us. (ii) There must be willingness to put away whatever God shows us to be wrong in our lives. (iii) Lastly, we must ask for, and then go on to take, the fulness of the Spirit. It is not enough just to ask. We must take what God offers and commands us to receive.

One of the early speakers at Keswick, G. H. C. Macgregor,[1] says that like all spiritual gifts, the reception of the fulness of the Spirit is subject to certain conditions, and the reason why so many Christians have not received it is that they have not fulfilled the conditions. (i) It can be received only by the obedient. In the Acts of the Apostles (v. 32) we are told that God gives the Holy Spirit to those that obey Him. He will never endue us with the divine power in order to do our own will. His power always goes for the accomplishment of His own purposes. We cannot therefore possess the power of God unless we are in line with the divine will. "Therefore until our consecration is complete, until our wills are yielded to God, until we have enthroned Jesus as Lord in our hearts, we cannot rightly claim, we cannot receive the fulness of the Holy Ghost." [2] (ii) It can be received only that it may be used for the glory of God—not for power, success, fame, or popularity. Until God is first in our lives and we are wholly yielded to Him, until we are wholly empty of self, we cannot be filled with the Spirit. (iii) "It can be received only when we are content to receive it moment by moment according to our need. As the possession of power for a holy life is dependent on never-ceasing faith in the Lord Jesus, so possession of power for service is dependent on unceasing reliance on the Holy Ghost. God never gives us a store of power to be used when and where we think fit." [3]

In his little book, *The Price of Power*, Dr. J. Stuart Holden gives what he regards as a few fundamental axioms governing the whole subject in its personal bearings.[4] (i) We can never have the power of the Holy Spirit until we are implicitly obedient to all that we know of God's will regarding our own personal lives. Power is always according to purity. God will not give His Spirit to anyone unholy,

[1] G. H. C. Macgregor, *A Holy Life and How to Live It* (London, Marshall, Morgan & Scott, Ltd., 1946), pp. 54–6.
[2] Ibid., pp. 54, 55.
[3] Ibid., p. 55.
[4] J. Stuart Holden, *The Price of Power*, pp. 11–17.

unclean, or unworthy. (ii) There must be a complete separation unto the divine purpose for which the power of the Holy Spirit is bestowed. The fulness of the Spirit is bestowed only for the work of the Kingdom of God. (iii) Part of the price of power is time spent in prayer and in study of the Word of God. (iv) We must be willing for complete identification with Christ in the consequences of a Spirit-empowered life and service. For Christ this meant suffering, rejection, scorn, and death; and we must be willing to endure the same treatment.

In a chapter called the "Secret of Power" in the same book, Dr. Holden sets forth five simple steps which, if honestly taken by a soul prepared to go all lengths with God, will bring the fulness of the Spirit.[1] (i) There must be a confession of past failure and present need. "Just as it is not until a man confesses his lost state that he can receive Christ as his Saviour, so likewise it is only the man who honestly confesses 'I am not filled with the Holy Spirit' who can ever receive the Holy Spirit in fulness."[2] (ii) The whole life must be yielded to God, thus practically acknowledging God's claim to possess His own. This yielding must be without reservation, and we must cease to live our lives as though they were our own. (iii) We must not merely ask for but claim the promise of the Holy Spirit. (iv) We must reckon that God fulfils His Word. But we must be careful not to look for feelings or a conscious realization of the fulfilled promise. (v) Finally, we must obey implicitly the known will of God. The Holy Spirit is bestowed to make the doing of the will of God possible to us, and hence it follows that any wilful departure from the divine will involves a loss of the enduement. It is absolutely essential that there be co-operation with the indwelling Spirit.

F. B. Meyer says that the enduement of the Spirit is governed by law.[3] It is not won primarily by an agony of prayer, or characterized by deep emotion. The primary condition is the "obedience of faith." The Holy Spirit is prepared to work only through the nature which is yielded to Him. It is not that we become automatons, for at every moment we are called upon to exercise our will and choice; but we cultivate the habit of asking the Spirit to illuminate our mind, suggest our thought, and direct our speech. That is what the fulness of the Spirit implies.

[1] J. Stuart Holden, *The Price of Power*, pp. 11–17.
[2] Ibid., p. 81.
[3] F. B. Meyer, *The Call and Challenge of the Unseen* (London, Marshall, Morgan & Scott, Ltd., n.d.), pp. 67–71.

Keswick speakers always emphasize that the fulness of the Spirit is related to the enthronement of Christ. It is when we enthrone Christ as Lord that we experience the mighty fulness of the Spirit. To the person who asks, "What, precisely, is meant by the fulness of the Holy Spirit?" W. Graham Scroggie replies that it is the lordship of Christ in the believer's life. All Christians know what it is to be delivered from the guilt of sin and from its ultimate penalty, but not many know what is meant by His lordship over their lives. The fulness of the Spirit means the domination of Christ as Lord.[1]

Much is said about the necessity of recognizing the personality and the sovereignty of the Holy Spirit. Evan Hopkins, for example, says that we will never be filled with the Holy Spirit unless we begin by honouring Him. We must recognize His personality, and not think or speak of Him as "it." If we say that we believe He is in us, then we must recognize Him—His personality, His sovereignty, His diety. The fulness of the Spirit is the indwelling of a divine Person who is allowed full control in the life.[2]

Another Keswick speaker, J. Oswald Sanders, Chairman of the Upwey "Keswick" Convention, Australia, in a very lucid address given at Keswick in 1947, spoke on the same subject.[3] There is a difference between knowing *about* the Holy Spirit and actually *knowing* Him. Christians are expected by God to know Him as a real, living Person, with whom they can have fellowship. To know the Holy Spirit is absolutely fundamental to a satisfying Christian experience and a fruitful Christian life. A great deal of the ineffectiveness of Christians can be attributed to a practical ignoring of the Holy Spirit. Perhaps He is not ignored wilfully; but for all practical purposes, He is ignored. He is worthy of equal worship, equal reverence, and equal love with the Father and the Son. He is a real, living Person, and not merely an impersonal influence.

Few people, he continues, know what they are praying for when they pray, "Lord, fill us with Thy Holy Spirit." The fulness of the Spirit is something very real, and has very practical implications— the possession and the mastery of the human spirit by the divine Spirit. We are filled with the Holy Spirit when the Holy Spirit has absolute possession and control of our spirit. The idea behind the words "filled with the Spirit" is not so much that of an empty

[1] W. Graham Scroggie, *The Fulness of the Holy Spirit* (Chicago, Bible Institute Colportage Ass'n, 1925), pp. 8, 9.
[2] *The Keswick Week*, 1907, p. 211.
[3] Ibid, 1947, pp. 194–8.

receptacle passively waiting for something to be put into it, but of a human personality which is to be controlled by a divine personality; that human personality brought under the domination and control of the Holy Spirit.

If that be so, then we could equally correctly render the command, "Be filled with the Spirit," by "Be controlled by the Spirit." The control of the Spirit is not automatic, but is dependent on a correct adjustment to Him. If we withdraw our yieldedness and our surrender, then the Holy Spirit's control is thereby broken, and His power cannot manifest itself.

We are filled with the Spirit when we allow Him wholly to possess and wholly to control us. He exercises this control right from the very centre of our personality. He dwells in every believer, and when He is granted full control, then He is able to carry out all His gracious offices.

G. Campbell Morgan suggests only two conditions for the filling of the Spirit—abandonment and abiding.[1] The blessing is first realized by abandonment; it is maintained by abiding. By "abandonment", Dr. Morgan means handing over to the control of God the whole life, in order that through that life His will may be realized and His work done. The life thus abandoned to God is a life that has given up its own plans, purposes, and hopes; and has taken instead the plan, the purpose, and the hope of God. By "abiding," he means continuing to live a life of abandonment: regarding Christ as Lord always, entering into no transaction of business or of pleasure without taking Him into account, treating Him as the ever-present King, by saying to Him at all seasons and hours and everywhere, "Master, is this Thy will?" "If men are filled with the Spirit by abandonment, they continue filled with the Spirit by abiding."[2]

It will be observed that although various suggestions are made above as a guide to those who desire the fulness of the Spirit, no hard-and-fast rules are set forth as the only condition of the fulness. The suggestions made are scriptural ones in every case. Although they differ in number—Andrew Murray, for example, offering seven, and G. Campbell Morgan only two—and although they are worded differently, they are essentially the same, and may be reduced to only one: the fulness of the Spirit may become the believer's experience if in all things he recognizes the sovereignty and the

[1] G. Campbell Morgan, *The Spirit of God*, pp. 228–33.
[2] Ibid., pp. 232, 233.

lordship of Christ in his life, and if he allows the Holy Spirit to become his Teacher, his Guide, his Power for sanctification and service. To be filled by the Spirit means to be controlled by the Spirit. Evan Hopkins used often to say that instead of seeking to have more of the Holy Spirit, we should yield ourselves to Him, that He might have more of us. The blessing consists in this, that we have been brought more completely under His power and control. It is when every room in the house of life, so to speak, has been yielded to Him, that we are full of the Holy Spirit. To exclude Him from even one room is to treat Him with disrespect and to grieve Him, and it means that we do not have the fullest confidence in Him and choose to run our own lives to some extent.

Two things are crystal clear in Scripture; that not all Christians are filled with the Spirit, and that God commands all Christians to be filled with the Spirit. The responsibility is not God's, but that of believers. The condition of filling is also made crystal clear. In the words of the apostles, God gives the Holy Spirit to them that obey Him (Acts v. 32). The Holy Spirit can control our members only in so far as we allow Him to do so by our obedience. That is the only way the blessing of the fulness of the Spirit can be made experimental in our lives.

D. The Results of the Blessing

Andrew Murray puts it very simply and succinctly, "The fulness of the Spirit is simply the full preparation for living and working as a child of God."[1] In other words, it enables us to be what God wants us to be, and to do what God wants us to do. We are not to expect that we will perform miracles, but simply that we will be able to lead a normal Christian life. Such a life will, of course, be quite different from that in which an attempt is made to serve both God and self, for God will be in full control.

Dr. W. Graham Scroggie enumerates some of the results of a Spirit-filled life.[2] If we have the fulness of the Spirit, we shall be at *rest*. Feverish service will be at an end. Not that we will cease to work, but there will be rest in toil, so that we may accomplish even incredible things quietly and restfully. Then we shall have *joy*, for "the fruit of the Spirit is joy." This joy will be beyond the reach of circumstances, and is abiding. Another product is *love* for the

[1] Andrew Murray, *The Full Blessing of Pentecost*, p. 110.
[2] W. Graham Scroggie, *The Fulness of the Holy Spirit*, pp. 19–21.

K

Lord and His people. "The fruit of the Spirit is love." There will be *power*—in Christian work, in secular work—wherever the Lord has put us. And then there will be *victory*—consistent victory—over sin.

G. H. C. Macgregor[1] tells us that while it is impossible to speak fully of the effect of the reception of the Holy Spirit in His fulness on our service, we may be sure that it will create a revolution in our Christian service. It will give us a new boldness in witnessing for Christ, so that we cannot but speak the things we have seen and heard (Acts. iv. 20). It will give us new attractiveness in witnessing for Christ, so that when we speak for Christ the attention of men will be arrested, and they will really listen. It will give us new power in witnessing for Christ. Words spoken in the power of the Spirit will make men think, and waken them to the reality and importance of spiritual things.

When we read what the New Testament has to say about the Holy Spirit and the relationship of the believer to Him, it seems almost as though such an experience is beyond the reach of present-day Christians. Just as Christians generally think that the day of miracles is over—that it ended with the apostolic age; so they usually think that such an intimate relationship between the believer and the Holy Spirit existed in the early Church, but is no longer possible now. The New Testament nowhere teaches, however, that the Holy Spirit is to have a lesser place in the latter-day Church than He did at the beginning of its history. If He holds the same place of honour today as He did then, the results will assuredly be very much the same. The Holy Spirit is Deity, and whenever a human being allows Deity to seize him and work in and through him, the results will be marvellous to behold. The results will be in proportion to the control of the Spirit in the life. They are assured if the control is assured.

Keswick is undoubtedly correct in making the Spirit-filled life the central, dominating theme of the Convention, and in making it the climax of the sequence of teaching during the week. A proper view of sin is indispensable in the Christian life. Equally important is a right understanding of God's provision for sin, especially that much-neglected aspect of it—the believer's identification with Christ in His death and resurrection. But unless the believer knows what God has to say about the place of the Holy Spirit in his life and in

[1] G. H. C. Macgregor, *A Holy Life and How to Live It*, pp. 52–4.

the life of the Church, and unless the fulness of the Spirit is an experimental reality in his life, he will find it impossible to lead a Christian life that is in conformity with the plan and intention of God. The cross clears the ground for the working of the Holy Spirit. Calvary provides for the death of the "old man," making possible the "new man" in the Spirit. But the "new man" cannot grow and develop and mature unless the Holy Spirit is allowed to have His way—as Teacher, as Guide, as Comforter, as Administrator and Director, as Power in service and sanctification. Serious students of the doctrine of the Holy Spirit frequently say that nothing is more needed than a study of the place of the Holy Spirit in man. That is true; but needed just as much is practical teaching on how ordinary Christians may become Spirit-filled Christians, and thus lead lives that come up to the New Testament standard. Keswick appears to succeed very notably in doing this, and there does not seem to be anything extreme or erratic in this phase of its teaching.

CHAPTER VII

CHRISTIAN SERVICE

The first four days of the Keswick Convention week are occupied in presenting a sequence of teaching, the object of which is to get Christians into a state of spiritual health. On the opening day a careful diagnosis of spiritual ills is made, so that Christians who are in a state of spiritual ill-health will know just where they stand, and why it is that they have been more or less powerless to overcome sin, and why they have been ineffective as witnesses of the gospel of Christ.

On the second day is taught the wonderful provision God has made in Christ, for the problem of sin. Calvary, it is shown, is God's answer to the whole problem of sin—its power over human beings as well as its guilt. That very much neglected aspect of the significance of the cross, the believer's identification with Christ in His death and resurrection, especially is stressed, since so few Christians have ever been taught it.

The third day is devoted to teaching on consecration, which is man's response to God's call for complete abandonment and surrender to Him—at once a crisis and a process; a crisis, because it involves the giving up of the right to oneself and the acceptance of Christ as the Lord and Master of one's life; a process, because the decision made must be maintained throughout life.

The fourth day is occupied with teaching on the Spirit-filled life. It is not enough to have the Spirit, which is true of all Christians; one must be completely controlled by the Spirit—an experience which has been made possible by the grace of God. The Holy Spirit is the power both for life and for service, and it is impossible to live the Christian life so as to please God without a right relationship to Him.

On Friday, the theme of the Convention is Christian Service. "To some," says W. H. Aldis, "it may seem that in the messages on the fulness of the Holy Spirit, we had reached the climax and goal of the Convention. There is a limited sense in which that is true, because to be filled unto all fulness of God is the greatest and highest and best thing God can do for any one of His children;

but there is also a sense in which this experience is far from being the goal of the Convention. The filling of the Holy Spirit is not, and cannot be, an end in itself: it is all in order to something, which might be summarized—*equipment for life and service.* Apart from the fulness of the Holy Spirit, life can never be at its best nor can our service be abundantly fruitful." [1]

"Keswick does not teach sanctification and holiness as an end in themselves," we are told in *The Keswick Week* for 1946, [2] "but rather that His people might be fit for the Master's use. Therefore, the instructional and hortatory messages of the Convention having reached their climax on Thursday, Friday morning is always devoted to the great missionary meeting, and the evening to the united communion service."

The missionary meeting on Friday morning is the longest meeting of the week, lasting over two hours, and is regarded as the climax of the meetings of the week. This, however, has not always been so. In the early years of the Convention the meetings began on Monday evening and ended on Friday, with addresses on the Spirit-filled life. Not that the early leaders of Keswick were not interested in practical service, but they felt that any Christian who got himself rightly related to God would inevitably ask the question, "Lord, what wilt Thou have me to do?" The Spirit-filled life is possible only if there is an outflow of the Holy Spirit through our lives to others.

Evan Hopkins often used to unfold the purpose of the Keswick Convention with the following little parable, which admirably illustrates the aim of the Convention with regard to service:

"A man . . . is anxious to cross a broad and rapid river. He can swim but poorly; but he fancies that, by doing his utmost, he will contrive to make the opposite side. He strikes out, and struggles hard to hold his head above the rush of the water. But his strength ebbs. The effort is too much for him. In a few minutes he must succumb from exhaustion, and be drowned in the stream. Then, when things are desperate, he hears a voice, 'Lay hold of the boat,' and, looking up, he sees, close to where he is, a pair of dipping oars which bring him deliverance. His hand grasps tightly the side of the boat. He clings to it, and is prevented from sinking, not by convulsive endeavours of his own, but by the floating power of the craft that has rescued him so timeously. But, secure himself, he

[1] *The Keswick Convention in Print*, 1941, p. 75.
[2] p. 229.

discovers another man, fighting just as he had done against the masterful current, and on the verge of being sucked under by it. What will he do in the new emergency? To go to the sufferer's relief would be to court a double failure. He could not save him, and he would himself perish. Again the voice speaks in a fresh imperative, 'Get into the boat.' He obeys. He leaves the experience of clinging for the better experience of resting. Borne up by the stout timbers underneath, he has no more troublesome distresses about himself. And his hands are free to rescue the 'lost complaining' victim of the angry flood." [1]

It is the function of Keswick, Evan Hopkins would say, to lead the struggling soul, and the clinging soul, on to the trust of the resting soul. Only a soul who thus rests in Christ's sufficiency for himself has liberty to toil for Him among his fellows.

And so in the early years of its history Keswick gave its attention to the promotion of Christian character, feeling that if character were sound, then fruitful service would follow. [2]

One of the early Keswick speakers said that he was sometimes asked whether Keswick was a great missionary meeting. No, he answered, Keswick is not a missionary meeting. *"It is a meeting for making missionaries.* And I do not hesitate to say that wherever its truths are really known, in other words, wherever Christ comes into full possession of a human soul, there you will find a missionary—whether his work lie in the East of London or the West, in Europe or in Africa, at home or abroad." [3]

But even in its early days there were some, notably Hudson Taylor and Reginald Radcliffe, who had a heavy burden for the missionary effort, and thought that missions should be presented at the Convention. The former more than once at Keswick set forth the claims of Christ to the service of His people in making the Gospel known to all nations. The latter at several Conventions invited friends to his lodgings for daily prayer on the subject of missions; and he tried to persuade Mr. Bowker, who presided over the Convention after Canon Battersby's death, to include in the programme a missionary meeting. The answer, however, always was No. "Missions meant secretaries quarrelling for collections, and Keswick could not stoop to that."

In 1886 and 1887 Mr. Radcliffe obtained Mr. Bowker's permission

[1] Alexander Smellie, *Evan Henry Hopkins—A Memoir* (London, Marshall Bros., Ltd., 1921), pp. 85, 86.
[2] C. F. Harford, *The Keswick Convention*, p. 77.
[3] Ibid., pp. 46, 47.

to use the tent for a missionary meeting on the Saturday of the Convention week, but on condition that it was to be a meeting unconnected with the Convention. In the latter year this meeting proved to have great results. Some of the speakers were Convention speakers. More than thirty persons applied to one or other of the speakers with a view to missionary service, and many did eventually become missionaries. As a result of this striking episode, the official programme for 1888 included a missionary meeting on the Saturday, which was attended by all the speakers; and a missionary meeting has been a part of the Keswick programme ever since. For years it was held on Saturday; for the last twenty years or so it has been held on Friday morning.

It was decided also to support individual missionaries—in all cases such as had accepted the Keswick message—who were already on the staff of recognized missionary societies, the money being paid direct to the different societies for their support, the missionaries themselves remaining members in each case of the society's staff and under its direction. The first so supported was Amy Carmichael, then working in Japan, who later founded a remarkable work at Dohnavur, India.

The great missionary meeting on Friday morning is given over almost entirely to missionaries themselves, who in brief addresses present the needs in their fields and show how God has been working with them. As they speak, they do not represent particular societies, but the world and its need of the Gospel, especially the spheres in which they themselves labour.

At the end of the meeting various groups are asked to rise—first, retired missionaries; then missionaries on furlough; finally accepted recruits. Those parents are asked to rise who would be willing to give·their children, if the Lord should call them to His service overseas. Young people are asked to rise to show their willingness to become missionaries if the Lord should call them. It is also made clear that every Christian who cannot go to the mission field is responsible to support missionary work by prayer and sacrificial gifts. Those who offer for service are given advice and guidance as to training and how to make their applications to various societies.

The results of Keswick on practical Christian service have been little short of amazing. It is said that when Mrs. William Booth lay dying, she remarked that Keswick had been one of the principal means of establishing the Salvation Army; because of the completed consecration into which many rich and influential people were brought.[1] Dr. Hudson Taylor gave as his reckoning[2] that two-thirds of the missionaries in the China Inland Mission were there as a result of Keswick.

An illustration, no more remarkable than others that might be given, of the practical results for Christian service of the meetings at Keswick, is the following testimony by Donald Fraser, the great missionary to Africa:

"When I went [to Keswick] I was entirely out of sympathy with the Convention, desiring to examine an interesting feature of religious life. . . . On the Wednesday I was more than ever irritated by the type of the preaching, but at the evening meeting a fearful sense of moral failure came over me, and when Mr. Hopkins began to expound 'where the Spirit of the Lord is there is liberty,' light broke, and that night I gave myself to God, and believed."[3] He volunteered for foreign service. The following Saturday Mr. Robert P. Wilder gave an address about the Student Volunteer Movement that had just been started in America. Donald Fraser and others went back to their universities in Scotland and England to tell their fellow students of the blessing they had received. Continues Dr. Fraser, "It is not easy to trace spiritual origins or growths. But my impression is that the Convention at Keswick created in our colleges the atmosphere which made the Student Movement possible."[4]

But it must not be thought that undue pressure is brought upon Christians to offer themselves to the foreign mission field. Christians are not told that the need constitutes the call, and that all should go if they are physically able to. It is made clear that God's workers are called by Him, and are appointed by Him to specific tasks in particular spheres of service. Every Christian is needed somewhere in some sort of work in the vineyard of God, and every Christian has been ordained to some task by God. No one—not even the weakest or apparently most incapable—is left without his share in God's work.

An illustration of this occurs to me, told by Eugene Stock,[5] for many years Secretary of the Church Missionary Society, of the Church of England, and also, for almost thirty years, Chairman of

[1] C. F. Harford, *The Keswick Convention*, p. 159.
[2] J. B. Figgis, *Keswick from Within* (London, Marshall Bros., Ltd., 1914), p. 134.
[3] W. B. Sloan, *These Sixty Years* (London, Pickering & Inglis, Ltd., 1935), p. 38.
[4] Ibid., p. 38.
[5] Eugene Stock, *My Recollections* (London, James Nisbet & Co., Ltd., 1909), p. 206.

the Missionary Meeting at Keswick. He says that one day a girl, the daughter of a clergyman, came to him and expressed her wish to join the Church Missionary Society and go to Palestine. On inquiring of her about her circumstances, he found she was an only child, and was helping her father in the charge of a mountain parish. He dissuaded her from leaving her parents in such a case, assuring her that she could serve God as well in her own community as in Palestine. She yielded, and continued as she was for two years. A visit to her home showed him the absolute necessity of her staying at home. Eventually she had her wish in an unexpected way. Her father resigned his church, and all three went to the Holy Land together—she herself as a missionary, where at length she died, deeply lamented by the natives as well as by her fellow-workers.

In 1927 Donald Fraser said, "At Keswick adjustments are made which make the appeal of God and of the world peculiarly suitable, and which must lead to a great response of life." [1] The response, it is pointed out by the speakers, will not necessarily lead to the mission field, whether foreign or home. But it will lead to sacrificial service of some kind, even though the field of service be restricted to the kitchen and the home. Christian service, moreover, will be viewed not as a charity, but as a debt. Loyalty to Christ can never be maintained without service. Salvation in its fulness means service as its outcome. Discipleship implies service.

When a Christian asks, "Lord, what wilt Thou have me to do?" he places himself unreservedly at the Lord's disposal, for the question involves a recognition of Christ's right to decide what shall be done with his life. He is clearly told, "Ye are not your own. For ye are bought with a price: therefore glorify God in your body, and in your spirit, which are God's" (1 Cor. vi. 19, 20). The question is related to the minutest activity of conduct: "Whether therefore ye eat, or drink, or whatsoever ye do, do all to the glory of God" (1 Cor. x. 31). Involved in the answer may be a journey to the uttermost parts of the earth, or perhaps remaining where he is, but at any cost it means obedience.

Implied in the question, "Lord, what wilt Thou have me to do?" is the belief in the possibility of an answer from Him. When Paul first asked the question at the time of his conversion, the reply of Jesus concerned both the immediate and the more distant future of his life. As for the next step, the Lord said, "Arise, and go into the city, and it shall be told thee what thou must do" (Acts ix. 6).

[1] *The Keswick Week*, 1927, p. 159.

This reply indicates that guidance is one step at a time. But the Lord went further, and told Paul what He planned for his life, "I have appeared unto thee for this purpose, to make thee a minister and a witness both of these things which thou hast seen, and of those things in which I will appear unto thee; delivering thee from the people, and from the Gentiles, unto whom now I send thee, to open their eyes, and to turn them from darkness to light and from the power of Satan unto God, that they may receive forgiveness of sins, and inheritance among them which are sanctified by faith that is in me" (Acts xxvi. 16–18).

The whole life of Paul after this event shows that it was a life guided and directed by the Spirit of God. His going into missionary work was not the result of his own desire to be of service to the non-Christian world, but was the result of an unmistakable call by the Spirit of God. The Holy Spirit guided him both negatively and positively, checking him when he was about to make a mistake, suggesting the right course to him.

Keswick holds firmly and teaches without equivocation that Christian service can never be effective unless it is guided by the Spirit of God in the same way that Paul was. This applies to all Christians alike, not alone to Christian workers. And it teaches just as clearly that we may always be sure of the Lord's guidance, and may know that He will answer the question we address to Him.

There are four ways, Keswick tells us, in which our Lord guides us in our life and work. First, He guides by the revealed truth of His Word, where we see what His mind is, so far as general principles are concerned. In the second place, He guides by our circumstances—by His outward providences, which indicate what is and what is not possible. In the third place, He guides by our conscience, when it is educated and informed by the Spirit of God, and readjusted by His written Word. Finally, He guides directly and immediately by the Holy Spirit. These four ways of guidance must be checked against each other in order to eliminate the possibility of mistakes. If they unite in their testimony, we cannot go wrong if we are abiding in Christ—permitting the cross to operate on the desires of the flesh, and determining to do the will of God at all costs when it becomes known. God does not treat us as mere machines, and His guidance is assured only if we are willing to pay the price for it.

Such guidance by the Holy Spirit of God can alone save us from projects that appear to be good, but are not really His directive will for us. It is terribly possible to be so busy in what we regard as the service of the Kingdom that it interferes with our fellowship with our Lord. Such service is bound to be vain and fruitless. Our works must be the works of God, not what we imagine to be His works. In the final analysis, the Christian life reduces itself to this—knowing God's will, and doing it. This, God in His grace gives us the power to do. It is not, Keswick says, an unattainable ideal that God holds out before us and demands that we reach. What He expects of us He gives us the power to do, both in sanctification and service. That is the message of Keswick.

PART III

BIOGRAPHICAL SKETCHES OF SOME KESWICK LEADERS

T. D. Harford-Battersby

In the chapter on the History of Keswick it was pointed out that the man primarily responsible for the founding of the Keswick Convention was T. D. Harford-Battersby. He was brought up an Evangelical in the Church of England, but while a student at Oxford he came under the spell of John Henry Newman, and adopted his Tractarian views. Following his graduation from the university he became a curate at Gosport. In two years he exchanged his High-Church views for the Broad-Churchmanship of the Rev. Frederick Myers, whose curate he became at Keswick in 1849, and whom he succeeded as rector of the parish when Mr. Myers died in 1851.

At Keswick he returned to the Evangelical fold, and became a leader of the Evangelicals in his diocese. But although he strove faithfully and diligently to live the Christ-life and to discharge his pastoral duties, he felt that there was something seriously lacking in his life, and was deeply conscious of the need of something fuller in his own life than he had yet experienced.

In the summer of 1874 he was on holiday with his family at Silloth, where the Rev. William Haslam was holding a mission. Haslam suggested that he attend the approaching Convention at Oxford, which he did. At first he thought the teaching one-sided and exaggerated, but on the fourth day, while listening to Evan Hopkins speak on the difference between seeking and resting faith, he received a blessing which not only changed his opinions but transformed his whole life. Two days later he gave the following testimony: "It was when I heard a dear brother clergyman speak of the faith of the nobleman whose son was healed, that the truth flashed upon my mind, and afterward God enabled me to trust and make a full surrender. It is a difficult thing to speak of my own experience, and very distasteful, yet perhaps for this very reason it may be right for one to do so, and to acknowledge the blessing I have received." [1]

Shortly afterwards, at the annual meeting of the Evangelical Union of the Diocese of Carlisle, where strong opposition was offered to the "Holiness Teaching," as it was called, a paper by him telling of his change and his blessing was read, and he thus publicly committed himself to the new teaching.

The following year, in June 1875, the first Keswick Convention was held, in a tent in the Vicarage grounds. The defection of Mr. Pearsall Smith almost wrecked the whole movement, but the following year it was decided to hold another Convention; and every year since, except for some war years, similar gatherings have been held at Keswick.

For eight years (1875–82) Canon Harford-Battersby presided over the Convention as Chairman. In the summer of 1883 he died.

Evan H. Hopkins

Evan Hopkins was for years the acknowledged leader of the Keswick teaching. He was the theologian of the movement. He had very unusual gifts both as a writer and a speaker. More than any other man, he kept the movement from being drawn into extravagance or excitement, and kept it on an even keel. For many years he was editor of the recognized Keswick organs, *The Christian's Pathway of Power* and its successor, *The Life of Faith*. It is said that his book, *The Law of Liberty in the Spiritual Life*, did more than anything else to explain the movement to those of the Evangelical School in the Church of England, who were at first inclined to look askance at it.

He was born in 1837 in South America, where his father, an Englishman, was a Civil Engineer. He was educated as a Mining Engineer, and for some years worked at his profession, gaining a considerable reputation in it. In 1863, after he was brought to Christ by means of a coastguardsman, he entered the Divinity School in King's College, London, and after his graduation was ordained in the Church of England.

In 1873 he was invited to an informal meeting in Curzon Chapel, where, after listening to Robert Pearsall Smith on the subject of Holiness, he entered into a new experience of surrender and faith.

[1] *Account of the Union Meeting for the Promotion of Scriptural Holiness, held at Oxford, August 29 to September 7, 1874*, p. 174.

What happened to him there may best be narrated in the words of his wife:

"How well I recall his coming home, deeply moved by what he had heard and experienced! He told me that he was like one looking out on a land wide and beautiful, flowing with milk and honey. It was to be possessed. *It was his.* As he described it all, I felt that he had received an overflowing blessing, far beyond anything that I knew; and it seemed as if a gulf had come between us. We sat up late that evening, talking, with our Bibles before us. O, I was hungry. At last, quite simply, but very really, I too took God at His word, and accepted Christ as my *indwelling Lord and life*, and believed that He did enthrone Himself in my heart.

"The text that had brought him such blessing was 2 Corinthians ix. 8; and I remember how he printed it clearly on a card, keeping it constantly before him, as he feasted on the facts it revealed. Now it would be, GOD IS ABLE, that possessed his soul in new power. Then it would be, *To make* ALL *grace abound toward* YOU; and ALL meant ALL in a fuller sense than it had previously done. Next it was, *That ye* ALWAYS—the perpetual present that is to be recognized—*having* ALL *sufficiency*—for there is no lack, no limit, no cessation of the abundant supply—*in* ALL *things*—heart-needs, trials, disadvantageous circumstances, Christian service —*may abound unto* EVERY *good work.* Christ had, indeed, become to him the 'Fountain within' springing up. It was not merely that his Lord would help him. It was that He would do *all*, and would live in him His own holy life—the only holy life possible to us, as he would often say." [1]

In the meetings for consecration that were held, during 1873 and 1874, in London, throughout provincial England, and across the Channel on the continent of Europe, Mr. Hopkins was a welcome speaker. He took a helpful part in the famous Conferences at Broadlands and Oxford, in 1874, and at Brighton, in 1875. As we have seen, it was an address given by him at the Oxford Convention that was the means of winning T. D. Harford-Battersby over to the Higher Life movement. He spoke at the first Keswick Convention, and appeared at Keswick as a leader for thirty-nine years without a break. No one was regarded with greater respect there than he.

Mr. Hopkins served two long pastorates, the first for twenty-three years, from 1870 until 1893, at Holy Trinity Church, Rich-

[1] A. Smellie, *Evan Henry Hopkins—A Memoir*, p. 54.

mond, Surrey; the second for thirteen years, from 1893 to 1906, at St. Luke's Church, Redcliffe Square, South Kensington, London. The remainder of his life, from 1906 to his death in 1918, he devoted to Convention work. When he died, the Convention lost one who was perhaps its most-used instrument and its best-loved leader.

For those who may wonder how the great blessing that Mr. Hopkins received at Curzon Chapel in 1873 lasted through the years, the following word of testimony with which he began an address at Keswick in 1913 may prove illuminating:

"I think I ought to be the most thankful man in this tent, because I am privileged to testify that the blessing lasts. It has lasted with me forty years. I shall never forget that sacred spot where the first consecration meeting was held, in London in May, 1873. I had been converted thirteen years, brought to the Lord through a coast-guardsman, and I had learned the need of my own heart during those years. At the time that I refer to I was immensely stirred to seek this blessing. We had heard about it, and there in Curzon Chapel, Mayfair, under the gallery, sixteen well-known Christian people met together. . . . This was just the beginning of the movement, and I ought to be one of the most thankful men in this tent, because of God's gracious keeping power for forty years. I want to bear testimony to that fact, and give Him all the glory. There have been many failures. I am not glorying in self, but what was revealed to me that day—the all-sufficiency of Christ—is as precious to my soul as it ever was."[1]

Charles A. Fox

Among the eminent men in the early days of Keswick, Charles A. Fox held a high place. He was one of the few who could really be called orators. And yet, after graduating from Cambridge, his Bishop earnestly tried to dissuade him from Holy Orders because of a bad stammer. He persisted, however, and triumphed over his handicap marvellously, although all through life the liability to stammer stood on the very edge of his public speaking.

He began work in Devonshire, and went afterwards to Eaton Chapel, London, where he exercised a ministry of rare influence.

He was not present at the Oxford Conference, but was at Brighton—as a listener, mainly. T. D. Harford-Battersby and H.

[1] *The Keswick Week*, 1913, p. 122.

F. Bowker were so impressed by him at Brighton that they came to him at the close of the meeting and said that they proposed to hold a similar gathering at Keswick that summer, and asked him to come. His poor health prevented him from accepting their offer, and it was not until 1879 that he was present at Keswick for the first time. Mr. Fox was, in fact, dogged by ill-health all his life; for ten years after graduating from the university he had been unable to engage in public ministry on this account. When he did come forth from this enforced seclusion, it was with a deep knowledge of God.

It is said that Mr. Fox's prayers at Keswick made, perhaps, an even greater impression on those who attended, than did his addresses. He had a way of lifting the hearts of the whole company up into the very presence of the unseen God. Someone said of him that he had a face as if he had looked into the face of God.

Mr. Fox was the poet of the Convention. Perhaps the best-known of his poems is the following, written while in deepest suffering, after he had become a victim of cancer in the face.

The Marred Face

Marred more than any man's! Yet there's no place
In this wide universe but gains new grace
Richer and fuller, from that marred Face!

O Saviour Christ! those precious wounds of Thine
Make doubly precious these poor wounds of mine;
Teach me to die with Thee the death divine;

All wounds and woes of earth, once made Thine own,
Add colour to the rainbow round the throne,
And save from loneliness saints else alone.

Pain trims the lamps at Nature's eventide,
Ere the King enters to bring home His Bride,
My King, by suffering perfected and tried!

Beloved ones are hastening past, and all
The ground is strewn with blossoms they let fall
In haste to gain Love's crowning festival.

Heaven beckons now—I press me toward the mark
Of my high calling. Hark! He calls! O! hark!
That wounded Face moves toward me through the dark!

L

In 1899 he was at Keswick for the last time. The next year he sent his final greetings to the Convention, "In thankful memory of five and twenty years' unbroken fellowship with beloved brethren at Keswick Convention." He died soon after.

George H. C. Macgregor

After a distinguished career at the University of Edinburgh and at the New College, Edinburgh, George H. C. Macgregor was called to the East Presbyterian Church, in Aberdeen, Scotland, in 1888. He remained there until 1894, when he left for the Trinity Presbyterian Church, Notting Hill, London. His ministry at both churches was notable.

He went to Keswick for the first time in the summer of 1889, at the close of the first year of his ministry in Aberdeen. He had been told by some fellow-ministers of the quickening and joy they had found in the gatherings at Keswick, and he resolved to begin his first summer vacation there. He was a theologian—and he did not forget that he was a Scottish theologian. He came as a matter of purely intellectual interest. He was surprised to find that sanctification was presented not so much theologically as practically. At first he felt angry, as a Scotsman, at being told anything new in theology by Englishmen! Before long, however, he was brought to a crisis. He faced the question, "Shall I yield, shall I confess, shall I acknowledge, that I have been without the blessing?" By the end of the week he had definitely committed himself to God to be filled with the Holy Spirit for his service.

That Sunday evening he wrote to his sister:

"The Convention is now over, and tomorrow we go back to the world. To say I have enjoyed it is to say nothing. To call it heaven may seem hyperbole, but it is perhaps the best and shortest way of speaking of it. I fear I shall never be able to speak of it. The joy is unspeakable and full of the glory. I have learned innumerable lessons, principally these: my own sinfulness and shortcoming. I have been searched through and through, and bared and exposed and scorched by God's searching Spirit. And then I have learned the unsearchableness of Christ. How Christ is magnified here, you can have scarcely any idea. I got such a view of the goodness of God today that it made me weep. I was completely broken down, and could not control myself, but had a fit of weeping. And I have learned the absolute necessity of obedience. Given obedience and faith, nothing is impossible. I have committed myself into God's hands and He has taken me, and life can never be the same again. It must be infinitely brighter than ever." [1]

He spoke at Keswick for the first time in 1892, but thereafter took an active part in the Convention each year until he died eight years later, at the early age of thirty-six.

In 1893, with Hubert Brooke and Charles Inwood, he went to Canada as Keswick missioners. Twice—in 1897 and 1898—he went to Northfield to speak at the Moody Conference there.

Macgregor's life and ministry were very short, but few men have left a more fragrant memory at Keswick than he. His addresses caught the ear of the Convention as few have done. He had the great gift of making as clear as crystal everything he said and wrote. His books are still read by those interested in a simple and scriptural presentation of the subject of holiness.

J. Elder Cumming

J. Elder Cumming was converted by a sermon of his own when he was a student of Divinity at Glasgow University. Part of a student's work was to write out a popular sermon. He had come to the application, when suddenly the question came to him, Have *you* done what you are asking others to do? He laid down his pen, knelt by his desk, and there and then gave himself to Christ.

He had been born in 1830—the son of a ship's captain—and until he went to Glasgow was schooled in the Isle of Man. He was in his second year of study of Theology when he found Christ.

His first charge was the East Presbyterian Church in Perth, where he served for six years. He then removed to Newington Parish in Edinburgh, where he gave twelve years of his life. In 1871 he went to Sandyford Presbyterian Church in Glasgow, and there the rest of his ministry was spent. While he was at the Sandyford Church a great shadow fell upon him—the loss of his wife, a bright, energetic woman who died after a few hours' illness. He went to various Conventions in search of consolation. At the Mildmay Conference a lady remarked to him that Keswick was the best of all Conventions. He went in 1882. Twice he was accosted on the street by ladies he knew who expressed surprise at finding him at Keswick. Speaking, years later, of his experience there, he said:

[1] D. C. Macgregor, *George H. C. Macgregor, M.A., A Biography* (New York, Fleming H. Revell Company, 1900), pp. 109, 110.

"I cannot tell you what pain and misery I experienced during the first three days—first, something like indignation; secondly, something very like perplexity, for my theological chart seemed to have certain things laid clearly down, and I did not see how other things could be put in without disarranging the former. I cannot tell how the arrow of God's Word was going home. I passed a very miserable time during the first days of that week. Then the way the Lord dealt with me was this. He told me, while on my knees in my solitude, of this, and this, and this. In perfect simplicity and innocence I said, 'Lord, these are not sins.' The answer that came by His Spirit was, 'Whatever they are, are they worthy of a son of God?' And at once I had to say, 'No!' 'Are you willing to put them away?' 'Yes, Lord.' I should have to go home to settle some of them. I took pencil and paper, and marked everything down and said, 'Now, Lord, I promise that by Thy grace I will.' It was all alone in the solitude of my room. . . ." [1]

He accepted the teaching of sanctification by faith. He went to Mr. Bowker, the Keswick Chairman, and told him that he was ready to organize meetings in Glasgow for the dissemination of this, to him, freshly discovered truth. A few weeks later the first Convention was held in Glasgow.

Dr. Elder Cumming became a speaker at Keswick in 1883, and he spoke from its platform for twenty-four years in succession. Failing health prevented his return after 1908, and he passed away in 1917.

He was sixty years of age when he began to write books. He wrote many, one of them, *Through the Eternal Spirit,* still being in print and still widely read.

His influence in Scotland was very considerable, and in his day he was regarded as one of the most able clergymen in his native land.

For many years the speakers at the annual Glasgow Conventions were, for the most part, his guests. In a testimony meeting at the close of one of the Conventions, his daughter, Miss Jenny Cumming, told the audience that she had been made to feel the reality of the fuller life taught there, not so much by what she had heard in the meetings as by observing the lives, lived in her own home, by those who were speakers on the platform. [2]

[1] *The Keswick Week,* 1895, pp. 125, 126.
[2] W. B. Sloan, *These Sixty Years,* p. 29.

H. W. Webb-Peploe

Prebendary Webb-Peploe was born in 1837. His father was a Prebendary in Herefordshire, and his mother the accomplished authoress of *Naomi*, and other popular writings of the time.

He was educated at Marlborough and Cheltenham Colleges, and at Pembroke College, Cambridge. At Cambridge, while practising in the gymnasium, he injured his back so severely that he had to be in bed for some time. On the morning of an important track event, however, when his doctor called, he asked, "Doctor, may I get up and go and jump?" The doctor ironically said, "Yes"; but as soon as the doctor left Webb-Peploe went to the athletic field in a cab, and came off champion both in the high jump and the long run. As the price of his victory, he was obliged to return to bed again for some time longer.

Next year he won the swimming championship, but again at the expense of his health. Thus it came to pass that at the examination period he had scarcely attended lectures, and therefore could not attempt honours. He took his examinations lying flat on his back, but nevertheless headed the ordinary degree list, coming out ahead of some four hundred others.

His conversion was due, under God, to a tract given to him one day when he was on his way to the famous "Derby" horse-race, at Epsom.

When he was ordained, in 1863, he was placed in sole charge of the church in his native place. Three years later he succeeded his father as vicar of King's Pyon with Birley, where he laboured for the next ten years. In 1876 he went to St. Paul's, Onslow-square, London, where he worked for more than forty years. When he first went there, there were some people who said that the Church Missionary Society would get no more out of that church "now that a revivalist had come!" It was little foreseen that the contributions would be multiplied nearly tenfold. Eugene Stock says that Webb-Peploe was universally recognized as the leading Evangelical clergyman in London, and one of the first half-dozen in the whole country.[1]

Prebendary Webb-Peploe was a genuinely extempore orator. The addresses of his which appear in the annual Keswick Reports were always printed as he delivered them, and were never revised.

[1] Eugene Stock, *My Recollections*, p. 264.

His books consist mostly of unrevised addresses delivered by him. He was one of the finest orators in England, with a voice reminiscent of Gladstone's in its resonance and compass.

He was not present at the Oxford Convention, but it was during the week of that Convention that he entered into an experience which changed his whole life. In one of his addresses he told how this happened.

"For many years I was a minister and a faithful preacher of the doctrine of justification, but I had no joy for every moment, no rest in the midst of trouble, no calm amid the burdens of this life; I was strained and overstrained until I felt that I was breaking down. I could believe the doctrine of justification, because I saw the facts in God's Book; I believed that it was accomplished, because it was history; but when God said, 'I can keep thee and bless thee every moment,' it seemed too good to be true. Thus a minister goes on in his self-energized efforts, seeking calm and rest and strength, and the consequence is perpetual fret, perpetual wear and tear, a life of strain instead of a life of calm, a gradual breaking down where there ought to be a building up, all because men do not believe God's word. Do not suppose that I despised the promised land. I wished for peace, for rest, for joy and calm." [1]

"It may be helpful," he continues, "to some to know how the Lord brought this blessing to me and showed me the life of privilege. Twenty-one years ago my wife and I went to the seaside. We were poor, and had several children. It was the year of the Oxford Convention; and on the day on which it opened I met Sir Arthur Blackwood, and after we had talked awhile he said, 'Do you know about the Oxford Convention?' I was a country clergyman then, and had not heard of it. He said, 'People are coming together there to seek for a blessing, to pray for the life of rest.' He looked me in the face and said, 'Have you rest?' I replied, 'Yes, thank God.' He said, 'What do you understand by rest?' 'I mean that my sins are forgiven, that I am accepted in the Beloved, that God will somehow take care of me in this world, and receive me when I die.' He said, 'I thought you would say that; but do you know what it is to have perfect rest in the midst of duties and difficulties, to have a joy that never is broken at any moment of your life, to have a calm that is never interrupted, and to have a strength for every duty, with a sense of repose in

[1] H. W. Webb-Peploe, *The Life of Privilege* (New York, Fleming H. Revell Company, 1896), p. 64.

the living God?' I said, 'No; I would to God I had; that is what I long for most.' He said, 'So do I. I will tell you what I will do. A friend is to send me every day an account of the Convention, and every morning we will go into the woods and read it. God can give us a blessing·here as well as at Oxford.'

"Four days afterward my little child that was with us at the seashore was taken sick and died. I had to carry the little coffin in my arms all the way home, where I buried my little one with my own hands. I returned from the burial and said to myself, 'Now you have lost your holiday, have come home in trouble, and you must speak to your people instead of letting your curate speak; you would better tell them about God and his love.' I looked to see what lesson was assigned for the Sunday, and found it was the twelfth chapter of Second Corinthians. I read the ninth verse, 'My grace is sufficient for thee,' and thought, 'There is the verse to speak on.' I sat down to prepare my notes, but soon found myself murmuring in my tent against God for all he called upon me to bear. I flung down my pen, threw myself on my knees, and said to God, 'It is not sufficient, it is not sufficient! Lord, let thy grace be sufficient. O Lord, do!'

"The day before I had left home my mother had given me a beautiful illuminated text, and I had asked the servant to hang it on the wall over my table, that I might find it there when I came back. As I opened my eyes I was saying, 'O God, let thy grace be sufficient for me,' and there on the wall I saw,

'MY GRACE IS SUFFICIENT FOR THEE.'

The word *is* was in bright green, *my* was in black, and *thee* in black. 'MY grace *is* sufficient for THEE.' I heard a voice that seemed to say to me, 'You fool, how *dare* you ask God to make what is! Get up and take, and you will find it true. When God says *"is"* it is for you to believe Him, and you will find it true at every moment.' That *is* turned my life; from that moment I could say, 'O God, whatever thou dost say in Thy Word I believe, and, please God, I will step out upon it.' The very farmers began to say, 'Mr. Peploe does not seem as fidgety as he used to be.' Men of business, your clerks will say, 'He is a changed man now.' You in the ministry who have two sermons a week to write, does it wear and tear you out? Two sermons a week were killing me then; now fifteen a week can be preached where God wills.

I may be wearing out—I care not for that—it is not tearing out." [1]

The following year at the Brighton Convention he delivered three addresses, and in one of these referred to his own experience of entering into the rest of faith: "There was a watching, waiting and struggling to do right, yet I constantly found myself overcome and generally unable to realize anything like St. Paul's experience, 'Not I, but Christ liveth in me.' Was his an ideal picture, I asked, or is it possible for me to realize it? After a time, I saw that if I believed it would be mine. When we believe that what God Almighty says will be fulfilled in our hearts, the soul drops into the hands of the Lord Jesus, for Him to use for His own glory. I know that there are many cares which bring the minister low, and which in former days made it seem to me impossible to obey the calls to service. But when the truth came—'Not I, but Christ that liveth in me'—the rest of faith was practically known in my ministerial life." [2]

When Canon Battersby and Robert Wilson found that Robert Pearsall Smith could not be at the first Keswick Convention, they turned to other speakers, Prebendary Webb-Peploe included. He had intended to go as a listener, but owing to the absence of the expected speakers, he had to take a large part in the ministry during the week. Indeed, he and another speaker shared the principal burden between them. After that, as long as he lived—he died in 1923—he was one of the most active speakers in the work of the Keswick Convention, speaking again and again not only at Keswick, but all through Great Britain and the United States.

About thirty years after the founding of Keswick, the Prebendary recalled the opposition the work was subjected to at the beginning, even from Evangelical clergy. "Surely," he said, "*no well-instructed* Christian of our day, who heard the teaching which I have briefly depicted, would think of condemning it as opposed to God's Truth, and yet it was only some twenty-eight, or twenty-nine, years ago that, when I had been asked to set forth 'Keswick teaching' before some fifty or sixty Evangelical clergy and I had heartily responded to the invitation, explaining from Romans vi–viii, from 1 Corinthians x. 13, and from 2 Corinthians xii. 9, guarded carefully by 1 John i. 8, 9, the blessed keeping power and purposes of the Lord Jesus

---

[1] H. W. Webb-Peploe, *The Life of Privilege* (New York, Fleming H. Revell Company, 1896), pp. 67–9.
[2] J. B. Figgis, *Keswick from Within* (London, Marshall Bros., Ltd., 1914), pp. 40, 41.

Christ for the people—the chairman of the meeting (himself perhaps the very centre of Evangelical Churchmanship) rose as soon as I had finished my address, and said: 'Heresy! Heresy! Damnable Heresy! I hold that it is for the glory of God that we should fall into sin, that He may get honour to Himself by drawing us out of it!' Thank God! further light was very soon given to the earnest, but misinformed, leaders of that last generation; and for the honour of our Lord and the good fame of the brethren, I may mention that each of the three great leaders, who most determinedly opposed the movement at first, afterwards invited me, as an exponent of Keswick teaching, to conduct missions, or to take special services in their parishes, and that, in each case, I was permitted to do what they asked, and to have these honoured fathers sitting humbly in their own parish churches, and listening earnestly, while I set forth 'the unsearchable riches of Christ.' "[1]

The pre-eminent service of Prebendary Webb-Peploe to the movement lay in the fidelity with which he brought everything to the test of the Word of God. He handled his Greek Testament as familiarly as his English. He knew the Scriptures so well that some thought he could almost reproduce the sacred volume entire if it were lost. He confined himself to Scripture exposition more exclusively than any other speaker on the Keswick platform. No shade of meaning escaped his eye. His addresses almost constituted a class in New Testament exegesis.

On one occasion, when some perfectionists tried to capture the Convention, Prebendary Webb-Peploe was asked to answer them. He did so in an exposition of the Scripture teaching on Sin. It was most masterly. As he went on the dusk began to fall, and he offered to stop, but the great audience urged him on. There in the gathering darkness they sat, in a hush, as he poured forth the treasures of God's Word. Never a breath of perfectionism was heard again. He was an Olympian and could, as Robert L. Stevenson puts it, heave a pyramid!

Handley C. G. Moule

Among the many leaders in the spiritual life who joined the Keswick group in the latter half of the eighties, was H. C. G. Moule, then Principal of Ridley Hall, Cambridge.

He was born in 1841, at Fordington, near Dorchester, where his father was Vicar. All of the seven boys in the family who grew

[1] C. F. Harford, *The Keswick Convention*, pp. 39, 40.

up to maturity achieved distinction. At Cambridge University J. B. Lightfoot was his first College tutor and lecturer. Later Moule said of him, "No man ever loitered so late in the Great Court that he did not see Lightfoot's lamp burning in his study window; and the most regular worshipper in morning chapel at seven o'clock always found Lightfoot there with him. . . . His strong points were unfailing thoroughness of knowledge and unsurpassable clearness of exposition and instruction. Great was my sense of loss when, in 1861, he resigned his tutorship to become Hulsean Professor of Divinity." [1]

At college (Trinity) he won various Latin and Greek prizes, and in the Classical Tripos Examination his name appeared second in the First Class. The next year he took a First Class in his theological examination, and became a Fellow of Trinity.

For four years he was a Master at Marlborough, and then for five years he worked with his father, as his curate. In 1873 he returned to Cambridge to become first Junior, then Senior Dean. In 1880 he became the first Principal of Ridley Hall, a new theological College of the Evangelical School, the counterpart of which at Oxford was Wycliffe Hall, opened three years before. He was Principal of Ridley Hall for eighteen years, and then became Norrisian Professor of Divinity at Cambridge University, which post he left in 1901 to become Bishop of Durham. His immediate predecessors in the See of Durham were Lightfoot and Westcott, and it was universally thought that he was no unworthy successor of these great scholars. This position he held until his death in 1920.

The year before he died Bishop Moule, in an address delivered at Keswick, told the story of his regeneration and entrance into the Keswick movement in the following words:

"I first take you back just fifty-two years, to the time when I began to understand and possess some of the possessions which Keswick loves to show us the way to. In the year 1867, at twenty-five, my mother led me to the Lord Jesus Christ. I had a good post as a form-master in a great public school. I was very well satisfied with life. To a certain extent, with all sorts of internal contradictions to the feeling, I was fairly satisfied with myself. And God in His great mercy kept me from what would be called wrong life, though not from a world of evil within.

"Then, one quiet day, I know not in the least how, nor shall

[1] J. B. Harford and F. C. Macdonald, *Handley Carr Glyn Moule, Bishop of Durham. A Biography* (London, Hodder and Stoughton, 1922), pp. 18, 19.

know in this life, there came on me conviction of sin, in its old-fashioned form, a sight of how richly I deserved the wrath of God and banishment from Him for ever, for I had kept Him out of my heart. With almost a fire in my brain I went to my mother. I will not dwell upon her holy memory. Enough to say that she led me with God-given wisdom to the feet of Jesus and by spirit-sight I saw the Lamb upon the Cross of Calvary, and knew that He and only He stood between me and the second death.

"Then in due time I was ordained to the holy ministry—thank God, not before I had come to know Christ. And then I went on, at times with college duty, at times with parish duty; and in due time I was made Principal of a Theological Hall at Cambridge, with which I remained connected many years.

"I had been about four years there, living as the head of a religious institution, when I learned about certain possessions I had not possessed. I was on a visit with my family that autumn, 1884, at the house of a dearly loved relative in Scotland, near Linlithgow, a place where year after year the generous master and mistress had opened a great barn on their estate for what we may call a series of Keswick meetings. We, my family and I, were paying a visit to our friends, and the Convention was due to be held.

"Was I anxious to go? Not at all. I had been strongly prejudiced, much by my own fault, against the whole Keswick ideal. I thought it meant a doctrine of sinless perfection, which could only lead to an attitude in which the Christ of the atoning Cross seemed to cease to be necessary, and honestly I was afraid. But there was a great deal also of mixed motive, of jealousy and prejudice, in my mind.

"I wished to get away during the days of the Convention, but there was no opportunity to do this without breach of courtesy, and so I stayed; and, again as an act of courtesy, I went to the first meeting. It did not please me at all, and a severe conflict of thought and feeling followed upon it. Then there came the next night, and with some difficulty I made up my mind to go again.

"I still see the great barn, the thronging people, and myself sitting in the audience, by no means on the platform, listening to what might come, partly as the critic, but partly, I will admit, with a heart hungry for some gracious thing, if it was to be found. For I had begun to feel, after my years of converted life and ministerial work, guilty of discreditable failures in patience, and charity, and humbleness, and I know not what. I knew that I was not satisfied, and I knew that I ought to find what would satisfy me; but I did not expect to find it there.

"Two addresses were given that evening, the first by the late Mr. William Sloan, of Glasgow, a noble specimen of the Scottish business man, out and out for God. He spoke on the first chapter of Haggai, in words which I do not think I shall ever forget, taking to pieces the Christian life which is not satisfied, and piercing into the reasons why it is not satisfied, all more or less reducible to our letting the self-life intrude itself into the work of God; the man feeling himself, after all, well-nigh as important in Christian work as his Master. Somehow or other that address, under the Spirit's good guidance, pulled me to pieces with a second conviction of sin, the sin of the converted life, the sin of the professing Christian man.

"I may humbly say, thank God, that I was not a hypocrite. The Lord had showed me myself and Himself, in reality, as I have told you, long years before. But I had misread His promise, or read it so imperfectly that in deed and in truth I had a world of special sin to be convinced of that September night of 1884. And I remember, at the close of that address, feeling indescribably that it had been an even awful thing to go to that meeting. I was no longer the critic; the prejudices, the fears that there would be something, from the point of view of sacred orthodoxy (which *is* sacred), wrong and out of line, all vanished away. I knew that *this* was orthodox, the conviction of my sin.

"Then the second address was given. The speaker was one whom I afterwards claimed, and claim still, for our relation is the same, though he has gone above, as my beloved friend, Evan Hopkins, of blessed memory. He rose up, and delivered an address as characteristic as possible, luminous as the light, perfect in arrangement, simple in expression, but with all the power of spiritual conviction in it. It was one long ordered piling up of the promises of God to the soul that will do two things toward Him—surrender itself into His hands, and trust Him for His mighty victory within. I will not—I must not—time flies—remind you what were the texts of the infallible Word which he piled up. It was as if there were two great weights in my balance. One was down heavily on the ground, loaded with the sins of my converted life and its grievous secret or open failures. Into the other balance the speaker now put promise after promise, aimed precisely at this, not for the unconverted man flying for refuge to the city where the guilty shall be safe under the protection of the high-priest, but the promises to that same fugitive, now dwelling in the city of refuge, who is starving there, and wretched, and miserable, because of himself. And as these promises were recited, grace enabled me to take them as meant, not to take them as read, but to take them as meant; to realize that they were meant to act; that I was to step on them with both feet, and to see if they did not bear.

"And so, in the great mercy of God, before I left that barn meeting, two consciousnesses had come in upon me. One was that I was in the hands of an absolute Master, so grasping and fettering me that I should have no interests outside His, seek no gain, or praise, or whatever it was, except for Him; that I was an illustration of the words of the ancient moralist, Aristotle, describing his theory of human slavery: 'The slave is but a part of his master, he exists but for his master, he has no interests of his own, and yet he is, as it were, a limb of his master, separate yet living with his life.'

"So I went out of that meeting, back to the hospitable house where we were staying. I recollect, as I walked up the stairs to my room for the night, the consciousness with which I knew, on the one hand, that I was the absolute bond-slave of a sovereign and irresponsible Master, on the other hand that I had found a Friend and Liberator, a Helper, a Deliverer, a 'goodness and a fortress,' who would, so long and so much as I used Him, make me more than conqueror over the oldest temptation, over the most inveterate subtlety of the approach and invitation of evil, so as to teach even me how to walk and to please God. In the meeting of the next night I felt constrained to put pride into the pocket; to rise and say before all the people how the last night had been a great blessing to my soul.

"Then in due time I had to go back to my responsible work at Cambridge. I knew there was in front of me a very difficult, laborious, perplexing term, with grave problems regarding movements of Christian life in Cambridge. And I was naturally a restless, impatient, and somewhat nervous being. But I recollect two things about that term. First, that, by a power certainly not my own, I was able to meet every threatened difficulty with a quiet mind, which was half the victory beforehand. Then, what was the very opposite to my nature, when I was hard at work in my study, and an unlooked-for knock at the door came—instead of the old thrill and twist of impatience, there was the pleasure the swimmer feels in climbing a wave, because it gives him a free sense of the lift of the water, and the delight at once of action and of rest. These things now did not put me out. I possessed my possession. A Christ submitted to, a Christ trusted, a Christ used, made life a different thing.

"All this was thirty-five years ago, dear friends in Christ . . . but it is to me as if yesterday. What have I to say as to the time since then? Has it been unbroken victory, has it been unbroken rest? No. By whose fault? Never the Master's. Every day and every hour He has been as full of help as ever, He has been as close at hand as ever. But did I never get indolent in the use of His helps to keeping awake? Did I never let myself get slack about regular prayer, when there was no excuse for slackness? Did I never let myself get careless over search of the Bible? Did I never let myself get indifferent about little bits of unpretending duty? Inevitably then something seemed as if it paralysed the fingers that were to use the Lord. And the Lord, unused, humbled the man again and again, by letting him feel what it would all be again if he did not possess his possessions and use what he possessed.

"But I know this well, that to this day, through these long years, with a Church and a world changed, with my life changed, as many a joy and many a sorrow has come over it, while God has often broken up the ground under my feet and clouded the sky above my head, and has put me to some of the greatest tests that human loss can bring, while also crowning me with mercies—all I can say is that, just as the old secret is used, the surrender of the spirit to the Lord, the same delightful results are assured, because He is the same. There is still a rest and a power for the soul, which means nothing less than this wonderful Christ, whom I saw in conversion, and who is indeed Christ for me now, in this after-blessing, as I ought to have seen Him from the first. Christ is still in me to make the weak strong, to make the easily defeated Christian conqueror, through Him that loved us." [1]

The above quotation by Moule of his spiritual experience, given at the end of a life richly fruitful in the service of God, may be rather long, but it is one of the fullest accounts we have by any of the Keswick leaders of how they came to be a part of Keswick.

Dr. W. H. Griffith Thomas, at one time Principal of Wycliffe Hall, Oxford, said of Moule's commentary on Romans, in the "Expositor's Bible" series, "In this will be found a statement of

[1] H. C. G. Moule, *Christ and the Christian* (London, Marshall Bros., Ltd., 1919), pp. 49–58. (The paragraphing of this quotation is my own, there being only five paragraphs in the passage as printed in the book.)

the doctrine of Sanctification as seen in Romans vi–viii, which contains the essential principles of holiness associated with Keswick, put forth with all the scholarship and spirituality characteristic of the author. As long as that book is studied, the theology of holiness as set forth at Keswick cannot fail to receive due attention."[1]

The adherence of Dr. Moule to the Keswick platform was a great accession of strength, for it brought into the movement one who had long been highly respected as a trusted Evangelical scholar and theologian. Keswick has had other great scholars, but there is no doubt that Dr. Moule was its greatest; and his books, though necessarily appealing to a far wider sphere than that represented by Keswick, have done effective service to the Keswick movement.

Andrew Murray

About the year 1820, the Dutch Reformed Church of South Africa, alarmed at the spread of rationalism in its midst and distrusting the clergymen that came from Holland, sent a sharp cry to Scotland for some godly ministers to come to them with the gospel. One of those who responded was Andrew Murray the First, who had received his college education at Aberdeen and, before going to South Africa, studied theology at Utrecht in the Dutch tongue. His labours and his zeal were apostolic. He married a South African Dutch girl, by whom he had seventeen children, of whom Andrew Murray the Second, the subject of this sketch, was one.

Andrew and his older brother, John, who later became professor of theology at Stellenbosch, like their father before them, went to Aberdeen and Utrecht for their schooling. Andrew was only twenty when he returned to South Africa. For seven years he worked as a missionary to the Orange Free State and the Transvaal, a parish about twice the size of England. In 1860 he accepted a call to Worcester, eighty miles from Cape Town; from there he went to Cape Town; and from Cape Town to Wellington, where he laboured from 1871 to the end of his life.

Andrew Murray was also greatly interested in education. His interest in young people led to the establishment of the Grey College at Bloemfontein, and, in 1873, of the Huguenot Seminary, which later developed into a college. In 1877 he established an Institute for the training of missionaries at Wellington.

[1] C. F. Harford, *The Keswick Convention*, p. 231.

He founded and for many years was president of the South Africa General Mission, and was a very active member of the mission committee of his own denomination, the Dutch Reformed Church.

It is as a writer, however, that Dr. Murray has become most famous. A bibliography of his books runs to about one hundred titles, written in Dutch and English. Many of them were first written in Dutch and later translated into English. All of his books are of a devotional character. Some consist of series of addresses given on missionary and conference tours and to his own congregations. His widely-read commentary on the Epistle to the Hebrews, *The Holiest of All*, was intended for the Dutch farmers who were not often able to get to church. It is amazing how many of his books are still in print, though written from fifty to seventy-five years ago.

Dr. Murray was present at Keswick for the first time in 1882, not on the platform, but in the audience. A testimony by him appeared later in *The Life of Faith*, over the initial M. It is too long to give entire, and so I will quote some excerpts from it.

"Let me also sound a note of praise to the glory of our blessed Lord Jesus for what He has done for me here at Keswick. It is not that the teaching has been new to me. In the distant land in which I have been working, 6,000 miles away from here, I had some years ago learnt something of the blessed life of faith for myself, and been privileged to lead others to it. But there was still a longing for something more. And even of what I had experienced the freshness and power got lost, the anointing with fresh oil was wanting. There was not that life in the perfect liberty and the continual clear leading of the Spirit to which the rest of faith was meant to be but the entrance. Self, seeking to do God's work, far more dangerous than refusing to obey, the flesh creeping in, learning spiritual truth, and doing spiritual work rendered it impossible for the life of God to reveal its full power in the soul.

"Some two years ago it pleased the Lord to lay me aside from work by an affection of the throat. In His good Providence I was brought to England some six weeks ago, and led to the faith-healing home in London. I cannot say what a blessing my stay there has been to me. I was brought to see that while I only thought of healing as the first thing, and faith as the means to it, the Lord's purpose was to make the healing the secondary thing, the means to lead on to fuller faith and fellowship with Himself. . . .

"On Tuesday evening, at the after-meeting, I rose with others to testify my desire, but could not rise a second time with those who could testify that they had realized that Christ was to them what they had believed. It was as if I only felt how utterly helpless every effort to grasp the blessing is, and could do nothing but bow in emptiness before the Lord. On Wednesday evening I was again in the after-meeting, and it was there the Lord revealed Himself. And as the words of the simple chorus were sung—'wonderful cleansing, wonderful filling, wonderful keeping'—I saw it all, Jesus cleansing, Jesus filling, Jesus keeping. I had for a year back been seeing what wonderful things God's word says about the power of the blood of Christ. It was *through the blood* that the God of peace brought again from the dead our Lord Jesus. It was *by His own blood* He entered into the holy place. It was with the blood of the better sacrifice that the heavenly things themselves were purged. It was thus through the blood that the power of sin and death had been overcome; through the blood alone that Christ had obtained and could hold His place in heaven as our Mediator. The blood that had obtained such mighty victories in the kingdom of sin and hell, and in the kingdom of heaven, too. Surely that blood that could cleanse the soul is a power but too little known. I believed and I received Jesus as my Cleanser. I look to Him to make the blood-sprinkling as glorious and effectual as the blood-shedding was. And I saw that the filling cannot but follow the cleansing. The vessel He hath cleansed He will not leave empty; the temple He hath cleansed, He will fill with His glory . . .

"I could say more, but this is enough just to give my grateful testimony to the love of our blessed Lord, and what He has done for me at Keswick." [1]

The year 1895 was made memorable at Keswick by Dr. Murray's first and only appearance at the Convention as a speaker. A very interesting service for testimony was held on Friday afternoon. Several speakers told at considerable length something of their own spiritual history. The first was Dr. Murray. It is rather long, but it is well-worth giving entire, as it appeared later in *The Keswick Week*.

"In Psalm lxxviii. 34 you have these words, 'When He slew them, then they sought Him.' When I was asked to give my testimony, I said I doubted whether it was desirable, and for this reason: We all know what helpfulness there is in the clear-cut testimony of a

[1] *The Life of Faith*, October 2, 1882, p. 221.

M

man who can say, 'There I was: I knelt down and God helped me, and I entered the better life.' I cannot give such a testimony; but I know what blessing it has often brought to me to read such testimonies for the strengthening of my faith. And yet I got this answer from those who wished me to speak: 'Perhaps there are many at Keswick to whom a testimony concerning a life of more struggle and difficulty will be helpful.' I replied: 'If it must be so, let me tell, for the glory of God, how He has led me.'

"Some of you have heard how I have pressed upon you the two stages in the Christian life, and the step from one to the other. The first ten years of my spiritual life were spent manifestly on the lower stage. I was a minister, I may say, as zealous and as earnest and as happy in my work as anyone, as far as love of the work was concerned. Yet, all the time, there was burning in my heart a dissatisfaction and restlessness inexpressible. What was the reason? I had never learned, with all my theology, that obedience was possible. My justification was as clear as noonday. I knew the hour in which I had received from God the joy of pardon. I remember in my little room in Bloemfontein, how I used to sit and think: 'What is the matter? Here am I knowing that God has justified me in the blood of Christ, but I have no power in service.' My thoughts, my words, my actions, my unfaithfulness—everything troubled me. Though all around thought me one of the most earnest of men, my life was one of deep dissatisfaction. I struggled and prayed as best I could.

"One day I was talking with a missionary. I do not think he knew much of the power of sanctification himself—he would have admitted it. When we were talking and he saw my earnestness he said, 'Brother, remember that when God puts a desire into your heart, He will fulfil it.' That helped me; I thought of it a hundred times. I want to say the same to you, who are plunging about and struggling in the quagmire of helplessness and doubt. The desire that God puts into your heart He will fulfil.

"I was greatly helped about this time by reading a book called 'Parables from Nature.' One of these parables represents that after the creation of the earth, on a certain day

A NUMBER OF CRICKETS MET.

One of them began, saying, 'Oh, I feel so happy. For a time I was creeping about looking for a place where to stay, but I could not find the place that suited me. At last I got in behind the bark of an old tree, and it seemed as though the place were just fitted for me, I felt so comfortable there.' Another said, 'I was there for a time, but it would not fit me'—that was a grass cricket. 'But at last I got on to a high stalk of grass, and as I clung there and swung there, in the wind and in the air, I felt that that was the place made for me.' Then a third cricket said: 'Well, I have tried the bark of the old tree, and I have tried the grass, but God has made no place for me, and I feel unhappy.' Then the old mother cricket said: 'My child, do not speak that way. Your Creator never made anyone without preparing a place for him. Wait, and you will find it in due time.' Some time after these same crickets met together again, and got to talking. The old mother said, 'Now, my child, what say you?' The cricket replied: 'Yes, what you said is true. You know those strange people who have come here. They built a house, and in their house they had a fire; and, you know, when I got into the corner of the hearth near the fire I felt so warm, and I knew that was the place God made for me.'

"That little parable helped me wonderfully, and I pass it on to you. If any are saying that God has not got a place for them, let them trust God, and wait, and He will help you, and show you what is your place. You know God led Israel forty years in the wilderness; and that was my wilderness time. I was serving Him very heartily, yet it was dark very often, and the great burden on my heart was, 'I am sinning against the God that loves me.'

"So the Lord led me till in His great mercy I had been eleven or twelve years in Bloemfontein. Then He brought me to another congregation in Worcester, about the time when God's Holy Spirit was being poured out in America, Scotland, and Ireland. In 1860, when I had been six months in the congregation, God poured out His Spirit there in connection with my preaching, especially as I was moving about in the country, and a very unspeakable blessing came to me. The first Dutch edition of my book *Abide in Christ* was written at that time. I would like you to understand that a minister or Christian author may often be led to say more than he has experienced. I had not then experienced all that I wrote of; I cannot say that I experience it all perfectly even now. But if we are honest in seeking to trust God in all circumstances, and always to receive the truth, He will make it live in our hearts. But let me warn you Convention Christians not to seek too much satisfaction in your own thoughts or the thoughts of others. The deepest and most beautiful

THOUGHTS CANNOT FEED THE SOUL

unless you go to God and let Him give you reality and faith.

Well, God helped me, and for seven or eight years I went on, always inquiring and seeking, and always getting. What we want is to trust God more. He helped me to trust Him in the dark and in the light. Then came, about 1870, the great Holiness movement. The letters that appeared in *The Revival* (now *The Christian*) touched my heart; and I was in close fellowship with what took place at Oxford and Brighton, and it all helped me. Perhaps if I were to talk of consecration I might tell you of an evening there in my own study in Cape Town. Yet I cannot say that that was my deliverance, for I was still struggling. I would say that what we need is complete obedience. Let us not be like Saul, who, after he was anointed, failed, in the case of Agag, to accept God's judgment against sin to the very utmost.

"Later on, my mind became much exercised about the baptism of the Holy Spirit, and I gave myself to God as perfectly as I could to receive this baptism of the Spirit. Yet there was failure; God forgive it. It was somehow as if I could not get what I wanted. Through all these stumblings God led me, without any very special experience that I can point to; but as I look back I do believe now that He was giving me more and more of His blessed Spirit, had I but known it better.

"I can help you more, perhaps, by speaking, not of any marked experience, but by telling very simply what I think God has given me now, in contrast to the first ten years of my Christian life.

"In the first place, I have learned to place myself before God every day, as a vessel to be filled with the Holy Spirit. He has filled me with the blessed assurance that He, as the everlasting God, has guaranteed His own work in me. If there is one lesson I am learning day by day it is this: that it is God who worketh all and in all. Oh, that I could help any brother or sister to realize this! I will tell you where you fail. You have never yet heartily believed that He is working out your salvation. You believe that if a painter undertakes a picture, he must look to every shade of colour and every touch upon the canvas. You believe that if a workman makes a table or bench he knows how to do his work.

But you do not believe that the everlasting God is working out the image of His Son in you, as any sister here is doing a piece of ornamental or fancy work, following out the pattern in every detail. Just think, 'Can God not work out in me the purpose of His love?' If that piece of work is to be perfect, every stitch must be in its place. And remember that not one minute of your life should be without God. We do not believe that. We want God to come in at times—say, in the morning; then we are to live two or three hours, and He can come in again. No; God must be

EVERY MOMENT THE WORKER IN YOUR SOUL.

"I was once preaching and a lady came to talk with me. She was a very pious woman, and I asked her, 'How are you going on?' Her answer was, 'Oh, just the way it is always; sometimes light and sometimes dark.' 'My dear sister, where is that in the Bible?' She said, 'We have day and night in nature; and just so it is in our souls.' 'No, no; in the Bible we read, "Your sun shall no more go down."' Let me believe that I am God's child, and that the Father in Christ, through the Holy Ghost, has set His love upon me and I may abide in His presence, not frequently, but unceasingly. The veil has been rent; the holiest of all has been opened. By the grace of my God, I have there to take up my abode; and there my God is going to teach me what I never could learn while I dwelt outside. My home is always the abiding love of the Father in heaven.

"You will ask me, 'Are you satisfied? Have you got all you want?' God forbid. With the deepest feeling of my soul I can say I am satisfied with Jesus now; but there is also the consciousness of how much fuller the revelation can be of the exceeding abundance of His grace. Let us never hesitate to say: This is only the beginning. When we are brought into the holiest of all, we are only beginning to take our right position with the Father.

"May He teach us our own nothingness and transform us into the likeness of His Son, and help us to go out and be a blessing to our fellow-men. Let us trust Him and praise Him in the midst of a consciousness of our own utter unworthiness, and in the midst of a consciousness of failure and of remaining tendency to sin. Notwithstanding this, let us believe that our God loves to dwell in us; and let us hope without ceasing in His still more abundant grace." [1]

[1] *The Keswick Week*, 1895, pp. 123–5.

Andrew Murray made only this one visit to Keswick as a speaker, but for many years he led a similar Convention in South Africa. At the 1914 Keswick Convention a missionary from the South Africa General Mission brought a message from him to the effect that eternity alone would reveal what South Africa owed to Keswick.

F. B. Meyer

F. B. Meyer was the best-known Baptist clergyman of his day. It is doubtful, indeed, whether any other minister of his time was better known throughout the world. Although an active pastor all his life to within a few years of his death, he travelled all over the world on preaching missions, making twelve journeys to America alone.

He was born in London in 1847, and after preparing for the Gospel ministry at Regent's Park College, was graduated from London University. He held pastorates at York, Leicester, and London—all of them notable ones. Twice he was President of the National Free Church Council, and once, President of the Baptist Union.

Like Andrew Murray he was a prolific author, writing literally scores of books, in every field of Christian literature, many of which are still in print. His books are not of a very scholarly nature, but all are carefully written and dependable, evincing not only an unusual talent for fluent writing, but rare spiritual insight as well.

Dr. Meyer was present at the famous Broadlands, Oxford, and Brighton Conventions, and could tell of light and help that had come to him in each of these gatherings; but a visit of two members of the famous "Cambridge Seven," Stanley Smith and C. T. Studd, to Leicester in 1885, when they were the guests of Dr. Meyer, was the incident that led to a definite step in his experience that finally equipped him to take his place on the Keswick platform. Let us allow him to tell the story in his own words:

"The visit of Messrs. Stanley Smith and Studd to Melbourne Hall will always mark an epoch in my own life. Before then my Christian life was spasmodic and fitful; now flaming up with enthusiasm, and then pacing wearily over leagues of grey ashes and cold cinders. I saw that these young men had something which I had not, but which was within them a constant source of rest and strength and joy. And never shall I forget a scene at 7 a.m. in the grey November morning, as daylight was flickering into the bed-

room, paling the guttered candles which from a very early hour
had been lighting up the page of Scripture and revealing the figures
of the devoted Bible students, who wore the old cricketing or
boating costume of earlier days, to render them less sensible of the
raw, damp climate. The talk we held then was one of the most
formative influences of my life. Why should I not do what they
had done? Why should I not yield my whole nature to God, working out day by day *that* which He would will and work within?
Why should I not be a vessel, though only of earthenware, meet for
the Master's use, because purged and sanctified?

"There was nothing new in what they told me. They said, that
'A man must not only believe in Christ for final salvation, but
must trust Him for victory over every sin, and for deliverance
from every care.' They said, that 'The Lord Jesus was willing to
abide in the heart which was wholly yielded up to Him.' They
said, that 'If there were some things in our lives that made it difficult for us to surrender our whole nature to Christ, yet if we were
willing to be made willing to surrender them, He would make us
not only willing but glad.' They said, that 'Directly we give or
attempt to give ourselves to Him, He takes us.' All this was simple
enough. I could have said it myself. But they urged me to take the
definite step; and I shall be for ever thankful that they did. And
if in a distant country they should read this page, let them be en-
couraged to learn that one heart at least has been touched with a
new fire, and that one voice is raised in prayer for their increase
in the knowledge and love of Him who has become more real to
the suppliant, because of their brotherly words.

"Very memorable was the night when I came to close quarters
with God. The Angel that wrestled with Jacob found me, eager to
make me a Prince. There were things in my heart and life which
I felt were questionable, if not worse; I knew that God had a
controversy with respect to them; I saw that my very dislike to
probe or touch them was a clear indication that there was mischief
lurking beneath. It is the diseased joint that shrinks from the touch
and tender eye that shudders at the light. At the same time I did
not feel willing to give these things up. It was a long struggle. At
last I said feebly, 'Lord, I am willing to be made willing; I am
desirous that Thy will should be done in me and through me, as
thoroughly as it is done in Heaven; come and take me and break
me and make me.' That was the hour of crisis, and when it had
passed I felt able at once to add, 'And now I give myself to Thee:

body, soul and spirit; in sorrow or in joy; in the dark or in the light; in life or in death, to be Thine only, wholly and for ever. Make the most of me that can be made for Thy glory.' No rapture or rush of joy came to assure me that the gift was accepted. I left the place with almost a heavy heart. I simply assured myself that He must have taken that which I had given, and at the moment of my giving it. And to that belief I clung in all the days that followed, constantly repeating to myself the words, 'I am His.' And thus at last the joy and rest entered and victory and freedom from burdening care and I found that He was moulding my will and making it easy to do what I had thought impossible; and I felt that He was leading me into the paths of righteousness for His name's sake, but so gently as to be almost imperceptible to my weak sight." [1]

Dr. Meyer often referred to this experience, and sometimes in speaking of it said that his early Christian life was marred and his ministry paralysed because he had kept back one thing from the bunch of keys he had given to the Lord. Every key save one! The key of one room was kept for personal use, and the Lord shut out. And the effect of the incomplete consecration was found in lack of power, assurance, joy, and peace. These things came to him only when he handed over the last key.

And yet, although this experience was a turning-point in his Christian life, Dr. Meyer saw the danger of living on it. One of his biographers tells us that on one occasion at Keswick someone asked him to recount the experience, and Dr. Meyer replied, "No, no, you cannot live on an experience."

After this experience Dr. Meyer grew in spiritual influence and power, and the Keswick Trustees invited him to the Convention, not at first to speak, but as a guest. When, the following year, 1887, he was asked to speak, keenly realizing his insufficiency and his need of the Holy Spirit, he went through another crisis experience that marked a definite point in his life. Again he himself must be allowed to tell what happened to him then:

"Before I first spoke on the platform I had my own deeper experience, on a memorable night when I left the little town with its dazzling lamps, and climbed the neighbouring hill. As I write the summer night is again casting its spell on me. The light clouds veil the stars and pass. The breath of the mountains leads me to

---

[1] W. Y. Fullerton, *F. B. Meyer, A Biography* (London, Marshall, Morgan & Scott, Ltd.), pp. 57, 58.

yearn for a fresh intake of God's Spirit. May we not count on the Anointing Spirit to grant us a fresh infilling when we are led to seek it? May we not dare to believe that we have received, even when there is no answering emotion? Do we not receive by faith? These were the questions which a few of us had debated far into the night, at a prayer meeting convened at which a number of men were agonizing for the Spirit.

"I was too tired to agonize, so I left the prayer meeting and as I walked I said, 'My Father, if there is one soul more than another within the circle of these hills that needs the gift of Pentecost, it is I: I want the Holy Spirit, but I do not know how to receive Him; and I am too weary to think, or feel, or pray intensely.' Then a Voice said to me, 'As you took forgiveness from the hand of the dying Christ, take the Holy Ghost from the hand of the living Christ, and reckon that the gift is thine by a faith that is utterly indifferent to the presence or absence of resultant joy. According to thy *faith*, so shall it be unto thee.' So I turned to Christ and said, 'Lord, as I breathe in this whiff of warm night air, so I breathe into every part of me Thy blessed Spirit.' I felt no hand laid on my head, there was no lambent flame, there was no rushing sound from heaven: but by *faith*, without emotion, without excitement, I took, and took for the first time, and I have kept on taking ever since.

"I turned to leave the mountain-side, and as I went down the tempter said I had nothing, that it was all imagination, but I answered, 'Though I do not feel it, I reckon that God is faithful.'"[1]

His hostess tells that that night she was sitting up for him, and he came in greatly agitated, and again and again as he walked up and down the room in deep self-examination, he said, "Can I have been wrong and wanting until now? Has my life hitherto been lacking power?" They prayed together, and he retired without any feeling of blessing, but the next morning all was peace. Later he wrote, "That was the high water mark! Alas, that tides like that should ever drop down to the beach!"

After this experience at Keswick, the Holy Spirit became more personally real than He had ever been before. He became quick and sensitive to every suggestion of the Spirit. The story is told that one day he and the officers of his church got together on some business. At such gatherings he always took the chair. On this

[1] W. Y. Fullerton, *F. B. Meyer, A Biography* (London, Marshall, Morgan & Scott, Ltd.), pp. 65, 66.

occasion, however, he was so filled with the conviction of God's presence that he could not now think of taking the chair. It was left for the Holy Spirit Himself. So the group sat with Dr. Meyer in the ranks, and transacted their business as in the very hearing of the Invisible Administrator and Guide.

It is doubtful whether any other Keswick leader ever did more than Dr. Meyer to make the distinctive Keswick message known throughout the world. There were other Keswick "missioners"— men who travelled to other countries as representatives of Keswick to promulgate the message of sanctification by faith and the Spirit-filled life; but no other—unless it be Dr. Charles Inwood—travelled more, and certainly no other was as well-received wherever he went. Speaking at Conventions seemed to be his special forte. His personality was magnetic; his message was appealing and attractive; and as a speaker he was second to none. He was perhaps the first to carry the message of Keswick to the United States. His death in 1929 left a gap in the ranks of Keswick leaders that has not yet been filled.

Some Observations on the Christian Experiences of These Men

In the nearly eighty years of the history of Keswick, scores of men have spoken at the Convention, some of them returning year after year for as many as thirty and forty years. The majority of them have been from the British Isles—and naturally so; but many have come from other lands throughout the world. Keswick's platform has been a cosmopolitan one. Moreover, as was noted earlier in this book, the leaders represent many denominational groups. At Keswick, denominational differences are put aside as of little importance in comparison with what all Christians hold in common. The motto of the Convention is, "ALL ONE IN CHRIST JESUS."

In the writing of these biographical sketches I have made no attempt to select men whose experiences, more than those of other Keswick speakers, fall into a peculiarly Keswick pattern. The subjects of these sketches have been chosen almost haphazardly. Their experiences are typical of the experiences not only of the other Keswick speakers, but of the rank and file of the movement as a whole.

I have related their experiences, mostly in their own words, and described their ministries in order, primarily, to illustrate how Keswick teaching works out in practice—how men come to it and are led to accept it, and the result of its acceptance in their lives.

We note certain resemblances in their lives and experiences. The religious background of the men in each case was a wholesome one—differing denominationally, but Evangelical in each instance. They were all university men, and all ministers of the Gospel—earnest and zealous in their work for the Lord. They were alike in this, too, that there were two stages in their lives—first, a stage in which, although they were sincere and earnest Christians, their spiritual experience was not an altogether satisfactory one; they were defeated by sin and were more or less powerless in their service. The second stage was one, not of perfection by any means, but one, nevertheless, of victory over sin and of power in service. These two stages were clearly marked, so that when they reached the second stage they could look back to the first as a kind of wilderness experience when they made little progress in the Christian life. Entrance into a fuller Christian life came in each case when they passed through a crisis in spiritual experience—a crisis created by the realization of personal failure to come up to God's standard of expected holiness, and the acceptance of His conditions for the living of a Spirit-filled life.

While, broadly, there was much that was the same in their experiences, in detail there was much that was different. We cannot help but be impressed by the varied nature of their experiences. The way they entered into a Spirit-filled life does not follow the same pattern. A long-continued illness was the means God used to bring Charles A. Fox to a realization of the all-sufficiency of His grace. The death of his little girl and the sudden and shocking realization that he was not finding true in his own experience the promise of God, "My grace is sufficient for thee," brought H. W. Webb-Peploe to a crisis of experience that transformed his whole life. A sermon on the healing of the nobleman's son, stressing the difference between clinging and resting faith, brought to an end the unhappy spiritual experience of the founder of the Keswick Convention. Some men entered the Spirit-filled life after passing through one great crisis; others, after more than one crisis. Some learned and accepted God's conditions of a Spirit-filled life gradually, over a period of years; others, within a few days, at a Convention for the promotion of practical holiness.

We note this, too—that although these men in their books and addresses suggest certain steps to the realization of a Spirit-filled life—Andrew Murray, for example, suggesting seven of them—not all of them, at *one* crisis experience, took the steps themselves. But let us not be deceived by this, and say that the steps they recommended were not in accord with their own experiences, for although all could not point to *one particular time* when they took the steps, they all did take the steps before they entered a life of spiritual fulness. Some took the steps over an extended period of time—of years, even; but that is why they had to wait years for the fulness of the Spirit. God tells us that He gives the Holy Spirit to them that obey Him. He cannot, morally, alter that condition. They met God's condition only little by little, receiving more and more of power as the condition was met; but it was not until it was fully met that they were really filled with the Spirit.

In their books and addresses, however, they tell us that there is no need for so long a delay as they experienced. If the steps they took over a long period of time are taken in an hour, the Spirit will come in His fulness in an hour. Consecration, and the conscious acceptance of the Holy Spirit as Teacher, Guide, and Strength, need not take years. They may be done in a moment; but they must be done before God will give us the fulness of the Spirit.

We find, therefore, that both in teaching and in practice Keswick proceeds on Scriptural lines. It tells us that practical holiness is possible. God has made it so. What He demands He makes possible. He has made it possible for us to fulfil His demands by His twofold provision of Christ and the Spirit. Christ and the Spirit are God's answer to the whole problem of sin. As we enter into a personal experience of the cross of Calvary in death to sin, choosing to identify ourselves with Christ's death to sin; and as we walk in the Spirit, permitting Him to work out in us the salvation purchased for us by Christ on the cross, obeying Him and being guided by Him, practical holiness will become a reality in our everyday living.

Bibliography

Abbott, Jacob J. Review of W. E. Boardman's book, "The Higher Christian Life," *Bibliotheca Sacra and Biblical Repository* (July 1860), 508–535.

Account of the Union Meeting for the Promotion of Scriptural Holiness, held at Oxford, August 29th to September 7th, 1874. Chicago: F. H. Revell, 1875.

Aitken, W. H. M. H. *God's Everlasting Yea. Divine Provision for Human Need. Mission Addresses.* London: John F. Shaw and Co., 1881.

The Highway of Holiness. Helps to the Spiritual Life. London: John F. Shaw and Co., n.d.

Mission Sermons. First Series. New Edition. London: John F. Shaw and Co., 1880.

Mission Sermons. Second Series. Brighton: "Brighton Pulpit" Office, 1876.

Mission Sermons. Third Series. Brighton: "Brighton Pulpit" Office, 1876.

Baird, John. *The Spiritual Unfolding of Bishop H. C. G. Moule, D.D. An Exposition.* London, Edinburgh: Oliphants Ltd., 1926

Balleine, G. R. *A History of the Evangelical Party in the Church of England.* London, 1908.

Blackwood, Sir Stevenson Arthur. *Forgiveness, Life and Glory. Homely Discourses on Eternal and Weighty Truths.* London, Glasgow, Edinburgh: Pickering & Inglis, 1865.

Heavenly Arithmetic. Addresses. London: James Nisbet & Co., 1880.

Heavenly Places. Addresses on The Book of Joshua. London: James Nisbet & Co., 1872.

Position and Progress. Addresses. London: James Nisbet & Co., 1880.

Things Which God Hath Joined Together. Addresses on Isaiah XLV. 21–25. London: James Nisbet & Co., 1880.

The Victory of Faith. A Sequel to "Heavenly Places." The Substance of Addresses on The Book of Joshua. London: James Nisbet & Co., 1875.

Blackwood, Lady S. A. *Some Records of the Life of Stevenson Arthur Blackwood, K.C.B.* London: Hodder and Stoughton, 1896.

Boardman, Henry A. *The "Higher Life" Doctrine of Sanctification, Tried by the Word of God.* Philadelphia: Presbyterian Board of Publication, 1877.

Boardman, W. E. *The Higher Christian Life.* Boston: Henry Hoyt, 1859.

In the Power of the Spirit, or Christian Experience in the Light of the Bible. London: Daldy, Isbister, & Co., 1879.

Boardman, Mrs. W. E. *Life and Labours of the Rev. W. E. Boardman.* New York: Appleton, 1886.

Brooke, Hubert. *The Great High Priest. Bible Readings on the High Priesthood of the Lord Jesus Christ.* London & Edinburgh: Marshall Brothers, Ltd., 1911.
  Personal Consecration; or, Conditions of Discipleship. London: James Nisbet & Co., Ltd., 1897.
  "They Might Be." (Jer. xiii. 11). London: Marshall Brothers, 1894.
Chilvers, H. Tydeman. *"But Jesus Answered." Christ's Replies to Vital Questions.* London: Stanley Martin & Co., Ltd., 1923.
Christian's Pathway of Power, The. (February 1874–December 1878) (In January 1879 the title of this monthly magazine was changed to *The Life of Faith,* which was henceforth published weekly; it is still closely associated with the Keswick Convention.)
Cumming, James Elder. *"Through the Eternal Spirit." A Bible Study on the Holy Ghost.* Stirling: The Drummond Tract Depot, n. e., 1937.
  "After the Spirit:" Being further Papers on The Eternal Spirit, His Person, and Work. Stirling: Drummond's Tract Depot, 1900.
  Consecrated Work and the Preparation for It. London: James Nisbet & Co., Ltd., 1897.
  The Blessed Life; Purity, Peace, and Prayer. London: Partridge & Co., 1891.
Dale, A. W. W. *The Life of R. W. Dale of Birmingham.* London: Hodder & Stoughton, 1899.
Dale, R. W. *The Atonement. The Congregational Union Lecture for 1875.* London: Congregational Union of England and Wales, 1904.
Davidson, Donald. *The Inner Circle. Studies in Christian Thought and Experience.* London: James Clarke & Co., Ltd., 1928.
  The Issues of Life. London: James Clarke & Co., Ltd. 1929.
Deck, Northcote. *Seeing Greater Things. Some of the Far Horizons of Faith.* London, Glasgow: Pickering & Inglis, n.d.
Dolman, D. H. *Simple Talks on the Holy Spirit.* London: Marshall, Morgan & Scott, Ltd., n.d.
Douglas, W. M. *Andrew Murray and His Message.* London, Edinburgh: Oliphants, Ltd., n.d.
Du Plessis, J. *The Life of Andrew Murray of South Africa.* London, Marshall Bros., Ltd., 1920.
Elliott-Binns, L. D. *Religion in the Victorian Era.* London: Lutterworth Press, 1936.
Encyclopedia of Religion and Ethics, VI, p. 749, IX, p. 736.
Figgis, J. B. *Christ and Full Salvation.* London: S. W. Partridge & Co., n.d.
  Keswick from Within. London: Marshall Brothers, Ltd., 1914.
  Visions; with Addresses on the First Epistle of St. John. London: James Nisbet & Co., Ltd., 1911.
Fletcher, Lionel B. *After Conversion—What?* London, Edinburgh: Marshall, Morgan & Scott, Ltd., n.d.
  Kneeling to Conquer. London, Edinburgh: Marshall, Morgan & Scott, Ltd., n.d.
  Life Quest and Conquest. London, Edinburgh: Marshall, Morgan & Scott, Ltd., n.d.

Mighty Moments. London: Religious Tract Society, 1931.

Flew, Robert N. *The Idea of Perfection in Christian Theology.* London: Oxford University Press, 1934.

Fox, Charles A. *The Spiritual Grasp of the Epistles; or, An Epistle a Sunday.* London: S. W. Partridge & Co., 1893.

Victory through the Name. London, Edinburgh: Marshall, Morgan & Scott, Ltd., n.d.

Fullerton, W. Y. *The Christly Life. A Study of the Christian Graces and How to Attain Them.* New York: Fleming H. Revell Company, 1931.

F. B. Meyer. A Biography. London: Marshall, Morgan & Scott, Ltd., n.d.

God's High Way. Old Ideals and New Impulses. London: Morgan & Scott, Ltd., 1919.

God's Intention. London: Marshall, Morgan & Scott, Ltd., n.d.

The Practice of Christ's Presence. London: Morgan & Scott, Ltd., 1916.

Garrard, Mary N. *Mrs. Penn-Lewis. A Memoir.* London: The Overcomer Book Room, 1930.

Girdlestone, R. B. *The Mission of Christ and the Title Deeds of Christianity.* London: Robert Scott, 1914.

Godet, F. *Commentary on St. Paul's Epistle to the Romans.* 2 vols. Edinburgh: T. & T. Clark, 1883.

Goodman, George. *The Epistle of Eternal Life. An Exposition of the First Epistle of John.* London: Pickering & Inglis, n.d.

Full Surrender. A Sevenfold Aspect of Surrender to God. London: Pickering & Inglis, n.d.

"I Live; Yet not I;" or, God's Open Secret of Liberty, from the Guilt, Reign, and Fruit of Sin. London: Pickering & Inglis, Ltd., n.d.

Gordon, A. J. *Grace and Glory. Sermons for the Life that Now Is and That Which is to Come.* New York: Fleming H. Revell Company, 1880.

How Christ Came to Church. The Pastor's Dream. A Spiritual Autobiography. Philadelphia: American Baptist Publication Society, n.d.

In Christ; or, the Believer's Union with His Lord. London: Hodder & Stoughton, 1939.

The Ministry of the Spirit. Philadelphia: American Baptist Publication Society, 1895.

The Twofold Life; or, Christ's Work for Us and Christ's Work in Us. New York: Fleming H. Revell Company, 1883.

Yet Speaking. A Collection of Addresses. New York: Fleming H. Revell Company, 1897.

Gray, James M. "The Keswick Idea." *Independent Magazine,* Vol. 48, 1896, p. 1159.

"Keswick Teaching." *Independent Magazine,* Vol. 48, 1896, p. 1785.

Hanbury, Charlotte. *Life of Mrs. Albert Head.* London: Marshall Brothers, 1905.

Harford, Charles F. (Editor). *The Keswick Convention. Its Message, Its Method, and its Men.* London: Marshall Brothers, 1907.

Harford, John Battersby, and Frederick Charles Macdonald. *Handley Carr Glyn Moule, Bishop of Durham. A Biography.* London: Hodder & Stoughton, 1922.

Harrison, J. East. *Reigning in Life. Heart-to-Heart Talks on God's Provision for Victory over Sin.* Philadelphia: Sunday School Times Company, 1922.

Haslam, W. *Building from the Top; and Other Readings.* London: Jarrold and Sons, n.d. (1878)

From Death into Life: or, Twenty Years of My Ministry. London: Morgan & Scott, n.d. (1880).

Notes from Keswick. London: Morgan & Scott, 1890.

"Yet Not I:" or, More Years of My Ministry. London: Morgan & Scott, 1882.

Hay, Archibald M. *Charles Inwood. His Ministry and Its Secret.* London, Edinburgh: Marshall, Morgan & Scott, Ltd., n.d.

Hodge, Charles. *Systematic Theology.* Vol. 3, pp. 108–113, 245–258. New York: Scribners, 1872–1875.

Holden, J. Stuart. *"Behold, He Cometh!" Addresses on the Second Coming of Our Lord.* London: Morgan & Scott, Ltd., 1918.

The Confidence of Faith. London: Robert Scott, 1916.

The God-Lit Road. London: Marshall Brothers, Ltd., 1926.

The Gospel of the Second Chance, and Other Addresses. London: Marshall Brothers, Ltd., 1912.

The Life of Fuller Purpose. London: Robert Scott, n.d. (1913)

Life's Flood-Tide. London: Robert Scott, 1913.

The Price of Power. New York, etc.: Fleming H. Revell Company, 1908.

Redeeming Vision. London: Robert Scott, 1908.

Some Old Testament Parables. Being Bible Readings Given at Portstewart and Addresses on New Testament Principles. London: Pickering & Inglis, n.d. (1935)

Supposition and Certainty. London: Thynne & Co., Ltd., 1930.

The Pre-Eminent Lord and Other Sermons. London: Hodder & Stoughton, 1909.

A Voice for God. London: Hodder and Stoughton, 1932.

Worship, Beauty, Holiness. London: Pickering & Inglis, n.d. (1913)

A Book of Remembrance: A selection of addresses, edited by M. Broomhall. London: Hodder & Stoughton, 1935.

Hopkins, Evan H. *Broken Bread for Daily Use; Being Thoughts and Comments on the Headline Texts of "Daily Light on the Daily Path. Morning and Evening Hour."* London: Samuel Bagster & Sons, Ltd., n.d.

Hidden Yet Possessed. London: Marshall Brothers, n.d. (1894)

The Law of Liberty in the Spiritual Life. London: Marshall Brothers, 1884.

Talks with Beginners in the Divine Life. London: Marshall Brothers, n.d.

Thoughts on Life and Godliness. London: Hodder & Stoughton, 1883.

The Walk that Pleases God. London: Marshall Brothers, 1887.

Hopkins, Mrs. Evan (Compiler). *Hymns of Consecration and Faith—for Use at General Christian Conferences, Meetings for the Deepening of the Spiritual Life, and Consecration Meetings*. New and Enlarged Edition. London and Edinburgh: Marshall, Morgan & Scott, Ltd., n.d.

Hovey, Alvah. "Higher Christian 'Life Examined," *Studies in Ethics and Religion*. Boston, 1892.

Howard, Philip E. *Charles Gallaudet Trumbull. Apostle of the Victorious Life*. Philadelphia: Sunday School Times Company, 1944.

Howden, J. Russell. *Victory in Life. A Series of Convention Addresses*. London: Morgan & Scott, Ltd., 1916.

Huegel F. J. *Bone of His Bone*. London: Marshall, Morgan & Scott, Ltd., n.d.

The Cross of Christ—The Throne of God. London: Marshall, Morgan & Scott, Ltd., 1935.

Fairest Flower. Grand Rapids. Zondervan Publishing House, 1945.

High Peaks in Redemption. London: Marshall, Morgan & Scott, Ltd., n.d.

Hunt, John. *Religious Thought in England in the 19th Century*. London: Gibbings & Co., Ltd., 1896.

Jackson, Edna V. *The Life That is Life Indeed. Reminiscences of the Broadlands Conferences*. London: James Nisbet & Co., Ltd., 1910.

Jewett, Paul K. *Is the "Victorious" Life Movement Scriptural*. Swengel, Pa.: Bible Truth Depot, n.d. (Pamphlet)

Johnson, E. H. *The Highest Life. A Story of Shortcomings and a Goal; Including a Friendly Analysis of the Keswick Movement*. New York: A. C. Armstrong & Son, 1901.

Keswick Convention, The. London: Pickering & Inglis, 1929–1939.

Keswick Convention in London, The. London: Marshall, Morgan & Scott, 1942, 1943, 1945.

Keswick Convention in Print, The. London: Marshall, Morgan & Scott, Ltd., 1941, 1944.

Keswick Week, The. London: Marshall Brothers, 1896–1928; London, Edinburgh: Marshall, Morgan & Scott, Ltd., 1946, 1947, 1948, 1949, 1950, 1951.

Koeberle, Adolf. *The Quest for Holiness. A Biblical, Historical and Systematic Investigation*. Minneapolis: Augsburg Publishing House, 1936.

Laidlaw, John. *The Bible Doctrine of Man; or, The Anthropology and Psychology of Scripture*. New Edition. Revised and Rearranged. Edinburgh: T. & T. Clark, 1895.

Foundation Truths of Scripture as to Sin and Salvation. In Twelve Lessons. Edinburgh: T. & T. Clark, 1897.

Studies in the Parables and Other Sermons. With a Memoir by H. R. Mackintosh. London: Hodder & Stoughton, 1907.

Langston, E. L. *God and Modern Problems*. London: Marshall, Morgan & Scott, Ltd., n.d.

N

How God is Working to a Plan. London: Marshall, Morgan & Scott, Ltd., n.d.

Lees, Harrington C. *The Eyes of His Glory.* London: Morgan & Scott, Ltd., 1916.

God's Garden and Ours. London: Robert Scott, 1922.

The Promise of Life. The Life That is in Christ Jesus. London: Morgan & Scott, Ltd., 1919.

The Starting Place of Victory. London: Marshall Brothers, Ltd., 1919.

The Sunshine of the Good News. London: Robert Scott, 1912.

Legters, L. L. *Freedom through the Cross.* Philadelphia: Pioneer Mission Agency, 1938.

God's Fellow-Workers. Philadelphia: Pioneer Mission Agency, 1937.

God's Provision for Christian Living. Philadelphia: Christian Life Literature Fund, 1932.

God's Provision for Victorious Living. Philadelphia: Pioneer Mission Agency, 1936.

Partakers. Philadelphia: Pioneer Mission Agency, 1938.

The Simplicity of the Spirit-Filled Life. Philadelphia: Pioneer Mission Agency, 1939.

Union with Christ. Philadelphia: Pioneer Mission Agency, 1938.

Life of Faith, The (1879–1892, 1944–1948).

Lockyer, Herbert. *Keswick: The Place and the Power.* Stirling: Stirling Tract Enterprise, n.d.

MacBeath, John. *The Life of a Christian.* London: Marshall, Morgan & Scott, Ltd., n.d. (1932)

The Second Watch. London: Marshall, Morgan & Scott, Ltd., n.d. (1926).

Taken Unawares. London: Pickering & Inglis, n.d. (1935)

McConkey, James H. *The Surrendered Life. Bible Studies and Addresses on the Yielded Life.* Pittsburgh: Silver Publishing Company, 1903.

The Three-Fold Secret of the Holy Spirit. Pittsburgh: Silver Publishing Society, 1897.

The Way of Victory. A Series of Studies upon Victory over Sin. Pittsburgh: Silver Publishing Society, 1943.

McCraw, Louise Harrison. *James H. McConkey. A Man of God.* Grand Rapids: Zondervan Publishing House, 1939.

Macfarlane, Norman C. *Scotland's Keswick. Sketches and Reminiscences.* London: Marshall Brothers, Ltd., n.d. (1916)

Macgregor, Duncan Campbell. *George H. C. Macgregor, M.A. A Biography.* London: Hodder & Stoughton, Ltd., 1900.

Macgregor, G. H. C. *A Holy Life and How to Live It.* London: Marshall, Morgan & Scott, Ltd., 1946.

Praying in the Holy Ghost. New York: Fleming H. Revell Company, n.d.

"Rabboni"; or, Personal Consecration. London: Marshall Brothers, 1904.

"So Great Salvation." Edinburgh: T. & T. Clark, 1892.

The Things of the Spirit: Teaching of the Word of God about the Spirit of God. London: Marshall Brothers, 1898.

McIntyre, David M. *Love's Keen Flame. Some Thoughts on Holiness as It is Described in the First Epistle of John.* Glasgow: John Smith & Son, Ltd., 1920.

Christ the Life. A Series of Brief Studies on the Believer's Life in Christ. London: Pickering & Inglis, Ltd., n.d. (1938)

The Prayer-Life of Our Lord. London: Marshall, Morgan & Scott, Ltd., n.d. (1927)

The Spirit in the Word. London: Morgan & Scott, Ltd., 1908.

The Upper Room Company. Glasgow: John Smith & Son, 1906.

MacNeil, John. *The Spirit-Filled Life.* Chicago: Bible Institute Colportage Association, 1896.

McQuilkin, Robert C. *The Baptism of the Spirit: Shall We Seek It?* Columbia, S.C.: Columbia Bible College, n.d.

"The Lord is My Shepherd." The Psalm of Victorious Life. Columbia, S.C.: Columbia Bible College, 1945.

The Message of Romans. An Exposition. Grand Rapids: Zondervan Publishing House, 1947.

Victorious Life Studies. Philadelphia: Christian Life Literature Fund, 1918.

Victory in Christ; or, Taking God at His Word. A Personal Testimony. Columbia, S.C.: Columbia Bible College, 1945.

Maclean, J. Kennedy. *Dr. Pierson and His Message: a Sketch of the Life and Works of a Great Preacher.* London: Marshall Brothers, 1911.

Mahan, Asa. *The Baptism of the Holy Ghost.* London: Elliott Stock, 1874.

Christian Perfection. London: F. E. Longley, 1875.

Out of Darkness into Light; or, The Hidden Life Made Manifest. Boston: Willard Tract Repository, 1876.

Mann, A Chester. *F. B. Meyer. Preacher, Teacher, Man of God.* New York: Fleming H. Revell Company, 1929.

Mantle, J. Gregory. *According to the Pattern.* London: Marshall Brothers, 1898.

'Better Things'. A Series of Bible Readings on the Epistle to the Hebrews. London: Marshall Brothers, 1896.

The Counterfeit Christ and Other Sermons. New York: Fleming H. Revell Company, 1920.

God's Tomorrow. London: Marshall Brothers, 1902.

The Way of the Cross. A Contribution to the Doctrine of Christian Sanctity. Brooklyn: The Christian Alliance Publishing Company, 1922.

Marshall, Walter. *The Gospel Mystery of Sanctification.* (Edited by Andrew Murray, and given by him the title, "The Highway of Holiness.") London: James Nisbet & Co., 1889.

Marston, Annie W. *From Mountain to Mountain. Bible Readings.* London: Marshall Brothers, n.d. (1889)

Martin, W. W. *Life Triumphant.* London: Marshall, Morgan & Scott, Ltd., n.d. (1930)

Maxwell, L. E. *Born Crucified.* Chicago: Moody Press, 1945.

Memoir of T. D. Harford-Battersby; Together with Some Account of the Keswick Convention, by Two of His Sons. London: Seeley & Co., Ltd., 1890.

Meyer, F. B. *Back to Bethel. Separation from Sin, and Fellowship with God.* Chicago: Moody Press, 1901.

The Call and Challenge of the Unseen. London: Marshall, Morgan & Scott, Ltd., 1928.

Calvary to Pentecost. London: Marshall Brothers, n.d. (1898)

The Christ-Life for the Self-Life. Chicago: Moody Press, 1897.

Christian Living. London: Morgan & Scott, Ltd., n.d.

Five "Musts" of the Christian Life and Other Sermons. London: Morgan & Scott, Ltd., n.d.

The Future Tenses of the Blessed Life. London: Morgan & Scott, 1894.

Light on Life's Duties. New York: Fleming H. Revell Company, 1895.

Meet for the Master's Use. London: Morgan & Scott, Ltd., n.d.

The Present Tenses of the Blessed Life. London: Morgan & Scott, 1889.

The Secret of Guidance. Chicago: Moody Press, 1896.

Steps to the Blessed Life. London: S. W. Partridge & Co., n.d. (1893)

Monod, Theodore. *The Gift of God. A Series of Addresses.* London: Morgan & Scott, 1876.

Moore, C. G. *"Things Which Cannot be Shaken."* London: Marshall Brothers, 1895.

Moore, E. W. *Christ Controlled; or, The Secret of Sanctity.* London: James Nisbet & Co., 1894.

Christ in Possession; or, the Yielded Life. London: James Nisbet & Co., Ltd., 1899.

Daybreak in the Soul; or, the Believer's Entrance upon Full Salvation. London: S. W. Partridge & Co., 1890.

The Overcoming Life; or, Thoughts on the Life of Christ in the Soul of the Believer. London: S. W. Partridge & Co., 1882.

The Spirit's Seal; or, Power from on High. London: James Nisbet & Co., Ltd., 1897.

Wanted, a Man! or, Bible Characteristics of the Ideal Man. London: Religious Tract Society, 1912.

Morgan, G. Campbell. *The Spirit of God.* New York: Fleming H. Revell Company, 1900.

Moule, H. C. G. *Christ and the Christian. Words Spoken at Keswick.* London: Marshall Brothers, Ltd., 1919.

The Cross and the Spirit. London: Pickering & Inglis, Ltd., n.d.

The Epistle of St. Paul to the Romans. (Expositor's Bible Series) London: Hodder & Stoughton, 1894.

The Epistle to the Romans. (Cambridge Bible for Schools and Colleges). Cambridge: Cambridge University Press, 1894.

Need and Fulness. London: Marshall, Morgan & Scott, Ltd., 1946.

Outlines of Christian Doctrine. London: Hodder & Stoughton, 1889.

Secret Prayer. London: Seeley and Co. Ltd., 1890.

Veni Creator: Thoughts on the Person and Work of the Holy Spirit of Promise. London: Hodder & Stoughton, 1890.

Murray, Andrew. *Abide in Christ. Thoughts on the Blessed Life of Fellowship with the Son of God.* London: James Nisbet & Co., Ltd.

Absolute Surrender and Other Addresses. Chicago: Moody Press, 1897.

Back to Pentecost. The Fulfilment of "The Promise of the Father" (Acts i. 4). London: Oliphants, Ltd., n.d.

Be Perfect! A Message from the Father in Heaven to His Children on Earth. London: James Nisbet & Co., 1895.

The Full Blessing of Pentecost. The One Thing Needful. New York: Fleming H. Revell Company, 1908.

Holy in Christ: Thoughts on the Calling of God's Children to be Holy as He is Holy. London: James Nisbet & Co., 1888.

Like Christ. Thoughts on the Blessed Life of Conformity to the Son of God. New York: Grosset & Dunlap, n.d.

The New Life; Words of God for Young Disciples of Christ. London: James Nisbet & Co., 1891.

Out of His Fulness. Addresses Delivered in America. London: James Nisbet & Co., Ltd., 1897.

The School of Obedience. London: Marshall, Morgan & Scott, Ltd., n.d.

The Spirit of Christ. Thoughts on the Indwelling of the Holy Spirit in the Believer and the Church. London: Nisbet & Co., Ltd., 1888.

The Two Covenants and the Second Blessing. London: James Nisbet & Co., Ltd., 1899.

What Full Surrender Means. Grand Rapids: Zondervan Publishing House, 1942.

Murray, Harold. *G. Campbell Morgan, Bible Teacher. A Sketch of the Great Expositor and Evangelist.* London: Marshall, Morgan & Scott, Ltd., n.d.

Nugent, Sophia. M. *Charles Armstrong Fox: Memorials.* London: Marshall Brothers, 1901.

Life Radiant: Some Memorials of the Rev. Francis Paynter, M.A. London: Marshall Brothers, n.d. (1908)

Packard, Edward N. "A Pastoral Experience," *Independent,* (July 8th, 1897).

Palmer, O. R. *Deliverance from the Penalty and Power of Sin.* Chicago: Moody Press, 1911.

Pardington, George P. *The Crisis of the Deeper Life.* Harrisburg: Christian Publications, Inc., n.d.

Paxson, Ruth. *Caleb, the Overcomer.* London: Marshall, Morgan & Scott, Ltd., n.d.

Called unto Holiness. London: Marshall, Morgan & Scott, Ltd., n.d.

Life on the Highest Plane. A Study of the Spiritual Nature and Needs of Man. Chicago: Moody Press, 1943.

Rivers of Living Water; How Obtained—How Maintained. Studies Setting Forth the Believer's Possessions in Christ. London: Marshall, Morgan & Scott, Ltd., n.d.

The Wealth, Walk and Warfare of the Christian. New York: Fleming
H. Revell Company, 1939.

Penn-Lewis, Mrs. Jessie. *All Things New. The Message of Calvary for
the Time of the End.* Bournemouth: Overcomer Book Room, 1931.

The Conquest of Canaan. Sidelights on the Spiritual Battlefield.
London: Overcomer Book Room, 1945.

The Centrality of the Cross. London: Overcomer Book Room, n.d.

The Cross of Calvary and Its Message. London: Marshall Brothers,
1903.

*"Face to Face"; Glimpses into the Inner Life of Moses the Man of
God.* Bournemouth: Overcomer Book Room, n.d.

*"Thy Hidden Ones." Union with Christ as Traced in the Song of
Songs.* Bournemouth: Overcomer Book Room, 1939.

The Overcomer (1909–1914, 1920–1948). This is a magazine edited
by Mrs. Penn-Lewis and her successors.

Soul and Spirit. A Glimpse into Biblical Psychology. Bournemouth:
Overcomer Book Room, n.d.

The Warfare with Satan and the Way of Victory. London: Overcomer Book Room, 1928.

Penn-Lewis, Mrs. J. and Evan Roberts. *War on the Saints. A Text
Book for Believers on the Work of Deceiving Spirits among the
Children of God.* Leicester: Overcomer Book Room, 1912.

Perkins, Harold W. *The Doctrine of Christian or Evangelical Perfection.*
London: Epworth Press, 1927.

Pierson, Arthur T. *The Believer's Life. Its Past, Present, and Future
Tenses.* London: Pickering & Inglis, n.d.

Forward Movements of the Last Half Century. New York: Funk &
Wagnalls Company, 1900.

*His Fulness. Four Bible Readings Given at Keswick in 1904 on
1 Corinthians i. 30.* London: Marshall Brothers, 1904.

In Christ Jesus; or, The Sphere of the Believer's Life. New York:
Funk & Wagnalls Co., 1898.

The Keswick Movement in Precept and Practice. New York: Funk
& Wagnalls Co., 1903.

*Shall We Continue in Sin? A Vital Question for Believers Answered
in the Word of God.* New York: Baker & Taylor Co., 1897.

Pierson, D. L. *Arthur T. Pierson. A Biography.* London: James
Nisbet & Co., 1921.

Pigott, Blanche A. F. *I. Lilias Trotter, Founder of the Algiers Mission
Band.* London: Marshall, Morgan & Scott, Ltd., n.d.

*Record of the Convention for the Promotion of Scriptural Holiness Held
at Brighton, 1875.* London: S. W. Partridge & Co., 1875.

Robinson, Henry Wheeler. *The Christian Doctrine of Man.* Edinburgh:
T. & T. Clark, 1911.

Robinson, Wade, "The Oxford and Brighton Conventions," *The Philosophy of the Atonement and Other Sermons.* London: J. M. Dent
& Sons, Ltd., 1912.

Romaine, W. *The Life, Walk, and Triumph of Faith.* London: George
Routledge & Sons, n.d.

Russell, George W. E. *The Household of Faith. Portraits and Essays.* London: Hodder & Stoughton, 1903.

A Short History of the Evangelical Movement. London, 1915.

Ryle, John Charles. *Holiness—Its Nature, Hindrances, Difficulties, and Roots; Being a Series of Papers on the Subject.* Fifth Enlarged Edition. London: Chas. J. Thynne, n.d.

Sanday, William and Arthur C. Headlam. *A Critical and Exegetical Commentary on the Epistle to the Romans.* New York: Charles Scribner's Sons, 1896.

Sangster, W. E. *The Path to Perfection.* New York, Nashville: Abingdon-Cokesbury Press, 1943.

Scroggie, W. Graham. *The Fulness of the Holy Spirit.* Chicago: Bible Institute Colportage Association, 1925. (Pamphlet)

Simpson, A. B. *The Christ Life.* Harrisburg: Christian Publications Inc., n.d.

The Epistle to the Romans. Harrisburg: Christian Publications Inc., n.d.

The Holy Spirit; or, Power from on High. Harrisburg: Christian Publications, Inc., n.d.

A Larger Christian Life. Harrisburg: Christian Publications, Inc., n.d.

The Self Life and the Christ Life. Harrisburg: Christian Publications, Inc., n.d.

Walking in the Spirit. Harrisburg: Christian Publications Inc., n.d.

Wholly Sanctified. Harrisburg: Christian Publications, Inc., n.d.

Sloan, Walter B. *These Sixty Years. The Story of the Keswick Convention.* London: Pickering & Inglis, n.d. (1935)

Smellie, Alexander. *Evan Henry Hopkins. A Memoir.* London, etc.: Marshall Brothers, Ltd., 1920.

Lift Up Your Heart. Four Addresses on Sanctification. London: Andrew Melrose, Ltd., 1915.

Service and Inspiration. London: Andrew Melrose, Ltd., 1904.

The Well by the Way. London: Andrew Melrose, Ltd., 1920.

Smiley, Sarah F. *The Fulness of Blessing; or, The Gospel of Christ as Illustrated from the Book of Joshua.* New York: Anson D. F. Randolph & Co., 1876.

Smith, Hannah Whitall. *Bible Readings on the Progressive Development of Truth and Experience in the Old Testament Scriptures.* Boston: Willard Tract Repository, 1878.

The Christian's Secret of a Happy Life. New York: Fleming H. Revell Company, 1941.

Every-Day Religion; or, The Common-Sense Teaching of the Bible. New York: Fleming H. Revell Company, 1893.

The Record of a Happy Life: Being Memorials of Franklin Whitall Smith, a Student of Princeton College. Philadelphia: J. B. Lippincott & Co., 1873.

Living in the Sunshine. New York: Fleming H. Revell Company, 1906.

The Open Secret; or, The Bible Explaining Itself. Chicago: Fleming
H. Revell Company, 1885.
The Unselfishness of God: A Spiritual Autobiography. New York:
Fleming H. Revell Company, 1903.
Smith, Logan Pearsall. *Unforgotten Years.* Boston: Little, Brown and
Company, 1939.
Smith, Robert Pearsall. *Holiness Through Faith. Light on the Way of
Holiness.* London: Morgan and Scott, 1875.
Stewart, James S. *A Man in Christ. The Vital Elements of St. Paul's
Religion.* New York and London: Harper and Brothers, n.d. (1947)
Stock, Eugene. *History of the Church Missionary Society,* Vols I and
II. London: Church Missionary Society, 1899.
My Recollections. London: James Nisbet & Co., 1909.
Stockmayer, Otto. *The Glory of the Lamb and the Lamb-life.* New
York: Y.W.C.L. Bookroom, 1915.
Storr, V. F. *Development of English Theology in the 19th Century,
1800-1860.* London: Longmans & Co., 1913.
Strachey, Ray. *Group Movements of the Past, and Experiments in Guid-
ance.* London: Faber & Faber, Ltd., 1934.
Strong, A. H. *Systematic Theology. A Compendium and Common-
place-Book Designed for the Use of Theological Students.* Philadel-
phia: Judson Press, 1946. (pp. 868-881.)
Taylor. Dr. and Mrs. F. Howard. *Hudson Taylor in Early Years. The
Growth of a Soul.* London: China Inland Mission.
*Hudson Taylor and the China Inland Mission. The Growth of a
Work of God.* London: China Inland Mission, 1921.
Hudson Taylor's Spiritual Secret. London: China Inland Mission,
1935.
Thomas, W. H. Griffith. *The Essentials of Life.* London, Glasgow:
Pickering & Inglis, n.d.
The Christian Life and How to Live It. Chicago: Moody Press, 1919.
Grace and Power. Some Aspects of the Spiritual Life. New York:
Fleming H. Revell Company, 1916.
The Holy Spirit of God. (Lectures on the L. P. Stone Foundation,
Princeton Theological Seminary, 1913.) London: Longmans, Green,
and Co., 1913.
*"Let Us Go On." The Secret of Christian Progress in the Epistle to
the Hebrews.* London: Marshall, Morgan & Scott, Ltd., n.d.
*The Principles of Theology. An Introduction to the Thirty-Nine
Articles.* pp. 208, 209. London: Church Book Room Press, 1945.
St. Paul's Epistle to the Romans. A Devotional Commentary. Grand
Rapids: W. B. Eerdmans Publishing Company, 1946.
Todd, John E. "Law of Spiritual Growth." (Review of W. E. Board-
man's book, *The Higher Christian Life.) The Biblical Repertory
and Princeton Review* (October 1860), 608-640.
Tozer, A. W. *Wingspread. A. B. Simpson, A Study in Spiritual Alti-
tude.* Harrisburg: Christian Publications, Inc., 1943.
Trotter, I. Lilias. *Parables of the Cross and of the Christ Life.* London:
Marshall Brothers, 1899.

Trumbull, Charles Gallaudet. *What is the Gospel.* Minneapolis: The Harrison Service, 1944.

Tulloch, John. *Movements of Religious Thought in Britain during the 19th Century.* New York: Scribners, 1885.

Unknown Christian, An. (A. E. Richardson) *How to Live the Victorious Life.* London: Marshall, Morgan & Scott, Ltd., n.d.

The Kneeling Christian. London: Marshall, Morgan & Scott, Ltd., n.d.

Victorious Christ, The. Messages from Conferences held by the Victorious Life Testimony in 1922. Philadelphia: Sunday School Times Company, 1923.

Victorious Life, The. Messages from the Summer Conferences at Whittier, California, June. Princeton, New Jersey, July. Cedar Lake, Indiana, August. Including also Some Messages from the 1917 Conference at Princeton and Other Material. Philadelphia : The Board of Managers of Victorious Life Conference, 1918.

Victory in Christ. A Report of Princeton Conference 1916. Philadelphia: The Board of Managers of Princeton Conference, 1916.

Walvoord, John F. *The Doctrine of the Holy Spirit.* Dallas: Dallas Theological Seminary, 1943.

Warfield, B. B. *Perfectionism.* 2 vols. New York: Oxford University Press, 1931.

Watt, Gordon. *The Challenge of the Cross.* Cleveland: Union Gospel Press, 1925.

The Cross in Faith and Conduct. Philadelphia: Sunday School Times Company, 1924.

The Meaning of the Cross. Philadelphia: Sunday School Times Company, 1923.

Webb-Peploe, H. W. *Calls to Holiness.* London: Marshall Brothers, 1900.

He Cometh! London: Marshall Brothers, 1905.

"I Follow After." London: Marshall Brothers, n.d.

The Life of Privilege. Possession, Peace, and Power. New York, London: Fleming H. Revell Company, 1896.

That Beautiful Name. Bible Readings given at the Keswick Convention, July, 1910. London: Marshall Brothers, Ltd., 1910.

The Titles of Jehovah. A Course of Sermons. London: James Nisbet & Co., Ltd., 1901.

The Victorious Life. London: James Nisbet & Co., Ltd., 1897.

Within and Without; or, The Christian's Foes. London: Marshall Brothers, n.d.

Webster, F. S. *Christians and Christians.* London: Marshall Brothers, n.d.

Spiritual Worship. London: Robert Scott, 1907.

Wrenford, J. T. *Reality.* London: Marshall Brothers, n.d.

INDEX

INDEX OF NAMES